Material Culture and Cultural Identity: A Study of Greek and Roman Coins from Dora

Rosa Maria Motta

Archaeopress Archaeology

Archaeopress
Gordon House
276 Banbury Road
Oxford OX2 7ED

www.archaeopress.com

ISBN 978 1 78491 092 1
ISBN 978 1 78491 093 8 (e-Pdf)

© Archaeopress and R M Motta 2015

Printed and bound in Great Britain by
Marston Book Services Ltd, Oxfordshire

This book is available direct from Archaeopress or from our website www.archaeopress.com

Preface

The ancient harbor town of Dor/Dora in modern Israel has a history that spanned from the Bronze Age until the Late Roman Era. The story of its peoples can be assembled from a variety of historical and archaeological sources derived from the nearly thirty years of research at Tel Dor — the archaeological site of the ancient city. Each primary source offers a certain kind of information with its own perspective. In the attempt to understand the city during its Graeco-Roman years — a time when Dora reached its largest physical extent and gained enough importance to mint its own coins, numismatic sources provide key information. With their politically, socio-culturally and territorially specific iconography, Dora's coins indeed reveal that the city was self-aware of itself as a continuous culture, beginning with its Phoenician origins and continuing into its Roman present.

Focusing primarily on the iconography and epigraphy of Dora's Greek and Roman coins, this study examines the evolution and outlook of the city and its society in these contexts:

a. The geographical and historical contexts of Dor and its physical transformations as reconstructed by archaeological evidence from Tel Dor and by literary sources.

b. Ethnicity, cultural identities, and cultural boundaries as starting points for the study of the changes that transformed the Phoenician city of Dor into the Hellenistic and Graeco-Roman Dora. The Hellenization and Romanization processes of the city will be examined within the larger frame of border studies. Dora's coin iconography will be used to determine that the city's milieu was not a product of Greek and Roman acculturation or assimilation, but a complex aggregation of three diverse systems that came into contact with each other. Since most samples are Roman imperial coins, the study will demonstrate the mechanisms by which Rome's imperial aspirations were articulated in the Middle East.

c. The value of mints as extensions of the governmental apparatus and the issuance of coins as an indication of the authority in charge. Dora's first year minting of quasi-autonomous Roman coinage in 65 BCE was done under the auspices of Pompey, who must have provided the impetus to initiate a new civic era. Minting continued, with several periods of inactivity, until the reign of Caracalla. Samples of each issuance will be analyzed within the larger context of the political and military developments in the eastern empire, especially under Trajan, when Dora's mint issued its largest output.

d. The relevance of material culture studies and semiotics to the study of coin iconography. Each of Dora's coin types will be examined as a semeion, i.e., a sign of the cultural self-understanding of the city and a primary vehicle through which the city constructed its ideology. Dora's coins will be viewed as records of the trends that contributed to the city's self-authoring narrative.

e. The relevance of Dora imperial images to the understanding of the role of visual media in the Graeco-Roman world. While the quasi-autonomous coins drew their iconography from local features, e.g., religious, economic, etc., all imperial coins have royal portraits — Augustus, Vespasian, Titus, Trajan, Hadrian, Antoninus Pius, Septimius Severus, Caracalla, Geta, Julia Domna and Plautilla. These imperial effigies will be analyzed and placed within the context of Roman imperial portraiture, since Roman imperial coinage reflects ideological claims within each reign.

f. Dora's exclusive use of the Greek language on its coins as a sign of identity construction. Dora's coin legends will be assessed according to linguistic and onomastic principles.

The study is obviously bounded within the timeframe of the material examined (205 BCE-210 CE). But if Dora's Graeco-Roman coins can be considered within the context of material culture and semiotic studies, the opportunity has been created of extending the same approach to bordering cities. With this in mind, I include a brief chapter comparing the numismatic issuance of Caesarea Maritima during the Flavian reign with coins issued in Dora during the same period, using the same approach.

Contents

Acknowledgments

This book is partially derived from my doctoral dissertation, presented at the University of Virginia in 2010. Since its acceptance, I have updated its information and added a new chapter and new references. My most heartfelt thanks and appreciation go first and foremost to Tyler Jo Smith, my PhD advisor, for first advising me to complete this research and then encouraging me to publish it with Archaeopress. I would also like to thank John Dobbins, who first introduced me to numismatics, Jane Crawford and Bernie Frischer.

During the initial phase of my studies, I traveled to Oxford to meet Chris Howgego and discussed research ideas. I thank him for taking time to talk with me when my ideas were in an embryonic stage. I also traveled to New York to meet Andrew Meadows at the American Numismatic Society; Andrew's advice, suggestions, and comments proved invaluable.

I am grateful to the entire crew of the Tel Dor Excavation Project, and especially to the directors Ilan Sharon and Ayelet Gilboa who trusted me with many boxes of materials and put the Tel Dor coins at my disposal during my stays in Israel. Ayelet most generously loaned me the use of her office at the University of Haifa. I would also like to thank Sveta Matskevich for her great support with the compilation and presentation of the images. Thanks also to Liz Block-Smith, who introduced me to Tel Dor, and to Ephraim Stern, who was director of the project long before I came Tel Dor and whose material I have used in this book. My gratitude extends to the late Y. Meshorer, whose work paved my own.

Haim Gitler and Gabriela Bijovsky at the Israel Antiquity Authority generously shared their knowledge and research that supported and expanded mine. Robert Kool and Donald Ariel provided me with office space and insights.

I am absolutely indebted to Arie Fichman, who generously entrusted his private collection of Dora coins to me and to my camera on several occasions during my stay in Haifa. Arie's collection provided the most important samples of Dora coinage, and his data became the basis for my own analysis.

The final draft of this book was written at the Albright Institute in Jerusalem, and I want to express my gratitude and deep appreciation to the many friends who cheered for me while I was living and working there. During the final revision of the book, I was helped by several others: Becky S. Martin who offered her expertise of Phoenician Dor, and John Hyland who kindly shared his knowledge of Persian history. I also thank two friends and colleagues, Jana Adamitis and Mark Padilla for their much-appreciated encouragement to finish the project. Finally, many heartfelt thanks go to my editor, Susan Holzman, who generously gave up time to review the manuscript. Her care, her competence, and her conscientiousness are truly appreciated.

Finding coins samples for the research was a difficult task that resulted in costly travel to several countries. This book would have not been possible, therefore, without the generous grants from the University of Virginia's Lindner Center for Art History, the Robert J. Huskey Travel Fellowship, The Albright's Carol and Eric Meyers Fellowship, and the Milton Bienenfeld Foundation award. I am grateful to Christopher Newport University for the Faculty Development Grant that allowed me to complete the final revision and to obtain all copyright clearance for the publication of artifacts housed in various museums around the world.

My loving family has been a source of inspiration throughout these years, and I thank all of them. *Das größte Dankeschön* goes to my husband Jens Bischof for his assistance in helping me decipher relevant German scholarship and for his patience as I completed the project on three continents. Thanks also to my children Karl and Christina, and their spouses Teresa and Edward for their encouragement and for their technical support. The smiles and hugs of little Gabriella and Anastasia helped me keep perspective on what is important in life. Lastly, *un grazie di vero cuore* to my brothers and sisters and their families who, although separated by geography and several time zones, cheered for me from Sicily. This book is dedicated to the memory of our parents Angelo and Angela Motta.

List of Abbreviations

BMC *British Museum Collection.* The Department of Coins and Medals. British Museum, London.

CIL *Corpus Inscriptionum Latinarum.* Deutsche Akademie der Wissenschaften. Berlin: G. Reimerum, 1863-2006.

FGrH *Die Fragmente der Griechischen Historiker by F. Jacoby.* Berlin and Leiden *1923*-1958.

LIMC *Lexicon Iconographicum Mythologiae Classicae.* 8 Vols. Zurich: Artemis, 1997.

RIC *Roman Imperial Coinage*, Vol 1-10. London: Spink and Son, 1923-1994.

RPC *Roman Provincial Coinage*, Vol 1-7. London: British Museum Press; Paris: Bibliothèque Nationale de France, 1998-2006.

N.B. Dora's coins have been numbered sequentially. Plate numbers are not used in the text when referring to the coins.

List of Classical References

Aeschylus. *Oresteia: Agamemnon.* Libation-Bearers. Eumenides. Alan H. Sommerstein. The Loeb Classical Library 146. Cambridge, MA: Harvard University Press, 2009.

Appian. *The Foreign Wars*. H. White. New York: The MacMillan Company, 1899.

Cicero. *In Catilinam 1-4; Pro Murena; Pro Sulla; Pro Flacco*. C. MacDonald. Loeb Classical Library 324. Cambridge, MA: Harvard University Press, 1976.

Cicero. *Epistulae ad Quintum Fratrem et M. Brutum*. Cambridge Classical Texts and Commentaries 22. D. R. Shackleton-Bailey: Cambridge: Cambridge University Press, 2004.

Dio Cassius. *Roman History, Books 61-70*. E. Cary. The Loeb Classical Library, 176. Cambridge, MA: Harvard University Press, 1925.

Dio Cassius. *Roman History, Books 71-80*. E. Cary and H. B. Foster. The Loeb Classical Library, 177. Cambridge MA: Harvard University Press, 1927.

Euripides. *Cyclops. Alcestis. Medea*. David Kovacs. The Loeb Classical Library 12. Cambridge, MA: Harvard University Press, 1994.

Eusebius. *Onomasticon. A Triglott Edition with Notes and Commentary*. Edited by R. S. Notly, and Z. Safrai, eds. 2004. Leiden: Brill Academic Publishers, 2004.

Herodian. *History of the Empire, Books 1-4*. C. R. Whittaker. The Loeb Classical Library, 454. Cambridge, MA: Harvard University Press, 1969.

Herodotus. *The Histories*. Translated by A. De Selincourt. London: Penguin Classics, 1996.

Herodotus. *The Persian Wars, Books 1-2*. A. D. Godley. Classical Library 117. The Loeb Classical Library 117. Cambridge, MA: Harvard University Press, 1920.

Herodotus. *The Persian Wars, Books 3-4*. A. D. Godley. The Loeb Classical Library 118. Cambridge, MA: Harvard University Press, 1921.

Herodotus, *The Persian Wars, Books 5-7*. A.D. Godley. The Loeb Classical Library 119. Cambridge, MA: Harvard University Press, 1922.

Hesiod. *Theogony. Works and Days. Testimonia*. Glenn W. Most. The Loeb Classical Library 57. Cambridge MA: Harvard University Press, 2007.

Homer, *Iliad Books 13-24*. A. T. Murray and W. F. Wyatt. The Loeb Classical Library 171. Cambridge, MA: Harvard University Press, 1925.

Homer, *Odyssey Books 13-24*. A. T. Murray and W. F. Wyatt. The Loeb Classical Library 104. Cambridge, MA: Harvard University Press, 1925.

Homer, *Homeric Hymns. Homeric Apocrypha. Lives of Homer*. M. L. West. The Loeb Classical Library 496. Cambridge, MA: Harvard University Press, 2003.

Horace. *Odes and Epodes*. N. Rudd. The Loeb Classical Library, 33. Cambridge, MA: Harvard University Press, 2004.

Jerome. *Select Letters, by Sophronius Eusebius Hieronymus*; F A Wright. The Loeb Classical Library 262. Cambridge, MA: Harvard University Press, 1933.

Josephus. *The New Complete Works*. Translated by W. Whiston. Commentary by P. Maier. Grand Rapids, MI: Kregel Publications, 1999.

Isocrates. *Volume I* (Part IV Panegyricus). G. Norlin. The Loeb Classical Library 209. Cambridge MA: Harvard University Press, 1928.

Livy. *History of Rome, Books 43-45*. A. C. Schlesinger. The Loeb Classical Library 396. Cambridge, MA: Harvard University Press, 1951.

Martial. *Epigrams, Books 6-10*. D. R. Shackleton Bailey. The Loeb Classical Library, 95. Cambridge, MA: Harvard University Press, 1993.

Pausanias. *Description of Greece*, Volume II. Books 3-5. W. H. S. Jones and H. A. Ormerod. The Loeb Classical Library 188. Cambridge, MA: Harvard University Press, 1927.

Pindar. *Olympian Odes. Pythian Odes*. W. H. Race. The Loeb Classical Library 56. Cambridge, MA: Harvard University Press, 1997.

Plato. *Laws, Books 1-6*. R. G. Bury. The Loeb Classical Library 187. Cambridge, MA: Harvard University Press, 1926.

Plato. *Republic, Books 1-5*. P. Shorey. The Loeb Classical Library 237. Cambridge, MA: Harvard University Press, 1930.

Pliny. *Natural History, Volume II, Books 3-7*. H. Rackham. The Loeb Classical Library 352. Cambridge, MA: Harvard University Press, 1942.

Pliny. *Natural History*, Volume III: Books 8-11. H. Rackham. The Loeb Classical Library, 353. Cambridge, MA: Harvard University Press, 1940.

Plutarch. *Lives, Volume VII. Demosthenes and Cicero. Alexander and Caesar*. B. Perrin. The Loeb Classical Library 99. Cambridge MA: Harvard University Press, 1919.

Polybius. *The Histories Books 5-8*. W.R. Paton. The Loeb classical Library 138. Cambridge, MA: Harvard University Press, 1923.

Polybius. *The Histories Books 16-27*. W.R. Paton. The Loeb classical Library 160. Cambridge, MA: Harvard University Press, 1926.

Saint Augustine. Select Letters. J. H. Baxter. Loeb Classical Library 239. Cambridge, MA: Harvard University Press, 1930.

Sidonius. *Letters, 3-9*. W. B. Anderson. The Loeb Classical Library, 420. Cambridge, MA: Harvard University Press, 1965.

Stephani Byzantii. *Ethnica: Volumen 1: Corpus Fontium Historiae Byzantinae* edited by Margarethe Billerbeck. Berlin: Walter de Gruyter, 2006.

Strabo. *Geography, Books 3-5*. H. L. Jones. The Loeb Classical Library, 50. Cambridge MA: Harvard University Press, 1923.

Suetonius. *Life of the Caesars, Volume II*. J. C. Rolfe. The Loeb Classical Library, 38. Cambridge, MA: Harvard University Press, 1914.

Tacitus. *Annals, Books 4-6, 11-12. J.* Jackson. The Loeb Classical Library 312. Cambridge, MA: Harvard University Press, 1937.

The New American Bible: St. Joseph Edition. New York: Catholic Book Publishing Company, 2003.

Virgil. *Aeneid, Books 1-6*. Latin Edition. Edited by C. Pharr. Boston: Bolchazy-Carducci Publishers, 1998.

List of Figures

List of Plates

List of Tables

Chapter 1
Tel Dor's Context

1.1 Introduction and Sources

The history of the ancient Phoenician harbor city of Dor (Fig. **1.1**) spanned for nearly two thousand years and can be reconstructed from historical and archaeological sources. However, since the city minted its own coins during the Graeco-Roman period, Dora's numismatic material is today one of the most valuable sources for reconstructing the city's history.[1] In fact, through an analysis of the city's coins, an understanding of various aspects of the society of ancient Dora, including the use of coins as medium of exchange, the religious and economic life of the city, and the architecture of at least one of the monuments as represented on the coins can be achieved. With their political, socio-culturally and territorially specific iconography, Dora's coins indeed offer valuable insights into the evolution and the outlook of the society that lived within the city's boundaries.

Some studies of Dora's coins already exist as part of coin catalogues. The earliest publication of a coin from Dora was completed in 1684 (P. Seguin, *Selecta Numismatica Antiqua*). Other coins of Dora appeared in J. Eckhel's *Doctrina Nummorum Veterum* in 1794,[2] and T. Mionnet's *Description de Médailles Antiques* in 1805.[3] De Saulcy's *Numismatique de la Terre Sainte*, published in 1874, also included some of Dora's coins,[4] while J. Rouvier's *Numismatique des Villes de la Phénicie* in 1901 included coins from Dora, Tyre and surrounding Phoenician cities.[5] In 1910 G.F. Hill published a catalogue of Dora's coins at the British Museum,[6] and in 1977 M. Rosenberger

presented a more complete list, which included 39 coins.[7] The most recent publication appeared as a chapter of the 1995 *Qedem Reports- Excavation at Dor* as a reprint of an article originally published in the *Israel Numismatic Journal* (1986-87) by Ya'aqov Meshorer. In this article, he catalogued Dora's coins with some iconographic descriptions.[8] The results of these studies are limited as they never attempted to place the coins minted at Dora within the material culture context of the city. In this book, aspects of cultural identities and cultural boundaries will be taken into consideration, as they are important factors in the evolution of the Phoenician city of Dor first into the Greek and then into the Roman city of Dora. These processes of Hellenization and Romanization have been often defined as processes of 'acculturation' that were based on a basic diffusionist model, i.e., the dissemination of Greek and/or Roman elements to other people.[9] In this study it is shown that these processes were, in fact, much more complex and not the "simple one-way influences and passive acceptance of Greek [or Roman] cultures."[10] According to A. C. Renfrew, most changes in society are due to trade and commerce and to the "operation of local economic factors,"[11] which lead to the adoption of aspects of the material culture of another group. An investigation of the economic and trading systems of Dora and an examination of the city's numismatic material are, therefore, of great value for the understanding of the changes that transformed Phoenician Dor into Greek and Roman Dora. This study examines all the sequences and series of coins produced by Dora's mint and sets its coinage within the wider economic-political and cultural-religious contexts of the city, such as they are known today. By analyzing the technical details of the city's mint and its production phases, the types and iconography of the coins, and the physical distribution of Dora's coins found within the wider geographical area, Dora's coins are turned into measures of contact or interaction between the various peoples who lived in Dora, and between Dora's people and the people of neighboring cities.

1.2 Geographical Identity of Tel Dor

Beginning at the foot of Mount Carmel, the coastal plain of Israel is a long strip of low seaboard land, varying

---

[1] The Phoenician name of the city was *Dor*, but was Hellenized to *Dora* by the Greeks, and the name appears as such on Roman coins. *Doros* also appears on some of the earliest sources. The remains are known today as Tel Dor, with the word *Tel* in Hebrew meaning 'mound' — a man-made hill covering the remains of an ancient settlement (Dahl 1915, 62). In this project, we will use Dora only to refer specifically to the Graeco-Roman city, Dor for the other historical periods of the city, and Tel Dor for the archaeological site.

[2] Eckhel 1775, 275-320. Joseph Hilarius von Eckhel (1737-1798) was professor of antiquities and numismatics at the University of Vienna, and is considered the father of numismatics for his scientific approach to the study and organization of ancient coins.

[3] Mionnet 1809, 375. Théodore Edme Mionnet (1770-1842) developed a scale still in use today to describe the size of coins, medallions, and similar flat round objects.

[4] De Saulcy (1807-1880) was the curator of the Museum of Artillery in Paris. Among his many works of Jewish interest are: *Recherches sur la Numismatique Judaïque*, 1854, and *Numismatique de la Terre Sainte*, 1874. See *The Numismatic Chronicle and Journal of the Royal Numismatic Society, Vol. IX*, 184.

[5] Other cities include Eboda, Marathus, Orthosia, Aradus-Berytus, Botrys, Gebal-Byblos, Caesarea-ad-Libanum, Sidon, and Tripolis.

[6] George Hill (1867-1948) was the editor of *Numismatic Chronicle* from 1904-1912. He was also the editor of the first numismatics festschrift, *Corolla Numismatica: Numismatic Essays in Honour of Barclay V. Head*, published in 1906 to honor Head at the time of his retirement as Keeper of Coins at the British Museum.

[7] Rosenberg 1975-78, 2:135.

[8] Meshorer 1995b, 355-365.

[9] The issues of acculturation, syncretization, hybridity and creolization have been studied at length. For studies focusing on early Greek colonies and trade, see Boardman 1999; Burkert 2004; Miller 1997; Martin 2007; Meirs 2012. For the Romanization of the East, see Millar 1993; Woolf 1998. For in-depth studies on hybridity and creolization, see Bhabha 1994; Young 1995 and 2002.

[10] Meirs 2012,

[11] Renfrew 1969, 160.

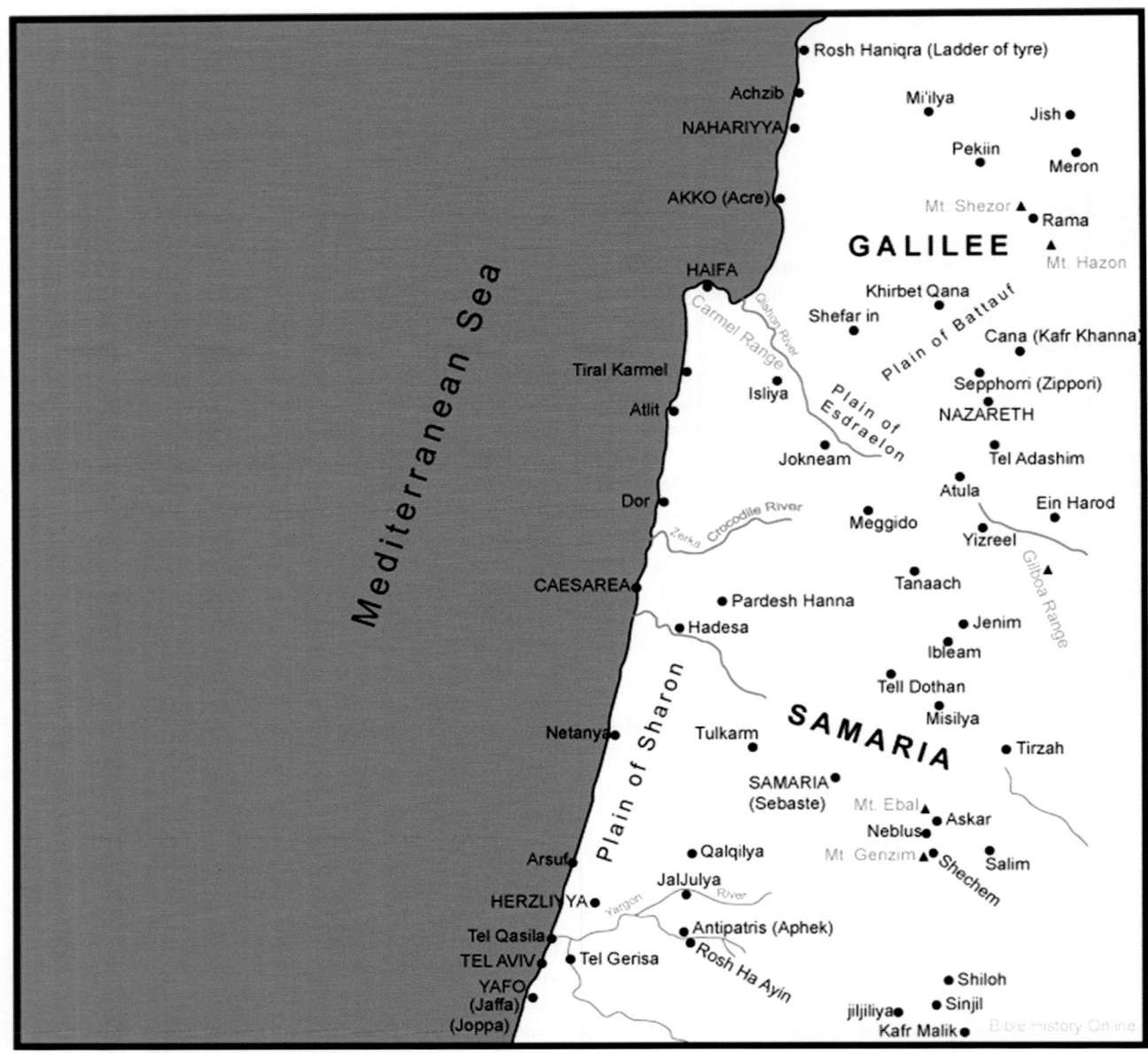

FIG. 1.1. MAP OF NORTHERN ISRAEL
MAP FREELY DISTRIBUTED - HTTP://WWW.BIBLE-HISTORY.COM/GEOGRAPHY/MAPS/MAP-OF-COASTAL-PLAIN-NORTHERN.GIF. ACCESSED 02/24/2009

in width and extending for about 170 miles along the Mediterranean Sea from the Lebanese border in the north to the Gaza strip in the south. Today the strip is divided into five sub-regions (Fig. **1.2**). The Western Galilee stretches from Rosh Ha'Nikra in the far north down to Haifa on the coast. It is a fertile region with many small islands scattered off the shore. South of Haifa is the Hof Ha'Carmel region which ends with the Nachal Hataninim and the town of Zikhron Ya'aqov. The Sharon plain is the third area, running from Zikhron Ya'aqov to Tel Aviv's Yarkon River. South of this, running to Nachal Shikma, is the Central Coastal Plain.[12] The last, the most southern part of the Coastal Plain, is the Plain of Judea, also known as the Western Negev, which extends south to the Gaza Strip.[13] The entire coastline is parallel to the inland mountain

ridge creating no promontories or deep embayments. The shore itself, however, is of two different types: precipitous cliffs, reaching 10-40m with rather shallow waters in front of them or a rather gently inclined shore, usually covered by sand dunes.[14] The high cliffs and the flat platforms were created by wave erosion that transformed the beach, creating vertical cliffs that increase in height as the water recedes. These vertical cliffs, made of coarse sandstone locally known as *kurkar*, protect the land from the sand blown in by the sea winds, making the area one of the most fertile areas of Israel (Figs. **1.3** and **1.4**). Although *kurkar* stones crumble easily, they harden underwater and have, therefore, been used over the years to build houses, breakwaters and jetties. Most of the remaining building and wall structures at Tel Dor are made of *kurkar*.[15]

---

[12] *Nachal* is the Hebrew word for small stream or river.
[13] Orni 1971, 37.

[14] ibid. 39.
[15] Bullard 1970, 125.

FIG. 1.2. MAP OF COASTAL PLAINS OF ISRAEL
BASED ON A PHOTO FROM HTTP://VISIBLEEARTH.NASA.GOV. ACCORDING TO
NASA COPYRIGHT POLICY, "NASA MATERIAL IS NOT PROTECTED BY COPYRIGHT
UNLESS NOTED". ACCESSED 10/02/2009

FIG. 1.3. KURKAR RIDGE (TEL DOR DIGITAL LIBRARY)
REPRODUCED WITH PERMISSION OF COPYRIGHT OWNER. FURTHER
REPRODUCTION PROHIBITED WITHOUT PERMISSION.

FIG. 1.4. KURKAR STONES (PHOTO BY C. MAJER
REPRODUCED WITH PERMISSION OF COPYRIGHT OWNER. FURTHER
REPRODUCTION PROHIBITED WITHOUT PERMISSION.

The remains of the ancient Phoenician city of Dor and the Graeco-Roman Dora, known as Tel Dor, el-Burj or Khirbet Tantura, are located in the southern part of the Hof Ha'Carmel region, about fourteen miles south of Mount Carmel and Haifa.[16] Adjacent to the ruins is Kibbutz

---

[16] The site is presently under the jurisdiction of *The Israel Parks and Nature Preserve Authority*, and was recently declared a national monument in order to assure the protection of both its antiquities and the endangered coastal ecosystems on the beaches north of it. For more information, see: www.parks.org.il.

Nachsholim, a thriving four-star beach resort that was built on the site of the Arab village al-Tantura after the latter was destroyed in 1948.[17]

The identification of al Tantura with ancient Dor/Dora has been long debated by historians and travelers. The British author and traveler James Silk Buckingham, writing in 1821, described al-Tantura as a small village on the coast, with a harbor located to the north, a few mud houses, a square, and one stone building, a khan, used as a guesthouse for travelers, but made no reference to Dor.[18] In 1855, Mary Rogers, the sister of the British vice-consul in Haifa, noticed blocks of marble and carved stones scattered around the shore and wrote that "ancient Dora stands a little beyond Tantura on a rugged promontory with ruined walls all round it at the edge of the cliff."[19] In his travelogue of 1859, the American clergyman William McClure Thomson wrote, "Tantura merits very little attention. It is a sad and sickly hamlet of wretched huts on a naked sea-beach.... Dor never could have been a large city, for there are no remains.... In front of the present village are five small islets, by the aid of which an artificial harbour could easily be constructed in ancient times."[20] In 1915 G. Dahl described al-Tantura as "the successor of Dor" and "a typical Palestinian coastal town of sailors and fishermen, with a population of a few hundred Moslem inhabitants."[21] Among modern scholars who believe that al-Tantura was the successor of Dora is M. Benvenisti, who writes that, as in ancient times, the villagers of *al-Tantura* drew freshwater from a well in the eastern part of the village.[22]

In the early twentieth century, al-Tantura was described as a small village on the coast, with a harbor located to the north, a square, and an estimated 1,200 residents who conducted a small trade with Jaffa.[23] The village seemed to have grown under the British Mandate from 1928 to 1944. In 1945, according to the land and population survey of the year, al-Tantura had a population of 1,490, a total land area of 14,250 square meters, and an economy based on fishing and agriculture, with the major agricultural products being grain, vegetables, and fruit, including citrus and olives.[24] In 1948, after the foundation of the State of Israel, al-Tantura was included within the area designated by the *United Nations Partition Plan* for the Jewish State. The kibbutz Nahsholim and the moshav Dor were soon built on land on the outskirts of al-Tantura by Jewish immigrants from Turkey, while the old Arab village, alleged successor of Dora, was abandoned.[25]

The identification of al-Tantura with ancient Dora has been a political rather than an archaeological debate, since the archaeological site is not on the location where the Arab village stood.[26] However, both cities overlooked the Tantura lagoon, and reference to the ancient Graeco-Roman city as Tantura may be coincidental. In fact, there is no historical or archaeological evidence demonstrating that the ancient city was inhabited through modern history, and both Eusebius (273-340 CE) and St. Jerome (390 CE) already referred to it as being ruined.[27] As M. Rogers writes, "This place [Dor] is now quite abandoned, as the walls are tottering and the cliffs are giving way; the stones are gradually being removed to build up Tantura."[28] If any continuation between the two cities did exist, it was perhaps in the structures of the new village built with the stones of the old one. Ancient stones from Dora can be seen, in fact, reused into masonry structures, roads, and public and private buildings in villages around Tel Dor.[29] In that sense, Dora might indeed have continued to exist in Al-Tantura.

1.3 The Historical Antecedent: From Canaanite to Persian Dor

The port city of Dor was founded around the beginning of the second millennium by the Canaanites, and its early history is therefore tied to that of the other littoral cities of Acre/Ptolemais, Tyre, Sidon, Byblos and Aradus. During the Late Bronze Age (c.1550-1200 BCE) these cities formed part of the trading network that linked Canaan to

---

[17] Khalidi 1992, 194. The name al-*Tantura* (in Arabic (الطنطورة)) means «The Peak,» a reference to its position on a cliff.
[18] Buckingham 1822, 121-123.
[19] Rogers 1862, 92. Mary Rogers' *Domestic Life in Palestine* contributes significantly to a distinctive tradition of British women's travel writing about the Middle East. In the book she also adds that the stones of Dora are gradually being used to build up Tantura (92).
[20] Thomson 1859, 498. An ordained Presbyterian minister, Thomson was a missionary in Syria and Palestine until 1849. Having devoted his life to the verification of the Scriptures, Thomson was accepted as an authority by biblical archaeologists.
[21] Dahl 1915, 8.
[22] Benvenisti 2000, 50. See also Raban 1988, 277.
[23] Khalidi 1992, 194. The author's information comes from Conder, C. R. and H. H. Kitchener (1881): *The Survey of Western Palestine.* London: Committee of the Palestine Exploration Fund. Sometime around 1880, Jewish pioneers from Zikhron Ya'aqov bought 30 hectares of the marsh-ridden land of *al-Tantura* for Baron Edmond de Rothschild, who financed the establishment of a bottle factory there for the developing wine industry in Zikhron Ya'aqov. A building was constructed and glass specialists were brought in from France; however, the factory was abandoned in 1895. The building today hosts the Tel Dor Archaeological Museum and the labs of the site.
[24] Hadawi 1970, 28. Hadawi (1904-2004) was born in Jerusalem to Arab Christian parents and worked as a clerk for the Land Registration Office for the British Mandate until 1948. In 1952 he became a land specialist for the United Nations Conciliation Commission for Palestine in New York.
[25] Benvenisti 2000, 19.
[26] The allegation that a massacre of the civilian population of al-Tantura was committed in 1948 by The Alexandroni Brigade in the War of Independence is under investigation by the Israeli authorities. See Benvenisti 2000, 19-25.
[27] Jerome's Latin translation of Eusebius' *Onomasticon* states, "Dor Nafeth, quod Symmachus transtulit Dor maritima. Haec est Dora in nono miliario Caesarea Palastinae pergentibus Tyrum, nunc deserta" (79, 8-10) – Dor Nafeth, which Symmachus translated as Dor-on-the-sea. This is the Dora at the ninth milestone from Caesarea of Palestina for those traveling to Tyre, and it is now deserted – my translation); in another passage (137, 16-17), he writes, "Dor autem est oppidum iam desertum in nono miliario Caesareae pergentibus Ptolemaidem" (Dor is however now a deserted town at the ninth milestone of Caesarea for those traveling to Ptolemais). Finally, writing about places in the Scriptures, Jerome writes in 404 CE that pilgrims visiting Philistia would see "ruinas Dor, urbis quondam potentissimae" – the ruins of Dor, once a most powerful city" (*Ep.* 108, 8). For more on Eusebius Onomasticon, see Notley and Ze'ev 2005. For inscriptions on Byzantine Dor, see Di Segni 1994, 183-186.
[28] Roger 1862, 75.
[29] The most important one is Fureidis, an Israeli Arab town established in the nineteenth century and only five km from Tel Dor. See Morris 1984.

Egypt, Mycenae, Syria-Palestine and Mesopotamia. The identification of the Canaanites with the Phoenicians has been discussed for centuries. Ancient Greek historians and geographers had already determined the features that defined these populations as Phoenicians — a name that appears for the first time in Homer and Hesiod (c. eighth century BCE)[30] and that has no equivalent in the eastern languages.[31] The original Greek name *phoinix* and its derivatives *phoinissa* and *phoinikes* were in fact used by the Greeks to designate the people of the Levant and in particular the eastern traders who frequented the waters of the Aegean.[32] The origin of the Greek word is still unknown, although one study draws its origin from the Greek word for red, *phoinix* — a possible allusion to the purple dye industry already famous during Homer's time. Other linguistic studies draw from the Ugarit and Hebrew or even the Egyptian languages.[33] The Hebrew Bible uses the name *kena'anim* or *kananaioi* to designate the inhabitants of the coastal plain area of northern Israel, where Dor was located.[34] In the sixth century BCE, Hecateus of Miletus mentions that *Phoinike* had previously been called *Chna*, and in the fifth century CE, Saint Augustine mentions that in his day the Carthaginians referred to themselves as *Chanani*.[35] According to nineteenth century scholar John Kenrick, "The Phoenicians appear to have known their country by no other name than that of Canaan,"[36] referring to themselves as Canaanites, [37] 'Punic' is an identity that is attested only in literary sources of people other than the Phoenicians themselves, and literary expression tells us more about the author(s) of the sources and their own culture than about the identity of "that social group as an historical or a social actor."[38] Today's scholars tend to use the term 'Canaanite' to designate the populations who spoke a North West Semitic language and lived in the territory of Syria-Palestine from the beginning of the second millennium until 1200 BCE; from that point on, the same people are then called 'Phoenicians.' In her book *The Phoenicians and the West,* for example, the Spanish author Maria Eugenia Aubet claims that the Canaanites and the Phoenicians were the same people since they "had a common historical, geographical, cultural and linguistic base" and that the separation of these peoples establishes "an artificial barrier between the Bronze Age and the Iron Age, conferring different chronological connotations on

the two terms."[39] Presently, it is customary to consider the Phoenicians the successors of the Canaanites from the end of the first millennium BCE – a period in which the Phoenicians first appear along the northern coast of Israel and at Dor.[40]

The earliest reference to Canaanite/Phoenician Dor appears on the *Onomasticon of Amenope*, a list of the coastal cities inscribed on the temple of El-Amra in Nubiaduring during the reign of Ramses II, who ruled Egypt from 1279 to 1213 BCE.[41] Another source is a papyrus from el-Hibeth in Egypt, dated to the 21st Dynasty – around 1100 BCE — that tells the story of Wen-Amon, an Egyptian official who was sent to Byblos to buy cedar logs for the sacred barge of Amon, making a reference to Tjeker, who supposedly inhabited Dor.[42]

Archaeological material from the nearly thirty years of excavations at Tel Dor reveals a continuous stratigraphic sequence of Phoenician material that stretches from the early Iron Age until the Assyrian occupation in the seventh century BCE.[43] Dor's city planning during the Phoenician Period seems to have followed the "modified contour plan," typical of most southern Phoenician towns, showing that most streets appear "to follow the contours of the mound, possibly encircling the town."[44] Many important public buildings were built during this period. Furthermore, this time saw the development of the typical Phoenician economy centered on trade, purple dye industry, shipbuilding, and fishing and there is ample evidence of overseas contact with Cyprus, Egypt, Philistia, and possibly Syria.[45]

Additionally, recent petrographic analyses of early Iron Age commercial containers in Cyprus verify that much of this pottery was in fact produced in the Carmel region, possibly at Dor.[46] In fact, the large amount of early Iron Age pottery in reliable contexts available at Tel Dor and the evidence of inter-regional ceramic types make it possible to build a framework of absolute chronology for the Phoenician Period, not just at Dor, but in all of northern Israel and Lebanon (Fig. **1.5**).[47]

The Assyrian army reached Palestine in 733 BCE when King Tiglath-Pileser III took military action against the Phoenician cities of southern Syria-Palestine and for

[30] Allen and Rambaut 1915, 85-99.

[31] Homer at times used the term 'Phoenician' to evoke a negative character, as he described the Phoenicians as "opportunistic merchants who populate bustling harbors," but used "Sidonian" in reference to makers of silver vessels. See J. Winter 1995, 256-7, 263.

[32] Aubet 1993, 9.

[33] According to P. King (2001, 161) the word 'Canaan' and 'Phoenician', are cognates meaning purple. The word 'Canaan' is Akkadian *kinahnu*, 'red purple', while 'Phoenicia' comes from the Greek *phinos*, 'dark red.' One theory has sought the origin of the Greek *phoinix* in the Ugarit *puwwa* or the Hebrew *pwt* – 'dye' or 'substance.' Another one connects *phoinix* to the Egyptian word *fnhw*; however, the Egyptians called Phoenicia *Retenu* or *Har'w*. See Aubet 1993, 10.

[34] According to Maisler (1946, 7), in biblical Hebrew, *cana'ani* or *kina'nu* means 'merchant,' so Canaan would be the 'land of merchants.'

[35] Saint Augustine, *Epistula* 13. See Aubet 1993, 10.

[36] Kenrick 1855, 42. See also Martin 2006.

[37] Exod. 6,15.16,35. Josh 5,12. Job, 40, 25. See Kenrick 1855, 42 fn. 3.

[38] Prag 2006, 30.

[39] Aubet 1993, 10. For further studies concerning the identification of Canaanites and Phoenicians, see Brody 1997, 1999; Moscatti 1968, 1988; Gray 1964; Prag 2006.

[40] Stern 1990, 27-34.

[41] Pritchard (1969, 25-29) notes that Ramses II (also known as Ramesses The Great) was the third Egyptian pharaoh of the nineteenth dynasty. He is often regarded as Egypt's most powerful pharaoh, having marked a place in history with his military campaigns, and is credited to have been the Pharaoh of the Exodus (Eusebius of Caesarea).

[42] Stern 1990, 28.

[43] Gilboa et al 2009, 113. Stern 2013.

[44] Shalev and Martin 2012, 89-94.

[45] Gilboa et al 2009, 117. The open area of the Persian period was riddled with pits, some containing refuse of the purple dye industry. See *Tel Dor Season Reports*, 2005.

[46] Ibid.

[47] Ibid.

FIG. 1.5 PHOENICIAN BICHROM VESSEL FROM TEL DOR (AREA D2

excavated at Dor show a distinct Assyrian style – two seals and pottery of the type known as Assyrian style, which was not only imported but also produced locally (Figs **1.6** and **1.7**).[50]

The precise date when the Levant was incorporated in the Achaemenid Empire is still the object of scholarly debate, but after the Achaemenid Kings of Persia conquered the coastal area of Syro-Palestine, the Persian satrap used local leadership to administer the small areas for the imperial Achaemenid government.[51] The northwestern area of Syro-Palestine, which extended along the Carmel and Sharon coast to Jaffa, fell therefore under the administration of the local city-states Sidon, Akko and Tyre.

Although designated as a provincial capital, Dor was under the administration of Sidon for much of the Persian period, as it appears that the city had been granted to the king of Sidon. The epitaph of Eshmunazar records that

The Lord of Kings gave us Dor and Joppa, the rich lands of Dagon which are in the plain of Sharon, as a reward for the deeds which I performed; and we added to the border of the land that might belong to the Sidonians forever" (Fig. **1.8**). [52]

Caubet and Prévotat describe the artifact as the "Sarcophagus of Eshmunazar II, King of Sidon Achaemenid Persian period, first quarter of fifth century BCE."[53] There is, however, a debate on the dating of the Eshmunazar II inscription, since the Persian king in the text is unnamed and there and there is no firm fixed point for Eshmunazar's reign. While V. Jigoulov's attempts to date the text to the reign of Xerxes based on scattered Herodotean references to the King of Sidon in the Persian navy, Josette Elayi favors an early date in the late sixth century.[54]

A date of the Eshmunazar II sarcophagus (Tl) at ca. 525 BCE could be tied to the reorganization and reoccupation of the coastal area and Dor, although there is very little material at Dor that can be dated to the period from 539-500.[55] Similarly, land grants to the Sidonian king could refer, according to Littman, to the Persian need for shipbuilding and manning of the fleet after the heavy loss of ships at Eurymedon.[56] Also possible is that the rich wheat

much of the eighth and seventh centuries, Dor and the neighboring cities were subject to Assyrian rule. The entire coastal area became an Assyrian province called Du'ru, with the city of Dor, which had been part of a short-lived Israelite kingdom, as the alleged capital of the province.[48] Dor's importance continued to be in its Phoenician fleet and its control of the maritime commerce, and its Phoenician identity is clearly visible in Dor's material culture. In the Assyrians' attempt to conquer and control Egypt, Dor became an important harbor to supply food and equipment for the army, and its port became a supply depot. Assyrian rule in Palestine came to an end, however, in the middle of the seventh century and Dor was abandoned through the sixth century and until the early fifth century when it was again reoccupied.[49] Despite the relative brevity of the Assyrian rule of Dor and the predominantly Phoenician character of the city during that period, two types of finds

---

[48] Millar 1993, 266. According to biblical sources (1 *Kings* 4:11) Dor had been incorporated into David and Solomon's Israelite kingdom, and was governed by the king's son-in-law, Abinadab, husband of Tafath. "And Solomon had twelve officers over all Israel, who provided victuals for the king and his household: each man had to make provision for a month in the year. And these are their names: ... Ben-Abinadab, in Naphoth Dor (all the height of Dor); Taphath the daughter of Solomon was his wife*."* For more on the Assyrian capture of Israel, see Orlinsky 1981, 1063.

[49] Leick 2003, 61. In 605 BCE when Babylonian army led by Nebuchadnezzar II defeated the Assyrian and Egyptian army at Carchemish, destroying the Assyrian Empire, Dor and other Levantine cities were abandoned as a consequence of Babylonian destruction. See Martin 2009, 94.

[50] Stern (2000, 131-145) notes that one seal, made of reddish granite, is engraved with the typical Assyrian motif of a king standing between two griffins, while the other, of certain Mesopotamian provenance, depicts the king of Assyria offering a gift to the god Asshur. The bulk of pottery consists mostly of bowls (or bowl fragments) that imitate Assyrian metal bowls. One complete vessel, a clay bottle with a pointed base, bears strong local characteristics, since the looped handles, according to Stern (146), represent a blending of local and Assyrian elements. See also Gilboa 1992.

[51] Martin 2009, 94.

[52] Gibson 1982, 107, 109.

[53] Caubet. and.Prévotat (Louvre Museum, AO 4806).

[54] Jigoulov 2010, 51-55; Elay and Elay 2004, 5-6.

[55] Martin 2009, 94.

[56] Betlyon 2005, 11; Littman 2001, 170. The naval Battle of the Eurymedon took place in 466 BC on the Eurymedon River in Pamphylia in Asia Minor, and was fought between the Athenian-led Delian League and Persia. The Athenians destroyed 200 Phoenician ships.

FIG. 1.6 ASSYRIAN CYLINDRICAL SEAL – TEL DOR PHOTO ARCHIVE

FIG. 1.7. SHERDS OF ASSYRIAN STYLE BOWLS (TEL DOR PHOTO ARCHIVE)

FIG. 1.8. SARCOPHAGUS OF ESHMUNAZAR II, KING OF SIDON. LOUVRE MUSEUM. AO 4806.

lands might have been granted to Sidon for the supply of food for the shipbuilders and the craftsmen during intense naval construction. [57]

Under the Persian/Sidonian rule, Dor's Phoenician affiliation remained very strong, and the Achaemenids used Dor's Phoenician shipbuilding and shipping to transfer luxuries and raw materials from abroad and to transport their armies during wartime. Phoenician building technique was used as well, and some of the Iron Age walls were incorporated into the city's external perimeter. Excavations of the later Persian phase, however, have revealed that the population also adopted Persian artistic styles, as shown by the wide parallel streets, intersected by narrower streets lined with domestic structures.[58] The well-

ordered street system of the Persian period had initially been ascribed to an orthogonal layout of the city, but more recent excavations have proved that Dor's urban plan is "a modified contour plan," with streets that follow the curves of the mound and possibly go around the town.[59]

1.4 Historical Identity: Greek Dora

The rivalry between the Persians and the Greeks for supremacy over the Eastern Mediterranean grew fierce over time, resulting in a series of wars that ended in 450 BCE and Persian intervention in the Spartan-Athenian conflicts (431-404 BCE). Since the Persians were primarily a land power, the Phoenicians provided the fleet, therefore playing a significant role in the Persian strategy against the Greeks.[60] This competition was not all destructive, however. It was during this three-hundred-year period in fact, that the impact of Greek culture started

---

[57] According to Herodotus 6.48, Darius ordered "tributary cities of the sea-coast to build warship and horse transport." Cited in Littman 2001, 170. Additionally, as suggested by John Hyland (personal interview 9/8/2014), "fleet of more than 100 triremes required crews of 20,000 or more, with substantial logistical needs after construction was completed and a campaign was launched."
[58] Stern et al 1995.

[59] Shalev and Martin 2012, 89.
[60] For an in-depth study of the Greek-Persian wars, see Green 1996.

to be manifested in the coastal regions of the Southern Levant and at Dor. According to W.F. Albright, numerous Greek emporia were established on the coast of Palestine and Syria in or before the sixth century BCE.[61] Unlike the Greek colonies of the West, however, the Greek population in these Phoenician cities did not constitute a majority of the inhabitants, and the Greek settlements were not real colonies, neither an *apoikia* nor a *klerouchia*; rather, each settlement had the character of an *enoikismos* — a coexistence of a foreign Greek element in an already populated city.[62]

The contact between the Greeks and other people and lands outside the Aegean sphere is documented in literary sources. Within the ancient Greek worldview, the authors, often historians or geographers, mapped the geographical periphery, the *eschata,* often describing landscapes that differed from the Greek *oikoumene* and cultures that they considered less civilized than their own.[63] Most often, Greek authors emphasized what made other people foreign and different.[64] Homer, for instance, uses the Phoenicians as the counterpoints of the Greek heroes.[65] The sea captain described by Odysseus is a man well versed in guile (*apatelia eidos*), a greedy knave (*troktes*) who had already wrought much evil among men, who tricks Odysseus with cunning persuasion (*parpepithon heisi phresin*), and who gives false counsel (*pseudea bouleusas*).[66] Although some scholars argue against interpreting Homer's epithets and attributes as negative stereotypes,[67] negative views of Easterners are also found in the works of Plato in the fourth century. In his *Laws*, we find Egyptians, Phoenicians, and other Easterners being accused of having a "narrow minded outlook" on life and wealth; and in the *Republic*, he also mentions the greed of the Egyptians and the Phoenicians.[68] However, the negative eastern stereotype coexisted with emulation of elite eastern society,[69] as Homer himself writes about a "well-wrought Phoenician silver krater" brought by a Sidonian craftsman as a gift to the king of Troy.[70] Homer's mention of the Phoenician silver krater is not far from reality, as exchange of eastern luxury goods was very common in Greek cities for high-status competition or ostentatious display of wealth, and Eastern

material culture has been found in various contexts and sites throughout the Greek world and especially in Greek sanctuaries as evidence of Greece's important trade with the East.[71] In reality, while describing 'the other,' i.e., the non-Greek, either in a positive or more often negative light, Greek writers were perhaps pondering their own ethnicity and their role as colonizers.[72] In fact, the engagement between Greeks and 'others' on a Mediterranean-wide scale, during the period of Greek overseas expansions reveals a deep complexity of intercultural contacts in all cities along the Mediterranean, including Dor.

Hecataeus of Miletus is the first Greek author to mention Dor in his section on Asia in the fifth century CE.[73] It is not possible, however, to establish for certain that the Dor mentioned by Hecataeus corresponds to the Phoenician Dor, or that an Athenian military or political presence existed in the city during the fifth century BCE. Nevertheless, clear contacts with Greek speakers are well attested by the discovery of abundant Cypriot and Attic material at Dor from throughout the Persian period.[74] Greek graffiti on Persian-period pottery attest that a part of the population of Dor at the beginning of the fourth period was Greek speaking, and it is even possible that Greek-speaking merchants might have settled at Dor, perhaps living in distinct quarters in the previously discussed style of an *enoikismos*.[75]

Although the city was, as previously discussed, heavily influenced by Greek culture prior to Greek military occupation, the Macedonian conquest in 332 CE was a turning point in the city's history, as evidenced by the ancient Semitic name of Dor being changed to the Greek-sounding name *Doros or Dora*.[76] Alexander the Great conquered the city on his march from Tyre to Gaza and Egypt in 332.[77] Following his death in 323 BCE and the

[61] Albright 1963, 124. For Greek colonies in the region, see Boardman 1999; Tsetskhladze 2006.
[62] Osborne 1997, 260. See also Figueira 2006, 427-521.
[63] Kroeber (1945, 9) notes that the "Greeks gave the name *oikoumene* to the world that stretched from the Pillars of Hercules to the Indians and the Seres." See also Whitley 2001, 376. For more on Greeks and others, see Romm 1992; Cohen 2000.
[64] For the Greek authors' views of the Persian Empire, see Briant 2002.
[65] Winter 1995, 247.
[66] Homer, *Odyssey* 14. 287-297. For more on Homer's view of the Phoenicians, see Winter, 1995: 256-57, 263. For racism in classical antiquity, see Isaac's *The Invention of Racism in Classical Antiquity* (2004). For a study of how the Phoenicians were viewed in ancient times, see Mazza 1988.
[67] Hall (2002, 117-118) offers counterpoint to Winter's arguments, definitely against interpreting Homer's Phoenicians as an ethnic stereotype. See also Hall 1997.
[68] *Plato, Law*, V. 747 and *Republic*, IV. 435-6. In *Panegyricus* (150-151), Isocrates also writes that Persians lack virtue because they are raised indulging "their bodies in the luxury of the riches." See Isaac 2004, 285.
[69] Martin, 2007, 6.
[70] In *Iliad* XIII.740-9, Achilles offers the silver krater to Patroclus as a prize at the funeral games.

[71] Burkert 1992, 14-24. There are individual imported pieces starting from the tenth and ninth centuries, although the number of pieces seems to increase in the eighth and seventh centuries.
[72] On his commentary of Herodotus' *Histories*, Hartog (1988, xix) calls Herodotus "the first historian, …a great artist … a liar."
[73] Hecataeus, mentioned by Stephanus of Byzantium, a sixth century CE Greek geographer, writes, "Ancient Doros, now however called Dora" (*FGrH*, 342). Dahl (1936, 62 – 65) explains that Hecataeus could have not known the name Dora, since the change occurred during the Hellenistic times. According to Dahl (1936, 65), later Greek authors mention the city as 'Dora' -- Apollodorus in 140 BCE and Artemidorus of Ephesus, who in 103 BCE writes, "adjacent to Strato's Tower comes Dora, a small town situated upon a peninsula, near the beginning of Mt. Carmel." Finally, Alexander Ephesius mentions "both Dor bordering the water and Joppa jutting into the sea" (Meineke 2010, 374).
[74] Stewart and Martin 2005, 79-94; Littman 2001, 161. For a thorough study of pre-Hellenistic material culture at Dor, see Stern 1995. For Greek expansion overseas, see Boardman 1999; 2002b. The numismatic evidence will be covered in Chapter 4.
[75] Albright's (1966) assumption that Greeks might have lived at Dor in its pre-Hellenic period is, however, highly disputed by Stewart and Martin (2005, 10), since the use of Greek fine wares does not prove the Greek ethnicity of the user.
[76] From this period on, the Greek/Roman name will be used to refer to the city.
[77] The 2009 Tel Dor Excavations produced a gemstone with the portrait of Alexander the Great. The gemstone was found in the remains of a large public building from the Hellenistic period in the southern area of the tell, and it is unpublished. The discovery might bring light to the theory that Alexander himself passed through Dor in 332 BCE, during his voyage to Egypt. It appears that the city fell to him without resistance.

FIG. 1.9. PERSIAN AND HELLENISTIC DOR (TEL DOR PHOTO ARCHIVE)

division of the Macedonian empire among his generals, Dora's destiny was tied to the Ptolemaic Empire of Egypt and under its rule from 296 to 201 BCE. During the various wars that ensued between the Ptolomies of Egypt and the Seleucids of the East, Dora was besieged several times and subsequently ruled by the Seleucids from 200 to 104 BCE, although there is little evidence of any major political distinction between the 'Phoenician' cities and the 'Greek' foundations of the Hellenistic world.[78]

Archaeological excavations at Tel Dor have revealed extensive evidence of the transformation of the Phoenician-Persian Dor into a Hellenistic city (Fig. **1.9**). The literary sources are few, but it can be discerned from Josephus that Dor was "a fortress difficult to conquer,"[79] and from Polybius that when Antiochus the Great laid siege to the city in 219 BCE, he failed to subdue it.[80] Indeed, excavations indicate that in the middle of the third century, an ashlar casemate wall with square towers at 45-m intervals fortified the city, which is divided in quarters by two intersecting roads (Figs. **1.10**). The houses are situated on the east and the south, the religious sanctuaries in the west, the warehouses and workshops near the southern port, and the public sports and recreational facilities in

the north.[81] The streets are narrow, with shops on both sides of the east-west street, which led to the sea, to the *agora*, and to the central sanctuary. The town reached the peak of its prosperity during this period, and although it is very difficult to establish exactly when the process of Hellenization took place or how quickly Dor could be considered 'Hellenized,' Greek and Greek-influenced material goods are very pervasive.[82] Pottery vessels of various types, from stamped wares to ordinary Hellenistic pottery (Fig. **1. 11**), including oil lamps, wine amphorae and braziers, have been found together with objects such as a marble herm, an *opus vermiculatum* mosaic of the mask-and-garland type (Fig. **1.12**), and an *akroterion* shaped like the goddess Nike. Military objects are also abundant, such as a small bulla imprinted with a phalanx, arrowheads shot from bows, a catapult-propelled spearhead, inscribed clay and lead sling projectiles, and many ballista and rolling stones, some of which are marked with Greek letters indicating their weight.[83]

In spite of the very large amount of Greek material culture, the character of the population continued to be Phoenician as is evidenced by the persistence of typical Phoenician ashlar masonry for private buildings. In fact, Greek construction styles in private buildings did not become predominant until after the middle of the second

See news release on the gemstone at http://dor.huji.ac.il/Dor_Alexander_gem.html.
[78] Grainger 1992, 66. See also Berlin 1997, 2-51.
[79] Josephus, *Antiquities* 13. 7. 12.
[80] Polybius, *The Histories*, V. 66.

[81] Nitschke 2001, 139.
[82] Stern 2000, 201-260.
[83] Martin 2007, 119 158; Ehrlich 2010, 15-26 (Hebr).

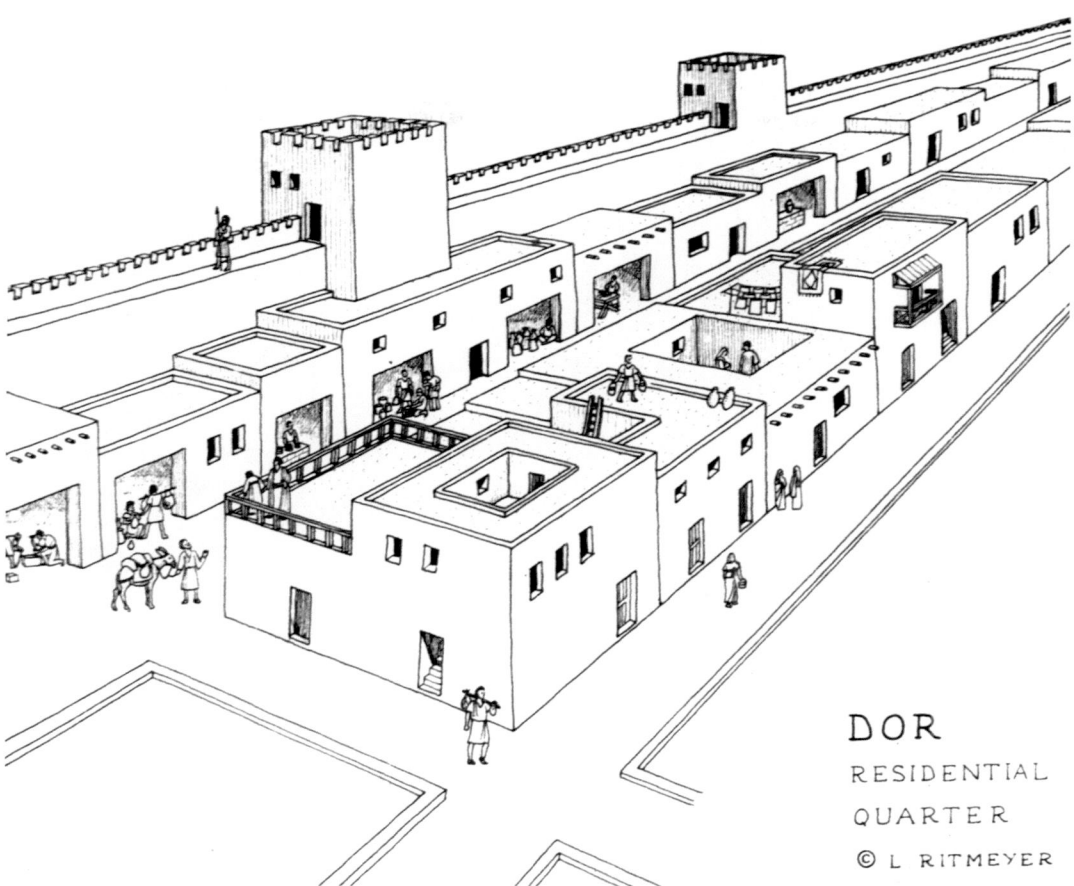

Fig. 1. 10. Reconstruction of Eastern Continuous Outer Wall During the Hellenistic Period

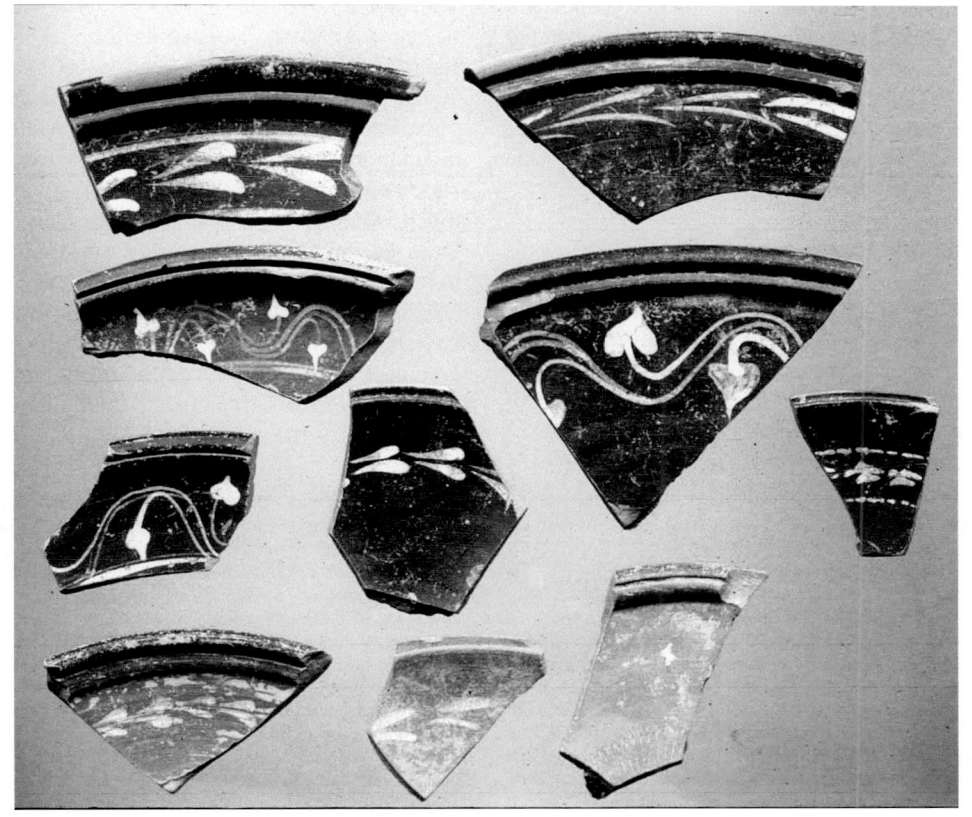

Fig. 1.11. Imported Hellenistic West Slope' Ware found at Tel Dor

FIG. 1.12. OPUS VERMICULATUM OF THE MASK AND GARLAND TYPE (TEL DOR PHOTO ARCHIVE)

century.[84] The Phoenician textile-dyeing industry also continued, as proved by the large quantities of loom weights, spindle wheels and dyeing installations. The local Phoenician language persisted even as the population became increasingly Hellenized and evidence points to a bilingual city for some time. A sling bullet, shot against the ruler Tryphon during the dynastic conflicts, is inscribed in both Greek and Phoenician (Fig. **1.13**).[85] These aspects of traditional Phoenician culture that persisted well into the Hellenistic period and even Roman times reveal the true nature of Dora's Phoenician society.

1.5 Historical Identity: Hasmonean Dora

After the Jewish revolt against Antioch IV in 167 BCE and the defeat of the Seleucid army by Judah Maccabeus in 165 BCE, the Jews achieved political independence.[86] The Roman Senate recognized the Jewish state in 139 BCE, de facto establishing the Hasmonean dynasty under the leadership of Simon Maccabeus.[87] Dora was itself the site of various battles during the dynastic wars between Tryphon, who took the rule from the infant son of

Alexander Balas, and Antioch VII Sidetes. At first Tryphon found allies in Judea; after marching into Judea, however, and murdering Jonathan the Hasmonean in a battle near Jerusalem, he fled to Dora. With the support of Simon Maccabeus, Jonathan's brother, Antiochus VII Sidetes besieged Tryphon, blockading the city both by land and sea.[88] The Hellenistic fortifications of Dora withstood the attack, and Dora did not fall to the Hasmoneans until 35 years later, when King Alexander Jannaeus, exploiting the disintegration of the Seleucid Empire, extended the Jewish state into Galilee and conquered the city in 104 BCE.[89] Not much is known about the size of the Jewish population of Dora during the forty years of Hasmonean rule and not much Jewish material culture has been excavated at Tel Dor. It can be assumed, however, that Jewish citizens must have moved there, since, according to Josephus, Pompey's conquest in 64/3 BCE "deprived the Jews of the cities, which they had conquered,"[90] and Dor is listed among those cities.

[84] Sharon 1987, 22. See also Sharon 2009.
[85] Gera 1985, 491-496. See also Shatzman 1991, 94; Fischer 1992, 30.
[86] Levine 1998, 38-45. The origin of the Hasmonean dynasty is recorded in the Books of Maccabees, considered part of the Biblical canon by the Catholic and Eastern Orthodox churches, but apocryphal by Protestantism and modern-day Judaism. The mentioning of 'Dora' in the text, however, sheds light on the annexation of Dora to the Jewish kingdom. For more on Jewish history, see Ben-Sasson 1976; Grant 1984; Learsi 1947.
[87] According to Livy, "Popilius...placed in [Antiochus'] hand the tablets on which was written the decree of the senate [to withdraw]...[and] drew a circle round the king with the stick he was carrying and said, 'Before you step out of that circle give me a reply to lay before the senate'" (*History of Rome*, 45.12).

[88] Josephus, *Jewish War* 1.7.7. The events are also mentioned in 15 Maccabees: "Wherefore being pursued by king Antiochus, he fled unto Dora, which lieth by the sea side ... Then camped Antiochus against Dora, having with him one hundred and twenty thousand men of war, and eight thousand horsemen" (Maccabees 15:11-13). Tryphon broke the blockade and made his way to Apameia, where he "was hemmed up in a certain place by Antiochus and forced to kill himself" (Strabo 14.5, 2) or was put to death (Appian, *Syriaca* 68). For more on the Seleucid empire, see Pomeroy 1988; Erskine 2003.
[89] Dora and neighboring Straton's Tower (later Caesarea) were at the time under the tyrant Zoilus. When Jannaeus attacked the cities, including Akko, the inhabitants sought help from Ptolemy VIII, but he immediately concluded a pact and ceded Zoilus' possessions to Jannaeus. The Hasmonean conquest is represented by coins of Alexander Jannaeus, which will be discussed later in this chapter.
[90] Josephus, *Jewish War* 1.7.7.

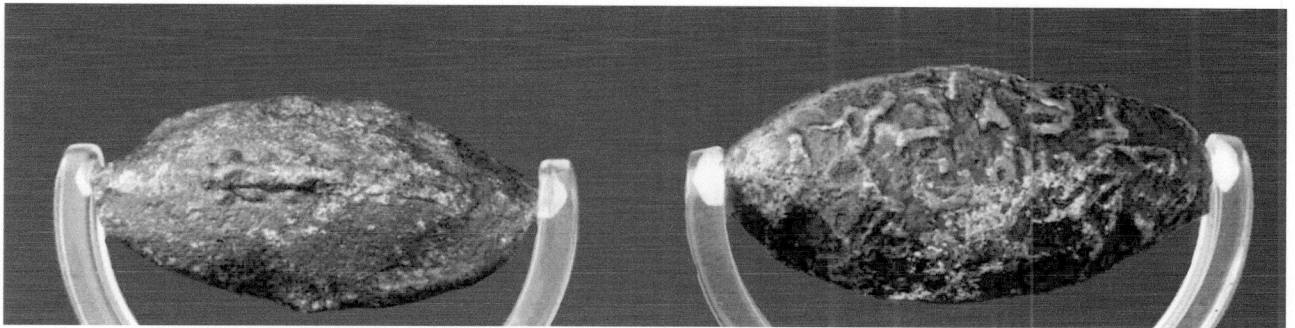

FIG. 1.13. LEAD SLING PROJECTILE INSCRIBED IN GREEK AND PHOENICIAN (TEL DOR PHOTO ARCHIVE)

1.6 Historical Identity: Roman Dora

The Roman history of Dora started in 63 BCE with the arrival of Pompey the Great in Syria, as a consequence of his military victory in the Third Mithridatic War (73-63 BCE).[91] During the later second and early first centuries BCE, Rome had extended her influence in the Eastern Mediterranean, and local rulers were wary of acting against Roman interests. Mithridates VI of Pontus, however, challenged Rome, waging three wars that ended with a final victory for Pompey the Great in the spring of 63 BCE. The conflicts, which had focused in Asia Minor and Parthia and involved several other states because of dynastic feuds, resulted in the annexation of Syria.[92] Aulus Gabinius was appointed proconsul of Syria by Pompey and restored Dora from Jewish Hasmonean rule to its autonomous status of a *polis* in 57 BCE, annexing it to the province of Syria.[93]

Pompey's victory over Mithridates was followed by decades of civil wars in the Roman world. During the civil war between Caesar and Pompey, most of the Roman troops in Syria were withdrawn to assist Pompey's cause and cities in the Near East were asked to supply money, recruits and ships.[94] Although there is no documentation of Dora's involvement in the conflict, it can be assumed that the port must have been used by Pompey's troops to some extent. Caesar toured the east shortly after the death of Pompey, honoring cities throughout the near east. After the death of Caesar and the ensuing battle between the republican armies and Caesar's supporters, the Syrian province was lost to the Parthians in 40 BCE.[95] Mark Antony sent a deputy, Publius Ventidius Bassus, to successfully recover it in 39 BCE. However, when a conflict broke out between

Octavian and Antony, the latter sought the support of the Ptolemaic queen Cleopatra, making territorial concessions to her. In 37-36 BCE, Cleopatra acquired the coastal cities between Orthosia, Berytus and Damascus, and according to Josephus, Dora was also awarded to Cleopatra in 35 BCE.[96]

Late in 30 BCE, after the death of Antony and Cleopatra and the annexation of Egypt to the empire, Octavian arrived in the East, forcing local dynasties to renegotiate their status within the Roman sphere. Herod, King of Judea, was successful in his affirmation of loyalty, and Octavian rewarded him by adding Jericho, the coastal region south of Dor and the region east of the Sea of Galilee to the kingdom of Judea. In 23 BCE, Herod was also given the Bashan, Horen, and Tarchon regions, and three years later, the Golan Heights (Fig. **1.2**); however, the city of Dora remained part of the province of Syria throughout Roman times and until it was abandoned in the third century CE.[97]

Much of the archaeological and historical analyses of the Roman province of Syria have revolved around the strong Greek influence and the small impact of Roman rule.[98] Some scholars argue that the region had such a rich Hellenistic heritage before the arrival of the Romans that it maintained a remarkable degree of independence in the Roman period.[99] The presumed superior Greek culture is seen as impenetrable and influencing Roman culture rather than the other way around. R. McMullen writes, "The Romans had nothing but respect for the Greek and Hellenized culture … the intruders would defer to the local custom, would already be converts to it."[100] This implication is, however, untenable.[101] As stated by De

[91] Butcher (2003, 33-35) notes that the Third Mithridatic War (73-63 BCE) was the last of the three wars fought between Mithridates VI of Pontus and his allies and the Roman Republic.

[92] During the occupation of Syria by Tigranes, son-in-law of Mithridates and king of Armenia, the Roman general restored Antiochus XIII to the throne of Damascus, but he was subsequently dismissed for fear that his rule would cause instability in the area.

[93] The coins minted at Dora, however, have 63 BCE as year 1 of the city's history.

[94] Butcher 2003, 36.

[95] Butcher (2003, 27, 49, 95) notes that the mints of Antioch and Apamea stopped issuing coins with the Roman dates, and reverted to dating by the Seleucid era.

[96] Josephus, *Antiquities* 14. 5. 3 and 15. 4.1; *The Jewish War* 1.7.7.

[97] According to Josephus, the city of Dora was given back to Herod, but the fact is not mentioned in other sources.

[98] Mommsen 1906, 127. Roman Syria is cited as a province where little or no Romanization occurred; rather, the Romans themselves were heavily influenced in their contact with the eastern province.

[99] Kennedy 1999, 79-80. See also Drijvers 1980, 77. For an opposing view see Colledge 1987; Downey 1988; De Jong 2007. According to their studies, the tradition of studying Syria as a hub of Hellenism has often obscured not only the Roman element but also the local pre-Hellenic diversity of the local cultures and communities.

[100] MacMullen 2000, 1-2

[101] That Romans considered Greeks superior is highly disputable. Roman literary sources attest to the opposite. Cicero's *Pro Flacco* attacks the character of the witnesses from Asia, whom he describes as typical

FIG. 1.14. AERIAL VIEW OF ROMAN DORA (TEL DOR PHOTO ARCHIVE)

Jong, alternative readings of material culture in the entire province show that Rome's coming to Syria resulted in definite changes in the economic, social, and material culture of the province.[102] According to Graf, the southern part of the province of Syria was less Hellenized than previously thought, with few signs of self-governing polis-structures.[103] Consequently, after the Romans annexed the province, a reshuffling of local structures took place; the Roman preference for the city as a government unit must have had a deep impact on the whole region.[104]

The Romanization that took place in the cities of Syria as well as in cities of Palestine-Judea is evident not just in the typically Roman constructions of military bridges and defense borders or in the imported material culture of the region — the huge quantities of pottery and imported Roman coins — but most importantly in the minting of Roman coins issued locally.[105]

There is no evidence that Dora, located in the southern part of the province of Syria and far from the legionary garrisons of the north, hosted any Roman legions. However, the very existence of a city mint issuing imperial coins and the far-reaching distribution of those coins as attested by coin finds throughout Israel are evidence of the importance of Roman Dora.[106] In fact, the city reached its greatest physical extent in the Roman period, and archaeological evidence shows that Dora's infrastructures

provincial Greek — fickle, irresponsible, dishonest, and completely unreliable (27.65). In contrast to Greek untrustworthiness and vices, Polybius' *Histories* presents the Roman military system, the Roman aristocratic funeral, Roman religious practices, and Roman financial probity as indication of a superior *politeia* based upon the exercise of reason (6.56.13-15; see also 18.34.7).

[102] Jong 2007, 2. In most Romanization studies, the model used is, according to Jong, problematic since it defines the term 'Roman' both in temporal (after the conquest) and geographical (coming from Italy) terms.

[103] Graf 1992, 3-5, 22. According to the author, the cities of pre-Roman Syria were a bunch of fortified towns and villages, dominated by petty kings, local tyrants and chiefs.

[104] Butcher 2003, 223, 270.

[105] Although coins had been minted in the Phoenician world much earlier than the arrival of the Romans, at this time coins are produced with the permission of Roman authorities.

[106] The coins from Dora are the topic of my discussion concerning cultural transmission and identifiable Roman characters in Chapter 4.

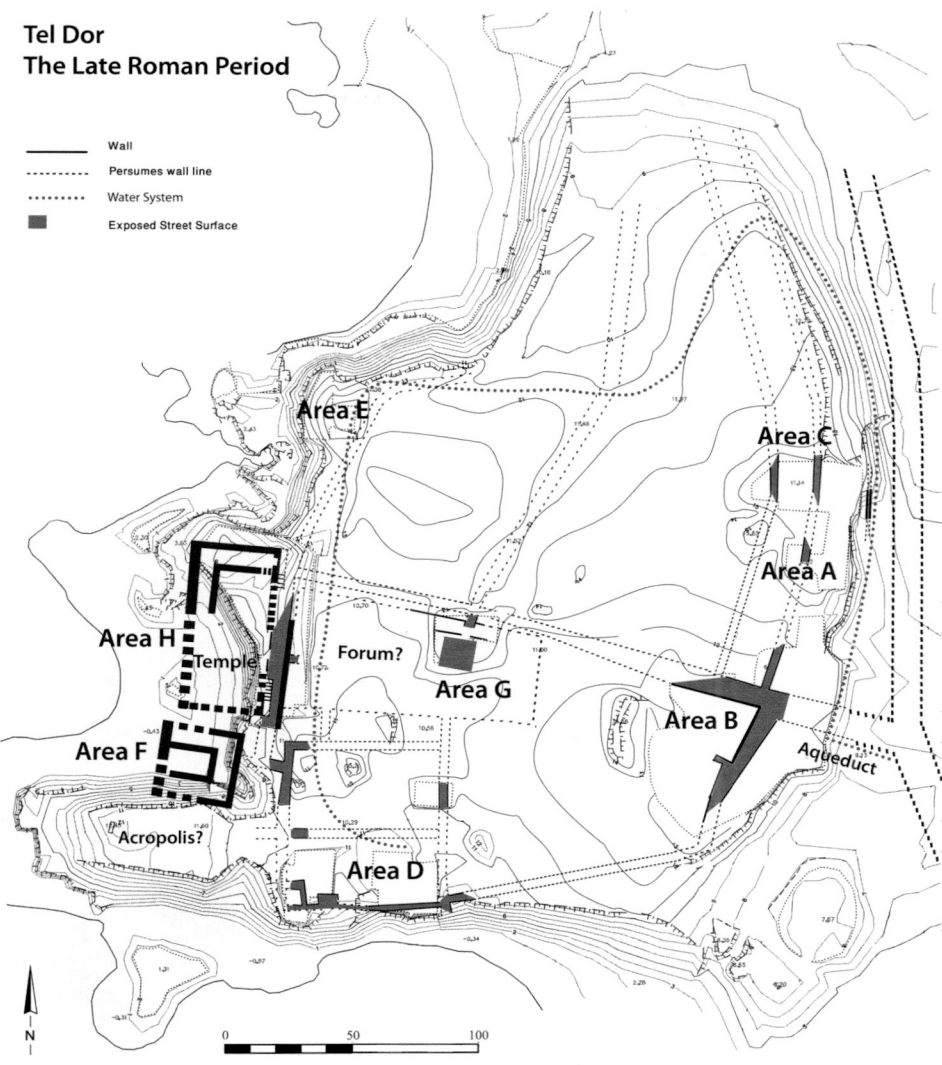

**Tel Dor
The Late Roman Period**

——— Wall

- - - - - - - - Persumes wall line

········· Water System

▇ Exposed Street Surface

Area E

Area C

Area A

Area H

Temple

Forum?

Area G

Area B

Area F

Aqueduct

Acropolis?

Area D

N

0   50   100

FIG. 1.15. EXCAVATIONS OF ROMAN AREAS (IFTAH SHALEV)

underwent a process of Romanization immediately after Pompey's conquest, when Gabinius restored its pre-Hasmonean Hellenistic pagan character.[107] The Hellenistic walls were abandoned early in the period, and the city spread into the plain below, reaching a size of 15 hectares (Fig. **1.14**). Dora's Roman plan shows enlarged streets and the wide use of cement and mortar in the construction of the structures. Among the better-preserved remnants of the Roman city are a sophisticated sewer system; a bathhouse occupying a large lot of land and a terrace above it with a thick Roman wall and concrete floors; a theater, which, although initially built during the Hellenistic period, shows only Roman remains; a large public building of uncertain function surrounding a courtyard; an aqueduct bringing water from Bir Tata in the Carmel Mountains; and ending with a solid concrete foundation, possibly for a *Castelum* (water-tower), from which water was distributed throughout the city in clay pipes. The main E-W street, perhaps the *decumanus maximus* was traced in the center

of the city where it intersected by the main N-S street--the *cardo maximus*, and then probably continued all the way to the main gate of the temple in area F. Both this temple and the one in area H are now considered Late Roman (Fig. **1.15**).[108] The Roman residential areas are best represented in area D2, where there are two phases of building remains, comprising parts of three *insulae*, crisscrossed by two streets,-- the southernmost E-W street (which continues to the west through D1), and the main N-S street(which bisects the town, leading from the southern harbor to area G). One *insula* (the southwestern one) seems to have been occupied by elegant residences, some with mosaic floors (Fig. **1.16**). In the northeast *insula*, a larger more public structure seems to have replaced a residential structure, while the third *insula* (the southeastern one) has industrial installations of indeterminate use.[109] Roman pottery includes clay vessels for everyday use, rhytons, and lamps, while metal objects are pots and pans of bronze

---

[107] Stern 2000, 270. Remains of the early Roman city can be found throughout all the excavation areas, from A to H.

[108] Tel Dor Excavation Reports 2006-13. See http://dor.huji.ac.il/periods_RM.html - accessed 9/7/2014.

[109] Raban 1988, 22.

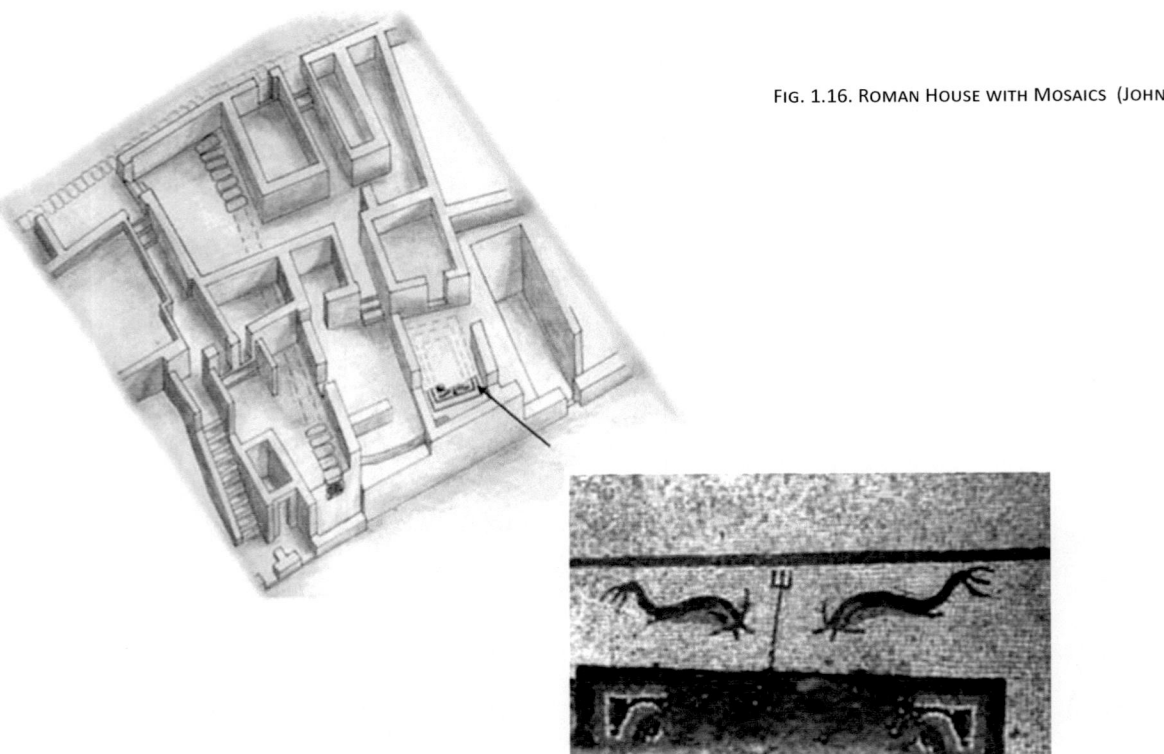

Fig. 1.16. Roman House with Mosaics (John Berg)

and some braziers.[110] Roman jewelry — three seal-stones of carnelian, a gold ring with an engraved carnelian seal-stone, and gold rings and earrings — denote very skilled craftsmanship (Fig. **1.17**).

Some scholars believe that the Roman administrator in the province of Syria often enacted an aggressive policy of actively suppressing any non-Greek cultural institutions in Near East cities in favor of civic Hellenism.[111] The reality must have been much more complex, and a mixing process might have taken place, forming a city whose culture reflected those of both the colonizer and the colonized.[112] Under Rome, Dora basically remained what it was before — a Hellenistic city with a prevalently Phoenician-Greek population and some Jewish presence.[113] The commercial port remained active throughout Roman times, but its importance was overshadowed by the rise of the neighboring city of Caesarea in Judea/Palestine. In fact, the building of an artificial deep-water harbor on the site of the small Phoenician Strato's Tower by Herod in 37 BCE may have been the beginning of the end for Dor.[114] It is very likely then that the larger port of Caesarea dominated the regional circulation of imported goods while the port

of Dora remained working for as long as it was connected to the purple dye industry, eventually losing its importance altogether.

It is commonly believed that Dora was no longer occupied by the mid-third century CE.[115] From the excavation records of the Christian basilica on the southeastern foot of the tell, however, it seems that Dora did not disappear from the map, but relocated from the ancient tell to the area east of it, around the Byzantine era church complex that "rose on a grid-patterned lower city."[116] According to Dauphin, the church had been built on the site of a pre-existing Hellenistic-Roman temple dedicated to Apollo, and "was the episcopal basilica of Byzantine Dora" (Figs. **1.18** and **1.19**).[117] Archaeological finds from the church's excavations attest that the city must have constituted a center of pilgrimage for people coming from Syria and Egypt well into the seventh century CE.[118]

1.7 Excavations of Tel Dor

Tel Dor was first investigated in the 1920s by John Garstang on behalf of the British School of Archaeology

---

[110] Recent analysis of a Roman-period pyro technological feature at Tel Dor has demonstrated the existence of a casting pit at Dor. See Eliyahu-Behar *et al.* 2009.

[111] Butcher 2003, 270.

[112] Bhabha (1994, 160) notes that hybrid subjects become a threat to the dominant culture of the colonizer, since similar-looking but subordinate individuals cannot coexist with the dominant colonizer.

[113] The literary evidence of a Jewish presence at Dora will be discussed later in the book.

[114] According to Josephus, Caesarea's port was constructed because the problematic sand movement of the lagoon around Dora impeded landing operations, forcing merchants to anchor offshore (*Antiquities* 15.9).

[115] One of the various theories on what may have caused the desertion of the population of Dora is the lack of potable water. For more on the geological analysis of the area, see Mart 1986; Bullard 1970; Raveh 1991.

[116] Dauphin 1999, 397.

[117] Ibid. For more on the Byzantine church, see also Dauphin 1981; 1982-1983; 1986; 1999; Dauphin and Gibson 1994-95.

[118] Dauphin 1982-1983, 30; 1984, 271-274. Dauphin (1999, 404) also notes that the church had "a memorial to Christ's death ... a fragment of Golgotha, the rock of Calvary, enclosed in a cross-shaped metal reliquary riveted into a column." For more on the Byzantine church, see also Dauphin 1981; 1986; Dauphin and Gibson 1994-95.

FIG. 1.17. PERSIAN, HELLENISTIC AND ROMAN PERIOD JEWELRY

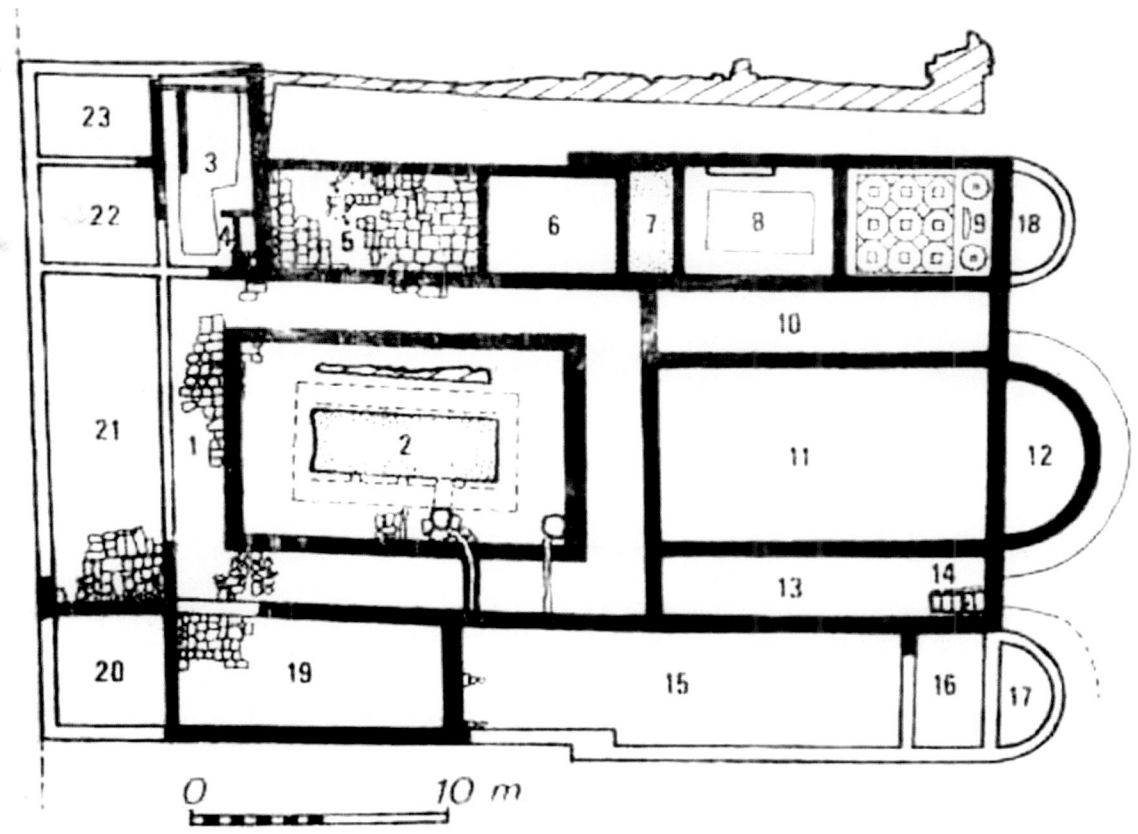

FIG. 1.19. LOCATION OF BYZANTINE CHURCH IN RELATION TO TEL DOR (GOOGLE MAP)
THE DESIGN IS A TRIPLE-AISLE BASILICA, 18.5M LONG BY 14M WIDE. THE LEGEND OF MAP OF THE CHURCH (BY C. DAUPHIN) IS: 1: PERISTYLE COURT; 2: CISTERN; 3: TOWER; 4: STAIRCASE; 5/19: VESTIBULES; 6: ANTECHAMBER; 7: BAPTISMAL; 8: ANOINTING ROOM; 9: ROOM FOR CELEBRATION OF THE EUCHARIST; 10 &13: AISLES; 11: NAVE; 12: CENTRAL APSE; 14: SAINT'S TOMB; 15: EXTERNAL AISLE; 17 & 18: SOUTH & NORTH APSES; 20-23: PORTICO.

17

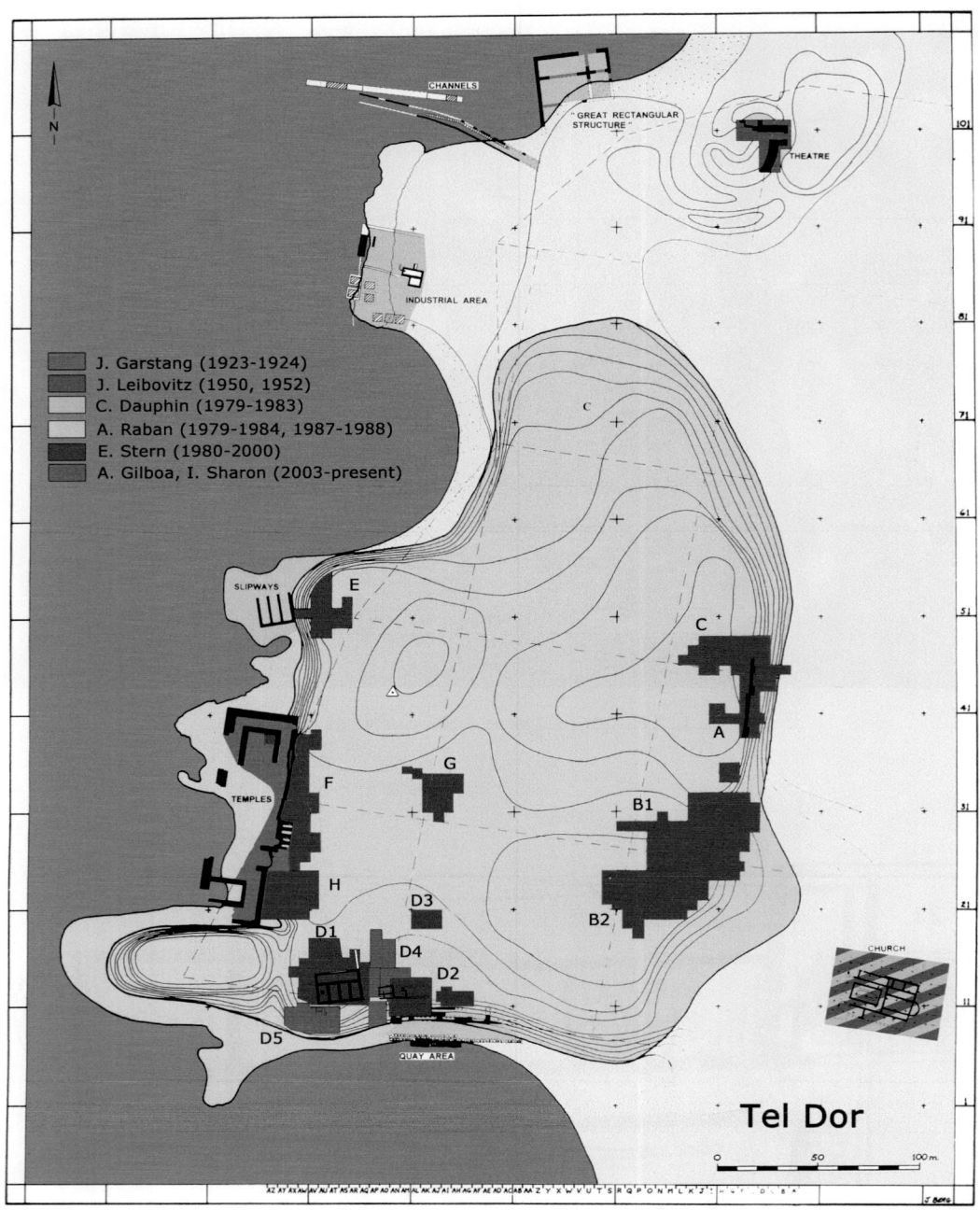

FIG. 1. 20. VARIOUS AREAS OPENED AT TEL DOR DURING THE COURSE OF EXCAVATIONS (DRAWING BY SVETA MATSKEVICH)

in Jerusalem;[119] the modern excavation project, however, dates back to 1980. During the nearly 30 excavation seasons, seven excavation areas were opened in different parts of the mound, each designated with letters, from A to G, with several sub-divisions (Fig. **1.20**). Area H was opened in 1996. Area A, on the eastern fringe of the tell, was excavated from 1980-1984, and is fully published in Volumes 1-2 of the final report. Area B, located south of area A, was excavated from 1980-1995 and was divided to two sub-areas: B1, comprising the actual city-gate

and everything to the north of it and B2, to the south of the gate. Area C, located on the eastern side of the tell, north of area A, includes parts of three different insulae: C0, C1 and C2--with slightly different stratigraphic sequences. Area C was excavated from 1980 - 1984 and published in Volumes 1-2 of the final report.[120] Areas D1, D2, D4 and D5 are on the southwestern corner of the mound and have been excavated consecutively from 1984 (D1) until recently (D2 and D4). Area D5 is the southwestern extension of area D1, on the southern slope of the mound. Area E, excavated from 1985 to 1989, is a step-trench on the northwest corner of the mound, above the rock-cut boat-slips and the small central bay. Areas F

---

[119] John Garstang (1876 -1956) was professor of archaeology at the University of Liverpool from 1907 to 1941. He served as the Director of the Department of Antiquities in the British Mandate of Palestine between 1920 and 1926, as well as Head of a British School of Archaeology in Jerusalem (1919-1926). See Albright 1956, 7-8.

[120] Stern 1995a. See also Stern 1985, 21-24.

and D2, on the west side of the mound, were the areas originally excavated by Garstang. Questions about his chronology and his architectural reconstruction of the two huge structures enclosed by *temenos* walls prompted a re-examination of the areas F and D2, which had been excavated from 1986-1997. Area G is in the exact center of the tell and was excavated from 1986-2000. Area H is located on the west side of the mound, between Area F and Area D1. It was opened in 1996 and excavated until 2000 with the purpose of investigating the connection between the southern temple and the town. The only remaining walls of podium H are the southern and eastern ones.

While archaeology in Israel has often attracted scholars who used the field to advance a particular agenda — either evangelical scholars in search of physical evidence of the Bible or Israeli archaeologists using ancient Israelite sites as physical confirmation of the new nation — the Tel Dor excavation project has had, from the very beginning, a purely academic goal.[121] The Renewed Tel Dor Project, launched in 2003, is presently concerned with several goals. One important goal is to contribute to the ongoing debate over the chronology of Iron Age in Israel through the analysis of Tel Dor's own Iron Age stratum. The conventional chronology, based on the biblical dating of David's and Solomon's kingdoms, places the Iron Age I/II transition around 1000 BCE; however, new research initiated by the minimalists, who regard the biblical narrative as myth, date the Iron Age I/II transition later, c. 900 BCE. Dor, although standing somewhat apart from these developments, can play a key role in this debate since it has an uninterrupted sequence of urban occupation levels spanning Iron Age I and Iron Age II. [122] A second goal is to investigate the westward expansion of the Phoenicians, with particular regard to the role of the Phoenician trading emporia and their long-standing interaction with the Western Mediterranean. Thirdly, the Tel Dor Project can shed light on the role of Mediterranean ports in the political and economic structure of the largely land-locked eastern empires--Assyria and Persia. Finally, the Persian to Roman Dor strata can also be used as the basis for studying the process of the Hellenization and later Romanization of Dor and the East. The analysis of the material culture portrayed on the city's Greek and Roman coins will undoubtedly contribute to the academic discussion of the city's past.

1.8 Coins Excavated at Tel Dor

The entire corpus of the coins found at Tel Dor consists of more than 2,000 coins, and ranges from the fifth century BCE to the late fourth century CE. The earliest specimens are fifth-century Athena-type silver *tetradrachma* (Fig. **1.21**), portraying the image of an owl, the iconographic

FIG. 1. 21. ATHENIAN COIN EXCAVATED AT TEL DOR (PHOTO BY R. MOTTA)

symbol of the Athenian *polis*. The Phoenician city-coins come mostly from the mints of Tyre and Sidon. The Sidonian coins are from the reign of Ba'al Sillem II (407-374 BCE) and Straton II (372-362) and portray the Persian king either killing a lion or struggling with two griffins, common motifs appearing also on Persian-era seals.[123] The coins from Tyre show Melqart, the most important god of the city, riding a mythological sea horse.[124] Coins issued in Palestinian cities were also found in the Persian-period strata, usually minted in the local Phoenician style or in a Phoenician-Greek style. The Hellenistic coins date back

---

[121] Excavation sites such as Hazor, Megiddo, or Masada conveyed a strong message of national rebirth. See Silberman 1989; Ben-Yehuda 2002, 1995;

[122] The Weizmann Institute of Science is carrying out an extensive 14C analysis program at Dor to establish the absolute date of the Iron Age I/II transition at Dor. For more information, see Gilboa, 2009 and 2014.

[123] Kindler 1967, 137. See also Betlyon 1982. Elayi (2004) dates the reign of Ba'al Sillem from 401-366, but the sequence of Sidonian kings is beyond the scope of this research.

[124] Recent work by J. Nitschke (2013, 261-282) has revised the numismatic imagery of Tyrian Melqart through the Hellenistic period, stressing his connections to a Herakles figure. For more on the social history of Achaemenid Phoenicia, see also Jigoulov 2010.

FIG. 1.22. PTOLEMAIC COIN EXCAVATED AT TEL DOR (PHOTO BY R. MOTTA)

FIG. 1.23. JEWISH COINS FOUND AT TEL DOR (STERN 2002)

to Philip II (359-336 BCE) and Alexander the Great (336-323 BCE), sometimes depicted as Herakles, wearing the lion skin around his neck.[125] Of the period immediately following Alexander's death, only coins of Ptolemy I and II have been found at Tel Dor, mostly from the mints of

Alexandria.[126] As with all Ptolemaic coin iconography, these coins also depict the king's head on the obverse and an eagle standing over a lightning-bolt on the reverse (Fig **1.22**). The city passed to Seleucid rule in 201 and remained

[125] An eagle clutching a lightning bolt is usually depicted on the reverse of these coins, with the inscription 'ΒΑΣΙΛΕΩΣ ΑΛΕΞΑΝΔΡΟΥ.'

[126] A hoard of silver *tetradrachma* was uncovered in 1986 under the floor of one of the rooms in Area B. Six depict Ptolemy I and four Ptolemy II. Nine were minted in Alexandria and one in Tyre. See Stern 2000, 258.

FIG. 1. 24. ROMAN COINS FOUND AT TEL DOR (STERN 2002, 184)

such until 103 BCE. More than 30 coins unearthed at Tel Dor belonging to that period and depicting Antiochus III Megas, the conqueror of the city, were minted in Antioch and Apamea in Syria.[127] The obverse of these coins depicts the head of Apollo, while the reverse shows various zoomorphic depictions and the inscription, 'King Antiochus'. The coins of Tryphon and Antiochus VII

Sidetes are, according to Stern, the most interesting of the collection, considering that the first king ruled for only three years (142-139 BCE) and was trapped when Dor was besieged by the latter.[128] The iconography of the Seleucid period goes from winged Eros to Isis together with the king's name, as well as a ship's prow and the symbol of the Dioscuri.

[127] Meshorer 1995, 461 - 472.

[128] Stern 2000, 259. The name of Tryphon was also engraved on a lead missile used during the conflict.

Alexander Jannaeus conquered Dor in 100 BCE, and coins of the Hasmonean period are among the coin finds of the city. The bilingual inscriptions on some specimens reveal the Judeo-Greek nature of the ruling class. The coins, minted in Jerusalem, have the Seleucid anchor and the Greek legend 'ΒΑΣΙΛΕΩΣ ΑΛΕΞΑΝΔΡΟΥ' on the obverse, while a star and the Hebrew inscription הלמך יהונתן (Yehonatan Hamelech) are depicted on the reverse (Fig. **1.23**).[129]

The Roman coins unearthed at Dor are by far the most numerous (Fig. **1.24**). The earliest specimens are three republican coins (an *as*, a *denarius*, and a *sestertius*) from the mint of Rome, dating to approximately 100 BCE, and the latest one portrays Valentinian II (375-392 CE). The Roman imperial coins analyzed thus far include imperial portraits, ranging from Claudius (41-54 CE) to Caracalla (235 CE); the originating mints are from nearby coastal cities such as Aradus, Berytus, Tripolis, Sidon, Tyre, Acre/Ptolomeis, Caesarea, Jaffa, Antipatris, Ashkelon, and Gaza. Other coins were minted in Antioch, Paneas, Gaba, Tiberias and Alexandria, while a few come from Rome and Nantes (Condivincum). Late Roman coins, depicting Maximianus Herculius (286-305), Maxentius (306-312), Constantine I (306-337), and Valentinian (375-392), mostly from the mint of Alexandria, Antioch, and Ephesus, are common enough to guarantee further research on coin circulation in fourth-century Dora, especially considering that the city was no longer inhabited.[130]

Most of these Roman period coins seem to be the work of very skilled artisans, as the imperial portraits closely resemble the images of the statuary or other coins struck in Rome. With the exception of a silver *tetradrachma* portraying Trajan, all imperial coins unearthed at Tel Dor are made of bronze, the most common being the *folles* and the *antoniniani*.[131] According to C. H. Sutherland, such types of lower-value imperial coins were used for the *stipendia* and the *donativa* of legionary soldiers on whose service the stability of the frontiers and the provinces relied, while the types of gold or silver coins were circulated among the better-educated, higher-income citizens who were also, like the soldiers, state employees.[132] This theory may in fact justify the larger quantity of low-value coins unearthed at Dor. Furthermore, the portraits of the emperors on these coins are of obvious historical interest, as are the images of buildings, mostly sacred ones, and the inscriptions. Information about imperial titulature and honors bestowed on these provincial cities can easily be gathered from the inscriptions on these coins.

All coins excavated at Tel Dor are an immense source of information, answering historical and economic questions about the city. However, since the city minted its own coins, in this study, the primary source of information about the culture of the city will be the coins struck at Dora and their semiotic function, i.e., those coins used as signs of cultural self-understanding, and the vehicles through which meaning was constructed in Dora.

---

[129] Meshorer 1982, 1: 35-87. Alexander Jannaeus was the first of the Jewish kings to introduce the 'eight-ray star' symbol on his bronze coins, in combination with the Seleucid symbol of the anchor. Romanoff (1943: 435-444) claims that these coins are the ones mentioned in Luke 21:1-4.
[130] The presence of fourth century coins may perhaps shed more light on Dauphin's theory (1999, 397) that Dora was not abandoned, but its inhabitants migrated to the southern slope, around the Byzantine church.

[131] The *follis* is a large bronze coin introduced in about 296 CE with the coinage reform of Diocletian. It weighs about 10 grams and is about 4% silver, mostly as a thin layer on the surface. The *follis* was apparently equal to 25 of the bronze *denarii* in 285 CE, or about 1/5 of a silver *denarius* from the time of Vespasian in 75 CE. The *antoninianus*, valued at 2 *denarii*, was introduced by Caracalla in early 215 and is a silver coin similar to the *denarius*. It was slowly debased to bronze. See *RIC* Vols. V-VIII.
[132] Sutherland 1986, 88.

Chapter 2
Material Culture, Coins and Cultural Identity

2.1 Definition of Culture

Culture plays a very important role in the modern theoretical discussion of identity, as the definition of national identity is commonly assumed to "foreground the self-conscious perception of having a shared culture" within a group.[1] Identity is understood not as something enduring, but as something that is constructed in particular historical contexts based on subjective rather than objective criteria.[2] Similarly, the formation of identity is seen as a process of self-definition that "relies as much on differences from other cultures as on similarities within a group."[3] This notion of culture as central to self-definition is of course very important for the study of the past, since culture and identity provide the framework for understanding the significance of ancient artifacts and practices. However, how does one define 'culture?' And can 'culture' be reified?

The concept of culture as a theoretical category goes back to the British anthropologist Edward Tylor who, identifying 'culture' with 'civilization,' described it in 1871 as "that complex whole which includes knowledge, belief, art, morals, law, custom, and any other capabilities and habits acquired by man as a member of society."[4] Perhaps influenced by the French Enlightenment of the late eighteenth century, which entertained an idea of civilization as a "transnational process of evolution … towards rationality and perfection," Tylor drew a contrast between the civilization of 'lower tribes' and that of 'higher tribes.'[5] According to Hall, "his aesthetic and idealistic" notion of culture was conceived from the Western canon of literary, artistic, musical and philosophical works, possibly as a defense against the influence of technology and materialism caused by the Industrial Age.[6] Tylor's understanding of culture was also shared by Matthew Arnold, who in 1869 defined 'culture' as "the pursuit of our total perfection by means of getting to know … the best which has been taught and said in the world."[7]

Today's more pluralistic understanding of culture as something particular to a specific human group, rather than something to be obtained by material progress or shared by a transnational educated élite, has its roots in the philosophy of German Romanticists Wilhelm von Humboldt and Johann Herder, who believed that cultural traditions, together with languages, are the ties that create a nation.[8] In particular, Herder, emphasizing that *Kultur* is in *Volksberiffs* and in *Volkslieder* — the spiritual essence of *Das Volk* — replaced the traditional concept of a political state with that of a nation, which is based on cultural and ethnic affinity and which "bears in itself the standard of its perfection,"[9] independently from any other nation.

Herder's concept of *Kultur* as the spirit of a *Volksnation,* and his belief that every nation has its own interpretation of *Humanität*[10] subsequently influenced the study of history. Historians began to shift their focus from remembrance of facts to reconstruction and from single facts to the spiritual and the universal in them. History was now described in terms of 'development,' 'process,' 'spirit of the age' (Zeitgeist), and 'spirit of a nation.'[11] In his *Reflection on History*, Jacob Burckhardt argued that the formation of historical societies was a process of interaction between three powers, State, Religion, and Culture.[12] However, while the first two powers might "claim authority at least over their particular people,"[13] the third is a realm that cannot be claimed by compulsive authority. "Culture," he wrote, "is the sum of all that has spontaneously arisen for the advancement of material life and as an expression of spiritual and material life — all social intercourse, technologies, arts, literatures and science."[14] In an era when "archaeological research … [was bringing] … revised results daily,"[15] it was therefore the duty of historians to dig beneath all the dead artifacts and discern the spiritual that forms the *Kultur* of a nation. In light of this, Burckhardt treated Greek history as the "history of Greek habits of thought and mental attitudes … [and sought] to establish the vital forces, both constructive and destructive, that were active in Greek life."[16]

---

[1] Preston 2007, 87. See also Hanson 2003, 6.
[2] Hall 2003, 23.
[3] Preston 2007, 87.
[4] Tylor 1920, 1. Edward Tylor (1832-1917) based his theories on the evolutionary theories of Charles Darwin. The first of his two volumes, *The Origins of Culture* (1871), deals with several aspects of ethnography, including social evolution, linguistics, and myth; the second, *Religion in Primitive Culture* (1873), deals with animism.
[5] Hall 2004b, 37.
[6] Hall 2004b, 37. Although the elitist view of this definition is criticized today, its legacy, according to Hall, persists in the field of sociology, where the study of 'mass culture,' 'subculture,' and 'counterculture' is still limited mostly to the sphere of art, fashion or music. See also Sewell 1999a, 41.
[7] According to Arnold (1883, xi), knowledge can be acquired by means of "reading, observing and thinking." *Culture and Anarchy* was first published in 1869, but the preface was added in 1875. See Storey 1998, 7-13.

[8] Both Humboldt and Herder proposed what is now called the Sapir-Whorf Hypothesis, i.e., the notion that language determines thought. See Hill 1989, 14.
[9] Barnard 1983, 231.
[10] Adler 2008, 94. For Herder, *Humanität* expressed his hopes regarding the progress of humankind and his belief regarding the ultimate purpose of humans' religious impulse. See also Barnard 1983, 240.
[11] Große 1999, 526.
[12] Sigurdson 2004, 10; 208. Burckhardt (1818-1897) was a historian of art and culture, and an influential figure in the historiography of each field. He is considered the father of cultural history.
[13] Burckhardt 1943, 107.
[14] Ibid., 33.
[15] Burckhardt 1998, 24.
[16] Ibid., 4.

Although Burckhardt's view of 'culture' was perhaps still concerned with the expressions and beliefs of the élite class, his study of gestures, customs and behavior patterns, festivals and other forms of popular expressions sparked a view of society that was multicultural and egalitarian, influencing later anthropological and archaeological theories.[17] Cultural history was in fact at the core of the works of Franz Boas (1858-1942), the father of modern anthropology. Grounded in the natural sciences, Boas used scientific methods of investigation and argued that what differentiated the study of humankind from geography or zoology was the study of culture. But culture to Boas was not a synonym for 'civilization,' i.e., a predestined linear upward progression, but rather "an accidental accretion of individual elements."[18] The differences among peoples, he argued, are the results of the historical, social and geographic conditions that formed various cultural boundaries.[19] The boundaries are not barriers to outside influences, however, but cultural distinctions. In fact, his student Robert Lowie defined culture as "hybrid and irregular collections of customs, techniques and beliefs, often borrowed by chance encounter with others."[20] Boas and Lowie's focus on the pluralistic understanding of culture easily crossed into archaeological theory, influencing Australian Marxist archaeologist Gordon Childe and British processual archaeologist David Clarke.[21] According to Childe, human groups conduct their lives in different ways from place to place, and the material residue that they deposit in the archaeological record displays spatial variation or archaeological culture, which can be identified by "a plurality of well-defined diagnostic types that are repeatedly and exclusively associated with one another."[22]

While the conventional archaeological understanding of culture is still predicted by the attestation of certain recurring features, such as pottery, coins, architectures, etc., in the 1960s the understanding of culture, especially in the study of material culture, moved away from Boas' definition. The new approach, embraced by Clifford Geertz, viewed culture as a "historically transmitted pattern of meanings embodied in symbolic forms by means of which men communicate, perpetuate and develop their knowledge about and attitudes toward life."[23] The socio-cultural as a system of symbolisms and significations in which ideas and meanings are expressed through symbolic action had already been at the core of the structural linguistics of Ferdinand de Saussure, and had easily crossed into anthropology and ethnology.[24] Deriving his theory from structuralism, Lévi -Strauss asserted in

fact that any culture is a "totality of symbolic systems" that seek to express certain aspects of physical and of social reality and that develop within a society at a supra-individual level.[25]

Although much of the theoretical writing on culture has adopted, a concept of culture as a system of symbols and meanings since the 1960s, Sewell notes that many scholars have recently criticized this concept in favor of a concept of culture-as-practice.[26] Yet the two concepts are not at odds with each other. Sewell writes,

System and practice are complementary concepts: each presupposes the other. To engage in cultural practice means to utilize existing cultural symbols to accomplish some end. The employment of a symbol can be expected to accomplish a particular goal only because the symbols have more or less determinate meanings–meanings specified by their systematically structured relations to other symbols.[27]

Specifically, system and practice constitute, according to Sewell, "an indissoluble duality or dialectic."[28] His definition of culture is therefore the articulation of system and practice, i.e., the human capacity to classify and represent experiences with symbols, and, using those symbols to communicate the encoded experiences of a social environment. As noted by Hall, not all customs and habits — even beliefs and values — are inherently cultural. In social practice, only certain elements are selected and endowed with a symbolic signification, acquiring a semiotic code that is intelligible to people of the same group.[29] It is the nature of the elements selected as symbols that provides a common, shared framework within a homogeneous culture and that determines the differences between various cultural groups.[30] Any group, for instance, can be bound by the same notion of religious dogmas and authority, attitudes toward biological gender, common origin, etc. —all behavioral traits that are endowed with symbolic signification in social practices.

Hall's definition of culture reorients in part the way in which ancient Graeco-Roman societies are seen today, since it seems clear that these people constructed, managed and understood their lives through a "system of shared beliefs and practices."[31] Moreover, the ongoing debate about culture in anthropology and archaeology has had a great impact on the study of cultural contacts and on

---

[17] Murray (1999, xvii) points out that Burckhardt's concept of 'cultural studies' is "fundamentally different from that prevalent in modern universities," where cultural studies are often equated with "popular culture or minority cultures."
[18] Stocking 1968, 214.
[19] Bashkow 2004, 443.
[20] Lowie 1920, 440. See Stocking 1968, 214.
[21] Hall 2004b, 38.
[22] Childe 1956, 123.
[23] Geertz 1973, 89.
[24] Ferdinand de Saussure (1857-1913) is considered the father of modern linguistics. See Holdcroft 1991; de Saussure 1998;

[25] Lévi-Strauss 1987, xix. For further reading, see Carrithers 1985; Lévi-Strauss 1974; 1987; Bohannan, 1969. Among the supporters of the culture-as-a-system theory was Ruth Benedict (1887-1948) who expressed her views most systematically in *Patterns of Culture* (Boston, 1934).
[26] Sewell 1999a, 45. James Clifford and George Marcus's collection *Writing Culture* (1986) was the first publication to criticize the concept of culture as a system of symbols and meanings. For more information, see Ortner 1984; Bourdieu 1977; Clifford and Marcus 1986. Particularly Bourdieu (1977, 5-6; 163-4) considered culture a medium of resources that shaped all human actions.
[27] Sewell 1999a, 47.
[28] Ibid.
[29] Hall 2003, 23
[30] Sewell 1999a, 48.
[31] Kurke 2003, 1.

the way archaeologists see material culture. As Eric Wolf suggests, culture is "a series of processes that construct, reconstruct and dismantle cultural material, in response to identifiable determinants."[32]

2.2 Material Culture, Semiotics, and Coins

Material culture is in fact the aspect of 'culture' that is most fundamental to archaeologists. The assumption that all objects made or modified by men reflect consciously or unconsciously, directly or indirectly, the beliefs of the individuals that came in contact with the objects is indeed one of the most important tenets of material culture studies.[33] For Marcel Mauss, objects were the most authentic and therefore reliable evidence of the characteristics of any civilizations.[34] Given the broad range of ecological, economic and socio-cultural factors involved in the production, diffusion, acceptance, longevity and use of any human creation, it is easy to understand that most material culture scholars, starting with William Morris in the nineteenth century, used artifacts as tools for the understanding of cultures and ethnography.[35] Likewise, in the early 1930s, Gordon Childe identified archaeological culture as "certain type of remains … pots, implements, ornaments, burial rites, house forms … constantly recurring together."[36] Under the influence of a neo-Marxist notion of socio-historical evolution,[37] Childe based his archaeological analysis on generalized types of artifacts and on different stages of social development of a culture, and he framed a functionalist notion of material culture within those developmental stages.[38] However, as he himself writes in *The Bronze Age* in 1930, he was unable to develop a sustainable theoretical linkage between archaeological cultures and ethnicity.[39] His theory therefore lacks the scope of a cultural identity analysis.

A more recent consideration of the relationship between material culture and cultural identity is Ian Hodder's 1982 ethnographic analysis of material culture in Kenya. In this and successive studies, Hodder perceives artifacts not only as tools or possessions, but also as signs of status and therefore as being actively engaged in the negotiations of identities based on age, gender and ethnicity.[40] Therefore, objects have meanings that archaeologists should be able

to read. Furthermore, since different cultures vary in their cognitive structures, producing different types of artifacts even when confronted with similar physical constraints, Hodder is critical of universal functions being attributed to artifacts.[41] Emphasizing a conceptual analysis of an object, Clive Gamble lists its "discrete parts" as production process, function, context, exchange, consumption and transformation — characteristics that sum up to what he calls the "common sense attitude of material culture."[42] Furthermore, according to Gamble, artifacts serve three contexts: material (coping with the environment), social (dealing with social organization), and ideational (coping with ideas, values and beliefs), and therefore all artifacts must be interpreted across these three contexts.[43] The role that artifacts play in society is also important in the conceptual approach of Carl Knappett, for whom artifacts reflect human properties. His "bio-psycho-social" paradigm asserts that the "ecological organism," the "psychological agent," and the "social person" have fuzzy boundaries that extend into material culture.[44] A critic of the "computational model of cognition,"[45] Knappett presents an alternative perspective that links cognition, perception and action, where brain, body, and world are integrated, and thus agent and object are mutually constitutive. Archaeology is, therefore, all about the interaction between objects and human beings, with the objects' sign-value (socio-semiology) as the real 'meaning' of material culture. As Colin Renfrew states, "material objects are employed to mediate in the interaction between human individuals, and between humans and their environment."[46]

When studying cultural identity through artifactual records, and through the process by which objects function as signs, Carl Sanders Peirce's general theory of signs has been used recently for analyses of identity, social organizations, linguistic practices and political performances. In contrast to Ferdinand de Saussure's semiology, which is mostly concerned with linguistic signs and their dyadic relationship,[47] Peirce's interest lies in the modes of inference and the inquiry process in general. He argues that every thought is a sign, and that every act of reasoning consists of the interpretation of signs.[48] Peirce's semeiotics is thus a triadic process

---

[32] Wolf 1982, 287. Dietler (1999, 485) notes, "Culture must be understood not only as something inherited from the past, but as a continual creative project."

[33] Prown 1982, 3.

[34] Mauss 1931, 6-7.

[35] The study of the materiality of culture was influenced by the Marxist philosophy that all products of human labor are social because of the mutual relations and interdependence between the product and the producer. In Marx's theory, in fact, an artifact that has use value, exchange value, and a price, is a commodity (*Ware*) with social qualities that are at the same time perceptible and imperceptible by the senses. See Evans 1982; Hodder 1982, 1999; Shanks and Tilley 1993; Hides 1996; Hodder and Hutson 2004.

[36] Childe 1929, v-vi.

[37] Marx's notion of 'commodification,' i.e., the transformation of goods into 'commodities' is the process that makes objects 'social.' See McGuire 1992, 103.

[38] Childe 1930, 8-11. See also Trigger 1980, 148-149; Wailes 1996, 6.

[39] Childe 1930, 232.

[40] Hodder 1982, 185.

[41] Hodder 2003, 16.

[42] Gamble 2001, 100. Other scholars, most notably James Sackett, reduced material culture to two contexts: utilitarian (such as tools and weapons) and non-utilitarian (such as artwork and ritual objects). For more on style of objects, see Sackett 1977, 369-380.

[43] Gamble 2001, 102.

[44] Knappett 2005, 35. The human characteristics are defined as biological animacy, psychological agency, and social personhood.

[45] The computational theory of cognition views the mind as a passive storehouse designed to receive external sensory information. The theory was proposed by Hilary Putnam in 1961 and developed by Jerry Fodor in the 1960s and 70s. See Knappett 2005, 25.

[46] Renfrew 2004, 23.

[47] de Saussure 1986, 66-67. According to de Saussure, the linguistic sign relationship is dyadic, comprising two elements - the 'signifier' (a sound or an image) and the 'signified' (a concept). For more, see also Ketner and Kloesel 1986; Gardin 1992; Lele 2006.

[48] According to Fisch (1978, 31-70), the spelling "Semeiotic" was Peirce's rendering of Locke's Σημιωτική. That spelling has been used by some of Peirce's scholars to distinguish Peirce's semiotic from others, but Deely (2003, 3-29) cites different spelling forms used by Peirce

of cooperation between a representamen (also called a 'sign' *sensu stricto*), an object, and an interpretant (i.e. the mental representation which is in turn another sign). The analytic relationship between the representamen and the object further produces, according to Peirce's theory, three general types of signs: icons, representing a formal shared similarity between the representamen and the object to be represented to the interpretant; indexes, representing continuity, contiguity, metonymy, relation between cause and effect, and other aspects of direct connection; and symbols, representing the relationship between representamen and object through some kind of arbitrary (instituted or imposed) convention.[49] Peirce's semiotic theories can easily be applied in the analysis of cultural identity through a people's coinage. In particular, his notion that "continuity is bound up with the possibility of thought"[50] is of great importance in the understanding of how social identity structured and manifested itself through coins in ancient pecuniary societies. In fact, within the semiotic interpretation of objects as signs, coinage can act as a "non-verbal mode of communication in multidimensional channels … [becoming] a material language with its own meaning tied to production and consumption."[51] Umberto Eco's description of a semiotic code as a set of rules for linking symbols with meaning can in fact be easily applied to coinage.[52]

From the perspective of Kuhn's *General Systems Theory*, the circulation of coinage, modern or ancient, can be compared with the flows of information at both national and transnational levels.[53] Indeed, in an ancient pecuniary society, coins functioned as 'markers' or 'signals' that can be considered similar to linguistic messages. De Saussure compared coins with words and showed how both units relate to dissimilar units, for which they are exchanged (commodities and concepts, respectively), as well as to similar units with which they may be compared (other coins or other words).[54] Polanyi, too, suggests that money is a "system of symbols"[55] that offers a "striking

resemblance"[56] to language and writings. Finally, according to Codere, "Money is a symbol. It functions as a sign; it is semiotic."[57] However, as de Saussure himself observed, while linguistic information flows according to established regular rules (e.g. sounds, letters of the alphabet, etc.),[58] money is employed to reproduce many elaborate cultural codes, and it can be given any meaning that the owner chooses to put into it.[59] Moreover, as signs, coins are significative of social space and time and it is therefore clear that a culture will generate different coinage at different times or places, as evidenced by Roman imperial coinage.[60]

When applying this analytical trend to ancient coins, it is easy to perceive each coin minted at Dora not simply as an ancient artifact, but as a semeion, i.e., a sign of the cultural self-understanding of the city and a primary vehicle through which Dora constructed its meaning. However, since Dora's was a cultural system formed through many ethnic contacts, it is important to assess which part of that cultural system was reflected on the coins. Furthermore, in order to see how the definition of Greek or Roman culture fit the reality of Dora, the issue of cultural identity in the Greek and Roman provinces will be examined.

2.3 Cultural Identity in the Greek and Roman Provinces

The definition of either Greek or Roman culture and identity that includes the provinces has recently led archaeologists to analyze the meaning of diversity within different categories of material culture and the connection between material culture and society.[61] Important considerations are the understanding of the basic meaning of culture and acculturation; of what it meant to be, become or behave like a Greek or Roman; of Greek or Roman behavior and its motivations; and of modern scholars' ability to define cultural boundaries from material culture evidence.[62] Recent ideas of hybridity and creolization, borrowed from cultural theories and post colonialism, have led many scholars to the belief that ancient societies had permeable, contradictory, and loosely integrated identities, and to the notion of interdependence between the different cultures that came in contact with each other.[63] All cultural systems were then constructed in what Homi Bhabha calls the "Third Space of Enunciation," where the culture of the colonizer is transformed by the necessity of

---

himself. See also Cobley 2001, 217. The use of Peircean interpretations of material culture has found a wide use in 'symbolic archaeology.' See Hodder, 1987, 1-3; Robb 1998, 329-346; Tilley 1999, 36-81; Lele 2006, 48-70; Gardin 1992, 251-275; Preucel 2010, 44-66; Keane 2003, 409-423.
[49] Lele 2006, 29-52.
[50] Parker 1998, 70. For more on the continuity of thought and the representation of knowledge in cognitive archaeology, see Flannery & Marcus 1996, 350-363.
[51] Tilley 1991, 186. On objects as signs and symbols, see also Csikszenmihalyi 1981; 1993; Pearce 1986; Hunt 1993; Gamble 2001.
[52] According to Eco (1994, 9), "Originally a symbol was a token, the present half of a broken table or coin or medal, that performed its social and semiotic function by recalling the absent half to which it potentially could be reconnected. This potentiality was indeed crucial because, since the two halves could be reconnected, it was unnecessary to yearn for the reconnection."
[53] Hornborg 1999, 152. See also Kuhn 1974, 154; 156. The General System Theory (GST) as described by Kuhn states that knowing one part of a system enables us to know something about another part. According to this theory all organizational and social interactions involve communication and/or transaction. Kuhn stresses that "*Culture* is communicated ... and *society* is a collectivity of people having a common ... process of culture" (156).
[54] Hornberg 1999, 153. According to de Saussure (1998, 178) "linguistics operates with units which are synchronically linked together."
[55] Polanyi 1968, 175.

[56] Polanyi 1968, 179.
[57] Codere 1968, 559.
[58] de Saussure 1998, 109-110.
[59] Baudrillard 1981, 34. See also Miller 1965, 350.
[60] Hornborg 1999, 159. This is of course evident in the distribution of Roman coins minted by different emperors or in different mints throughout the empire.
[61] Material culture theories have only recently been applied to Roman archaeology. *FACTA, A Journal of Roman Material Culture Studies* was founded in 2007 for the specific purpose of promoting material culture approaches to Roman archaeology.
[62] There are several studies that address these concepts. See Brah and Coombes 2000; Modood and Werbner 1997; Young 1995. For Greek multiculturalism, see Dougherty and Kurke 2003.
[63] Hall 2004b, 23; and Sewell 1999a, 47. For a complete look at these issues, see also Carr and Neitzel 1995; Chilton 1999. Damaskos and Plantzos 2008.

communication and negotiation with the colonized.[64] This notion can easily be adapted to Greek and Roman cultures when analyzing how material culture "was manipulated, combined, and deployed in practice to express identities — and how [material] cultural encounters shaped identity."[65]

According to some scholars, any notion of a coherent, internally consistent culture, even in the original Greek communities, was questionable, and Greek culture, as a system, possessed only "a thin coherence."[66] However, in spite of the hundreds of *poleis* and the marked local diversities, a Greek national identity did exist. It was sustained, according to Càssola, by the frequent and regular contacts of the many people who guaranteed reciprocal comprehension between the cities — from traders who created commercial networks to physicians who worked for different patrons in different cities, sometimes over great distances; to painters, sculptors and architects whose works were commissioned throughout the Greek world.[67] While moving from city to city, these people created a 'connective tissue' that embraced the entire Greek world; thus Càssola writes,

Queste attività bastavano a creare un tessuto connettivo che abbracciava tutta la grecità e provocavano uno scambio di esperienze tale da garantire, non l'omogeneità della cultura, ma la reciproca comprensione e il reciproco interesse fra tutti i centri abitati.[68]

The *tessuto connettivo* is therefore the unified notion of Greekness (*grecità*), which becomes apparent in the pan-Hellenic cults, the common sanctuaries and the similar material culture accessible to and accessed by both Greeks and non-Greeks, who "shared much in the way of culture, both literal and material."[69]

And yet, as Hall points out, when studying shared behavioral patterns of cultures, archaeologists have to ask whether the style and categories that they regard as similar or distinct were regarded as such in antiquity.[70] He writes, "Culture in any meaningful, analyzable sense, whether viewed emically or etically, has no existence independent of its reification. And those to whom this reified semiotic code is intelligible constitute a cultural group."[71] Hall's use of the terms etic, i.e., externally observed, and emic, i.e.,

internally perceived, is concerned with their application to a society's physical perceptions as 'units' that are considered as appropriate in particular contexts by native participants vs. those same units as described by outside observers.[72]

The concepts of cultural reification, hybridity, and creolization also offer new insights into the process of Romanization. Just as with the process of Hellenization, classical scholars also believed for a long time that Romanization was a uniform process that molded diverse people into 'new Romans' throughout the Roman Empire. Haverfield, writing in 1923 claimed:

One uniform fashion spread from the Mediterranean throughout central and western Europe, driving out native art and substituting a conventional copy of Graeco-Roman or Italian art, which is characterized alike by technical finish and neatness, and by lack of originality and dependence of imitation."[73]

However, he also argued that the process of Romanization differed from one province to another in response to the local political and economic structures.[74] His notion was challenged in the early 1930s, when Collingwood, studying the material culture of Roman Britain, asserted that "the civilization … even in the most Romanized parts of Britain is by no means a pure, or even approximately pure, Roman civilization bodily taken over by the conquered race."[75] A "fusion," he argued, took place in a sort of sliding scale, with the upper classes and the larger cities at the top as the most Romanized, and the peasantry and the small villages at the bottom, as the least Romanized.[76] Collingwood's idea of a 'Romano-British' culture as a syncretistic or hybrid culture was itself challenged in the 1970s by scholars who supported a position of resistance to Roman culture, stressing the integrity of indigenous cultural traditions in the formation of a post-conquest identity, at least in some Roman provinces.[77] More recent scholars dismiss Romanization as acculturation, i.e., the process by which Roman provinces were "given civilization,"[78] and prefer the concept of creolization — a perspective that "offers insights into the negotiation of post-conquest identities from 'the bottom up.'"[79] However, as Woolf points out, acculturation has its merits when applied to the provincial élite that adopted Roman symbols to build its own Roman identity.[80] But how did the Romans perceive the nature of their culture? What did it mean to be Roman?

---

[64] Bhabha 1994, 219.
[65] Antonaccio 2003, 59.
[66] Sewell 1999a, 49.
[67] Càssola 1996, 10. Among the most traveled physicians was, for instance, the physician Democedes of Croton, in Southern Italy, who worked in Aegina, Athens, and Samo and finally at the court of Darius (Herodotus 3.131).
[68] Càssola 1996, 10. "These activities were sufficient to create a connective tissue that spanned the entire Greek world and provoked an exchange of experiences as to ensure, not the homogeneity of culture, but the mutual understanding and mutual interest of all the towns" (my translation). For more on the concept of Greekness in Herodotus, see Thomas 2000, 102-134.
[69] Antonaccio (2003, 58) notes, "The circulation of culture took place by means of circulation of persons and culture, and its practice created the framework for circulation."
[70] Hall 2002, 196.
[71] Hall 2003, 25.

---

[72] In defining the features of an emic unit, Kenneth Pike (1990, 28) offered a precise description: "An emic unit... is a physical or mental item or system treated by insiders as relevant to their system of behavior ... in spite of etic variability." The etic variability is of course a reference to the generalized classification done by observers from their point of view. See also Pike 1993, 78.
[73] Haverfield 1923, 18.
[74] Ibid. 23.
[75] Collingwood 1932, 92.
[76] Ibid.
[77] Webster 2001, 210. For an overview on the rise of 'nativism' in North Africa, see Mattingly 1996, 49.
[78] Haverfield 1923, 11.
[79] Webster 2001, 209.
[80] Woolf 1998, 1-23; 48-76.

Roman writers give us the best insight into the Roman perception of their own identity. *Romanitas* was defined in terms of having a common set of values, common religious practices, and the common conception of a world order that regarded the spread of civilization as their divine duty.[81] Moreover, since Romans did not claim a common ancestor, being Roman was not a matter of ethnicity or geography, but a matter of behavior. The basic Roman values, *virtus, pietas, fides, constantia,* and *dignitas* were not automatically inherited, but had to be acquired. *Romanitas* was therefore "negotiable,"[82] and anyone could become Roman by simply adopting Roman values and customs.

This Roman self-identification in terms of common customs and morality (*mores*) had a large impact on the provinces, where the success of Roman rule depended in large part on the degree of assimilation of the local élite, especially during the imperial period. Since it was easy for provincials to become Romans, acculturation of the ruling class became, in fact, an essential tool for maintaining political control. Most élites adopted *Romanitas* as a degree of collaboration with the imperial power, and political power was placed in their hands.[83] Furthermore, according to Woolf, the fact that the élite adopted Roman cultural traits may have been a catalyst for the spreading of Roman culture throughout local societies, since the new styles were no longer just considered an emulation of Roman traits, but a symbol of élite status and wealth.[84] In other words, certain Roman traits spread among indigenous peoples because these traits acquired a semiotic code that was intelligible to them, contributing to the formation of a post-conquest local hybrid identity.

However, the extent of this hybridization was different for different provinces, and not all the cultural patterning visible in a province can be regarded as solely the product of intersecting realities of Roman and indigenous peoples. The cultural influence on the Greek-speaking provinces, for instance, provides an example of a cultural resistance to Rome by people that were "extremely reluctant to admit the civilized status of non-Greeks or to surrender their sense of identity, even when they acquired Roman citizenship and high office within the empire."[85] Furthermore, the Roman imperial political élite's fascination and interaction with Greek culture and customs resulted in the Roman

adoption, imitation, and adaptation of many Hellenistic traits. Throughout the Asian provinces, the Romano-Greek culture remained in fact Greek in language and culture, and Roman in its political and social structure. Hybridization occurred, however, and is evident not only in the material culture of nearly all Romano-Greek cities, which display "an eclectic blend of Roman, Greek and other origins,"[86] but also in the religion. In fact, the imperial cult that was celebrated in cities of Asia Minor was a new form of worship with little resemblance to Greek celebrations of the Hellenistic kings.[87] Moreover, those who took part in the political and administrative life of the Greek cities, either at a local or imperial level, were rewarded with citizenship and therefore considered Roman by the Romans themselves. It is feasible to assume, then, that these people developed some sort of Roman identity without compromising their original Greek identity.

Both concepts of acculturation and cultural hybridity, as discussed earlier in the chapter, have strong appeal in the study of Dora, a city that, although definitely removed from the binary opposition between colonizers and colonized throughout its history, reached the status of a mini-Rome, minting its own imperial coins during the Roman period. As illustrated in Chapter 1, Dora developed as an aggregate of various ethnic groups from its very inception. It can be assumed, therefore, that both Hellenization and Romanization brought changes to the local identity and the self-understanding of the city and that Dora perceived both her own Greekness and *Romanitas* that are etically observed on her Roman coins.

2.4 Expressing Dora's Identity in a Provincial Setting

According to Plutarch, "Alexander established more than seventy cities among savage tribes and sowed all Asia with Grecian magistracies, and thus overcame its uncivilized and brutish manner of living."[88] The Greek language and literature presumably brought people of the Asian provinces to such an advanced stage of social, cultural, and moral development that the cities of the Asian provinces changed their names or adopted "a form of name designated to be more intelligible to those who are settled among them."[89] It would be likely, therefore, that Greeks and non-Greeks formed a well-integrated society even in Phoenician Dora. According to Pierre Briant, however, Hellenistic foundations functioned as nuclei of social segregation and dominance, as the Greeks of the fourth century did not intend to integrate in any way with the indigenous peoples and cultures.[90] As previously stated, it has always been the view of classical scholars that the encounter between the two cultures resulted in the imposition of the Greeks' (colonizers') culture on the colonized;[91] that cultural features flowed

---

[81] The mission was for Rome to disseminate *humanitas* to the *barbaroi*. As Vergil writes, "It is for you, Roman, to rule the nations with your power, (that will be your skill) to crown peace with law, to spare the conquered, and subdue the proud" (*Aeneid* VI. 850-853 – my translation); and according to Pliny the Elder, Italy was "chosen by the power of the gods ... to give civilization to mankind" (*Natural History* 3.39).
[82] Isserlin 1998, 146.
[83] Butcher 2003, 270.
[84] Woolf 1994, 10. Nearly perfect examples of Woolf's theory are the catacombs of Beit She'arim, in Galilee, where marble sarcophagi favored by wealthy Romans were also adapted for Jewish use by incorporating a relief image of Jewish symbols like the *menorah*, the Arch of the Torah, as well as symbols of the festival of *Sukkot*, together with other symbols taken from the contemporary Hellenistic-Roman world, like lions and a bull, Roman eagles, and Roman six-leaf rosettes. See Goodenough 1953-68 (1), 236.
[85] Woolf 1994, 16.

[86] Ibid.
[87] Price 1985, 45-47.
[88] Plutarch, *Lives. De Fortuna Alexandri*, 5. 395.
[89] Josephus, *Antiquities* 1.121.
[90] Briant 1978, 60. See also Momigliano 1975; Préaux 1965, 1978; Hengel 1980.
[91] Gosden 2001, 242.

from more advanced to less developed groups; and that indigenous peoples were more than happy to accept those more advanced cultural traits.[92] According to this view, then, the Greek merchants who traveled to or settled at Dora imposed the 'Greekness' described by Càssola on the people of Dora. Modern scholars disagree, however, further questioning whether the characterization of Greek culture "as a way of living signaled in the archaeological record by artefacts … would have been recognized by the Greeks themselves."[93] When two cultures come into contact, according to Hall, the symbolic significations that the indigenous population invests in the adopted cultural features are emically associated with a local identity (civic or ethnic), creating from the very beginning a "hybrid signification."[94] Hall's view of hybridization is of course highly relevant to material culture. Since, as Hodder points out, artifacts' engagement in the negotiations of identities is based on class, age, and gender, 'objects' become relevant to locals only because their messages acquire local or regional significations.[95] To modern scholars, Dora's Hellenistic culture etically expresses a mixed identity, but there can be no doubt that the ancient city's culture must have been constructed and emically perceived as hybrid by its own citizens. In fact, unlike other cities in Phoenicia, Dora did Hellenize its name from Dor to Doros or Dora,[96] and its two most important cultural criteria — language and religion — were both Phoenician and Greek throughout its Hellenistic history.

The process of Romanization of Dora followed the same pattern of Hellenization, although Hellenism and Latin culture remained more distinct than Phoenician and Greek.[97] On the one hand, for instance, the Romans allowed the Greek language to operate as the official language of the city; on the other hand, the diversity and flexibility of Hellenistic Dora allowed the city to accept the changes brought by the Romans, especially in its material culture. [98]

As seen in Chapter 1, archaeological records show that the impact of Rome was great. The entire physical appearance of Dora in fact changed, and new structures, i.e., *villae*, a theater, aqueducts, monuments, etc. were built with new materials and in new ways. The issue is, of course, determining how the people of Dora perceived their new Roman identity, and how the concept of *Romanitas* permeated their pre-existing identity.

The Roman belief that cities should be autonomous, although under gubernatorial surveillance, allowed Dora, for instance, to mint its own Roman coins immediately after the arrival of Pompey — a fact that must have greatly contributed to the city's self-identification as part of the larger Roman sphere. In particular, the iconography of the Severan coins presents a city that seems to have achieved the status of a 'mini-Rome.'[99] And yet, since Dora was on the outskirts of the Syrian province, most of the Romans defending or settling the city, both military and civilian, were probably not from Rome but from Antioch, thus spreading what Peter Wells calls a "filtered" version of *Romanitas*.[100]

In a city such as Dora, with a long Greek/Hellenistic history, it can be assumed that identity could not have been a simple matter of choice between Greek and Roman. On the contrary, Roman identity must have been a superstructure that slowly changed the city, once the local élite, Greek and Phoenician in origin, assimilated to Roman standards. And this assimilation must be considered as a slow process, whereby the local élite imitated Roman officials present in the city by being part of the local administration and political life in a Roman fashion and by acquiring Roman juridical rights. As suggested by Woolf, becoming Roman is not exactly acquiring "a fixed package of thoughts considered to be Roman,"[101] but rather acting in various "Roman ways,"[102] without necessarily losing one's own identity. The citizens of Dora, therefore, could have easily considered themselves both Greek and Roman, as demonstrated by the persistence of the Greek language and the local religious traditions side by side with Roman traditions.

Dora's Graeco-Roman identity, present in all material culture of the city, is most evident in its Roman numismatic material. Like several other Hellenistic cities, Dora had minted coins during its Ptolemaic period,[103] and the Romans respected the custom and continued the long-standing tradition. However, while the Ptolemaic silver coins of Dora are examples of late Hellenistic royal coinage with little local autonomy, the Roman imperial bronze coins express Dora's true hybrid identity. Together with imperial portraits and other Roman symbols, the iconography and

---

[92] Hall 2003, 39. About the early Greek contacts with the Italian indigenous peoples, for instance, John Boardman wrote, "When the Greeks arrived [in Sicily], the Sikel culture had perhaps only just admitted painted pottery beside the plain incised ware … the impact of Greek ideas and culture was immediate… On many Sikel sites near the early colonies we find Greek vases, and often two vases which are native in shape but quite Greek in decoration" (*The Greek Overseas*, 1999). And later he added, "The Etruscans accepted all they were offered [by the Greeks] without discrimination. They copied — or paid Greeks and perhaps immigrant Easterners to copy — with little understanding of the forms and subjects which served as models" (*The Greek Overseas*, 1999). One wonders, along with Hall, how it is possible that the Chigi Vase meant nothing to its Etruscan owner; whether the symbolic significations that the Etruscan owner invested in the object were in accordance with those of its Greek manufacturer; and whether this is not an example of mutual hybridization, which Hall calls the "Etruscanization of Greek culture" (2003, 39).

[93] Hall 2004b, 43.

[94] Hall 2004b, 44. An example to illustrate mutual hybridization is what Hall describes as the Africanization of Coca-Cola used in western Kenya as a special-occasion luxury drink.

[95] Hodder 1982, 185.

[96] The only other Phoenician city that Hellenized its name was Acre, which became Ptolemeis in 250 BCE. The cities of Arados, Tyre, Sidon, Botrys, Berytus, Sarepta and Joppa kept the same names throughout the Hellenistic period. See Schürer 1979, 122.

[97] For material culture displaying both Phoenician and Greek language, see discussion in Chapter 1.

[98] Stern 2000, 261- 318.

[99] The coins will be discussed in Chapter 4.

[100] Wells 1999, 127. Antioch was already one of the largest cities of the Greek world and further developed as the center of Roman administration of the region and later as an imperial residence. See Millar 1993, 91.

[101] Woolf 1998, 245.

[102] Ibid.

[103] According to Butcher (2001, 212), nearly all the Hellenistic cities minted their own coins.

the iconology of these coins, in fact, present a great variety of local images, each one a clearly recognizable sign of communal identity to its users. Furthermore, the visibly non-Greek deities represented on the coins are evidence of the survival of a pre-Greek identity even under Roman rule.

The remaining chapters will therefore reflect on these ancient coins as artifactual records of cultural and social trends in order to arrive at that common understanding that made each Dora coin a semeion, i.e., a sign, to the people of the city. It is inevitable that the investigation aims at being a study of numismatics written for non-numismatists. In fact, I will discuss not so much the numismatic evidence as such, but rather all possible interpretations that contribute to the Dora narrative. In addition, the study will be relevant to the understanding of the role of visual media in the ancient world. The chronological parameters of the study will be restricted since the medium — presently available coins — is limited. Moreover, because the Hellenistic minting period was short-lived with only one specimen from the rule of Ptolemy V (205-199 BCE), most of the study will focus on coins from the Roman period, beginning in 64/63 BCE and ending in 211/212 CE. The dates are not significant in the archaeological history of the city, but will obviously determine the scope of the investigation. Each of the following chapters will then be a study of limited scope, bound by the chronology and the iconography of the available coins.

Chapter 3
The Mint of Dora

3.1 The Concept of Money

Historians and economists, including Karl Marx have long studied the institutional role of ancient mints, and the "store of value" and "medium of exchange" functions of the coins within the ancient circum-Mediterranean monetary economies.[1] Recently, however, ancient coin studies have transcended the studies of history and economics, and coins have become objects of study as important semiotic phenomena. As stated in the previous chapter, the ancient use and exchange of coins is not just a social convenience, but also a triadic event, in which the symbol of money, i.e., a piece of currency, "allows … people to share in a common understanding of the world."[2] But before looking at this particular role of coins, it is natural to ask how and why coinage originated in the West, and how it arrived in Dora. The minting of coins in Dora was in fact firmly rooted in a tradition that had operated mints throughout the Greek world from about 600 BCE.

Most classical scholars agree that the earliest coins came from Lydia and the East Greek area and were probably issued around the third or fourth quarter of the seventh century BCE.[3] According to Herodotus, who quotes the sixth century philosopher Xenophanes as an authority, the Lydians were the first retail traders and "the first of men whom we know, [that] struck and used currency of gold and silver."[4] Regardless of where the earliest coins were minted, however, the earliest archaeological context for electrum coinage is the Temple of Artemis in Ephesus, with a secure *terminus ante quem* of c. 560 BCE.[5]

Very little is known about the early function of coins or the authorities issuing the earliest coinage, but many hypotheses and theories have been advanced by scholars who have based their ideas on literary sources, ethnographical and anthropological analyses, and even modern economic considerations on how ancient economies might have

worked.[6] Writing in 1892, Carl Menger, an economist, traced the origin of coinage in the early civilization's desire for the special attributes of precious metals, first as personal ornaments and subsequently as choice materials for architectural decoration and vessels of every kind. He adds,

It cannot be doubted that, long before [precious metals] had become the generally acknowledged media of exchange, they were, amongst very many peoples, meeting a positive and effective demand at all times and places, and practically in any quantity that found its way to market. Hence arose a circumstance, which necessarily became of special import for their becoming money.[7]

The function of coinage as a universal medium of exchange does not refer, according to Menger's theory, to a "general commercial convention or a legal dispensation … [but to] their saleableness [that] is far and away superior to that of all other commodities."[8] Writing in 1933, the British numismatist Charles Seltman suggested, however, that coins of precious metal must have originated as a medium of exchange, perhaps with "some Ionian merchant, who made a private mark on electrum dumps so that when in the course of circulation they returned to him, he would not have to weigh them again."[9] In the same tone, in 1958 the classical archaeologist R. M. Cook suggested that coinage was invented among traders to allow "uniform payments of considerable value in a portable and durable form."[10] Writing in 1964, Kraay challenged the economists' assumption that coins originated to facilitate trade by noting that the early denominations were too large, that circulation of coins was too narrow, and that use of coins was limited to Greeks while trade had existed for thousands of years without coins. Coins,

---

[1] The "store of value function" of money is its ability to be saved, stored, and retrieved in a predictably useful manner. The "medium of exchange function" is the durability of money when used in trade. See Bernstein 2008, 29-39.

[2] Dyer 1989, 505.

[3] Kraay 1976, 313; Casey 1986, 12; Kurke 1999, 3. The earliest coin type, the Lydian *stater* with a roaring lion facing right and a reverse incuse, was made of electrum, an alloy of gold with 20% silver. See also Jenkins 1990, 14; Wallace 1987, 386; Robinson 1951, 159. There are some scholars who argue for different sources for the origin of the first coin. Thompson (2003, 67-87) and Chandler (1992, 42-43) both believe the origin to be in Jerusalem; and Balmuth (1971, 1-7) argues for northern Syria.

[4] Herodotus' *Histories*, I. 94.

[5] Howgego 1995, 2. The coins under the Artemision were in lumps of electrum, with the most common type depicting a lion's head. See Karwiese 1991, 10.

[6] Casey 1986, 12.

[7] Menger 1892, 253. Carl Menger (1840 -1921) was the founder of the *Austrian School of Economics*. In his 1871 book *Principles of Economics (Grundsätze der Volkswirtschaftslehre)* Menger advanced the theory of "total utility" vs. "marginal utility" of goods. He asserted that the marginal utility of goods is the source of their value rather than the labor that goes into making them. For more on Menger's marginalist theory, see O'Driscoll 1986.

[8] Menger 1892, 253.

[9] Seltman 1933, x

[10] Cook 1958, 257. Modern economic historians still maintain the view that coinage came into existence to serve trade and commerce, and that it evolved without any government intervention due to its convenient accounting properties (Murray 1993, 237-240). Finley (1973, 166) argued, however, that the ancient Greek economy should not be studied using the concepts of modern economic science because economic actions in antiquity were determined primarily by social and not economic concerns. Other recent scholarship suggests that some cities in Magna Graecia and in Ptolemaic Egypt used coin minting to increase their state coffers by exchanging their lighter weight standard coins with heavier foreign coins and thus making a profit. See Le Rider 1989, 159-172; Martin 1985, 225-226.

he argued, were "not invented for the purpose of any sort of trade … [but] rather for the convenience and profit of the issuing authority."[11]Finally, in an article published in 1970 about money and exchange in the Roman world, Crawford argued, "coinage was probably invented in order that a large number of state payments might be made in a convenient form and there is no reason to suppose that it was issued for any other reason than … for financial reason."[12]

But while Crawford used the correlation between the output of silver coinage and military expenditure in the Roman republican period to make his argument,[13] other numismatists and cultural historians have been reluctant to impose modern economic thinking on early societies and have looked at other, not necessarily practical, reasons to justify the minting of coins in ancient cities. Finley ascribed "civic pride" as one of the most important motives. Coinage, he wrote, was essentially a "political phenomenon, a piece of local vanity, patriotism or advertisement with no far-reaching importance."[14] Starr also shared the point of view that early issues of coins were "occasioned by the public needs of the *polis*,"[15] and he added that coin minting in Greek cities was "to advertise the growing pride and power of the minting *poleis*."[16] Similarly, Helmut Engelmann believes that Greek coinage was "ein politisches Phänomen" (a political phenomenon) with the specific function of making the city's sovereignty "greifbar und sichtbar" (visible and palpable).[17] Martin was not, however, convinced that coins were a matter of state sovereignty, pride and power, and did not agree that ancient cities were in the business of minting coins much like "modern states produce national flags."[18] The adoption of coinage, he argued, was connected to the evolution of a "tradition that obligated wealthier citizens to contribute to the well-being of the city state."[19] In

fact, in cities with no kings or rulers in charge of public spending, the development of community-wide events and the need for large public structures created a sort of shared responsibility, which "entailed a reconfiguration of social and financial relations"[20] among the citizens. Coinage became necessary because it gave the citizens of the *polis* a way of pooling resources for public projects in order to share financial burden, pay workers, and accumulate the money needed for an army or a navy. In other words, those who could afford it contributed to the well-being of the entire community. The fact that the Greek word for coins *nomismata* ('customary things') derives from νόμος ('law or custom') implies that the coinage's function was indeed sanctioned by the *polis* and intended for the benefit of the entire community.[21]

But if one view of coinage's purpose is that of "a source of revenue in support of *ta koina* (common concerns),"[22] more recently scholars are approaching the subject from an analysis of the literary texts of the period, without any economic considerations. Kurke, for instance, argues that the minting of coins was mostly for the benefit of the state and arose as a counterweight to the power of the *symposia* and other institutions that maintained élite power; thus:

The minting of coin would represent the state's assertion of its ultimate authority to constitute and regulate value in all the spheres in which general-purpose money operated simultaneously—economic, social, political, and religious. Thus, state- issued coinage as a universal equivalent, like the civic *agora* in which it circulated, symbolized the merger in a single token or site of many different domains of value, all under the final authority of the city.[23]

Howgego also uses literary sources (inscriptions, papyri, and law codes) as evidence that the development and spread of coinage was dependent on the development of the *polis*, writing:

The explanation is rather to be found in the receptive ground provided by the radical transformation of the *polis* in the sixth century BCE. The interactions of economic, social and political changes were complex. The spread of coinage may itself be seen both as caused by such changes, and also as an agent of the process.[24]

Emphasizing that the spread of coinage "furthered the role of commodification and social and political changes"[25] that had caused its invention, Howgego argued that the transfer of coinage eventually became the dominant means of exchange in the Roman world where "the use of

---

[11] Kraay 1964, 91. He also argued that coinage "remained essentially a Greek phenomenon, which … the Etruscans, Phoenicians, Carthaginians and Egyptians were slow to adopt" (Kraay 1976, 317). Kraay's view that coin circulation was narrow has been questioned. The discovery of Corinthian and Aeginetan coins in Sicily, for instance, would be examples of broader circulations of coins. See Arnold-Biucchi 1988, 1-35.

[12] Crawford 1970, 40. The same concept was expressed in *La Moneta in Grecia e a Roma* (Crawford 1982: 120-2).

[13] His argument has been dismissed as being too limited in time (c.157 to c. 80 BCE) and as having speculative figures for military expenditures. See Mattingly 1977, 199-215; Hopkins 1980, 111; Howgego 1995, 2. Other scholars argue that the Roman monetary policy, which controlled money supply in order to influence production and exchange or to maintain a closed currency system, runs against ancient evidence on the origin of coinage. See Lo Cascio 1981, 76-86; Howgego 1985, 88-92; Burnett 1987, 99-92.

[14] Finley 1973, 166.

[15] Starr 1977, 112.

[16] Starr 1983, 431.

[17] Engelmann 1985, 165.

[18] Martin 1996, 260. The idea that coins were a symbol of sovereign identity has given justification to the common understanding that Hellenistic monarchs restricted or suppressed Greek cities from minting coins. Martin argues, however, citing Barclay Head, that the right to mint coins was monopolized by the states as "a source of considerable profit" (Head 1911, vii). Davis also states, "since minting was profitable, all kings … attempted to control minting within their own territories, to the point where the issue of *tetradrachma* was a symbol of sovereignty maintained … or autonomy conceded" (Davis 1984, 280) as cited in Martin 1996, footnote 13. See also Martin 1985, 219, 242, 245.

[19] Ibid., 267.

[20] Ibid., 269

[21] Greeks had no word for money, neither before nor after coinage, but used the term *chremata* (i.e., useful things) a word that referred "to all the goods that a person might possess." See von Reden 1995, 177; Schaps 2004, 16.

[22] The background would be that of wealthy citizens "performing *leitourgiai* (sacred services) for the benefit of the entire civic community" (Martin 1996, 264).

[23] Kurke 1999, 12-13.

[24] Howgego 1995, 16.

[25] Ibid., 18.

money was embedded in the structure of the economy."[26] However, he also claimed that "we have no firm criteria for answering such general questions"[27] as to the reasons behind the invention and spread of coinage in the ancient world.

The difficulties involved in questioning why coinage was invented in the first place do not of course minimize its impact on civilization. The introduction of coinage and its effects, although not uniform for all societies, changed the thought and behavior of the peoples who adopted it in a permanent manner.[28] When analyzed in the perspective of human development, the invention of coinage was indeed a technical innovation that not only changed societies from a nonmonetary to a moneyed status, but also became a manifestation of different social systems in flux.[29] In fact, as the number of cities issuing coins increased, the use of coins spread throughout the Greek and Roman world with little change or innovation, but always reflecting and illuminating different historical periods in multifaceted ways.

Considering the rapid spread of coinage in all cities of the Graeco-Roman world, a number of issues remain unresolved. The city of Dora did not operate a mint until the Hellenistic period, and one wonders whether there was a need for a mint in Dora at all, given the relatively small size of the city and its proximity to larger cities such as Tyre, Sidon, and, later, Caesarea where large issues were the norm. Since coin losses — and consequent archaeological finds — are considered to be proportional to the volume and value of the coins originally issued and to the political and economic factors prevailing during the lifetime of the coins, one also wonders whether it is possible to arrive at an approximate output of the Dora mint.[30] Lastly, since no physical evidence of a mint has ever been unearthed among the archaeological structures of Dora, the question arises about the possibility that the minting for the city of Dora was actually done elsewhere.[31]

3.2 The Mint of Dora and its Production History

Although no archaeological excavations at Tel Dor have ever produced remains of a building complex dedicated to minting coins,[32] there is numismatic evidence that coins were issued by the city of Dora during the reign of Ptolemy V Epiphanes (204-181 BCE).[33] Coins had been circulating in the city from the fourth century on, the oldest specimens being Phoenician coins minted at Tyre in the fourth century BCE,[34] and Ptolemaic coins issued in cities along the coastal areas were in circulation in large numbers, mostly from the reign of Ptolemy I and Ptolemy II.[35] Ptolemy V came to the throne after the death of Ptolemy IV Philopater in 205 BCE as a five-year old, and his accession was followed by much violence. During the Fifth Syrian War (202-199 BCE), in fact, Antiochus III of Syria conquered the territories in Phoenicia and Palestina, including the city of Dora. It is during Ptolemy V's brief rule of Dora, however, that a single *tetradrachm* type, representing the young king, was issued probably between 202-199 BCE (**No. 1**). The positive attribution to the mint of Dora has been established on account of the letters ΔΩ, inscribed on the left field of the reverse, and representing the initials of the city's name, much like the ΣΙ found on the coins from Sidon.[36]

The Ptolemaic coinage unearthed at Tel Dor includes two hoards of forty-seven and ten silver *tetradrachma* respectively with a total of 135 specimens. Although this number does not offer any conclusive evidence for a ratio of circulation, the number is large enough to guarantee that it is not just due to the vagaries of circulation and excavation; rather, it indicates that Ptolemaic coinage from neighboring cities had broad use within Dora's territory.[37]

---

[26] Ibid., 22.

[27] Howgego 1995, 25.

[28] Schaps 2004, 15.

[29] Von Reden 1997, 154

[30] Newton 2006, 211-227; Casey 1986, 69. There are presently nearly one thousand known specimens of Dora's coins available in museums and private collections throughout Europe, Israel, and the United States, including: Tel Dor Excavation (300), Israel Antiquity Authorities (64), Israel Museum Jerusalem (28), Eretz Israel Museum Tel Aviv (25), American Numismatic Society New York (36), British Museum London (49), Bank of Israel Jerusalem (8), Hebrew University Museum (20), and private collections, i.e., the A. Sofaer private collection New York (41), the A. Fichman private collection Haifa (150). The 50 coins in the present catalogue come from the various collections and were selected for either their uniqueness (**No. 16**) or their fairly good condition.

[31] This question arises from the knowledge that the city of Neapolis in southern Italy, struck silver coins for other cities in the Campania region in the fifth and early fourth century BCE. See Rutter 1997, 75, 82-83, 102; Forsythe 2005, 338. Furthermore, in his book *Das System der Kaiserzeitlichen Münzprägung in Kleinasien: Materialen und Entwürfe* (1972), Konrad Kraft, finding evidence of die links among coins of different cities in Asia Minor, proposed the existence of a provincial *'Werkstätte'*, a sort of atelier that supplied the entire province. For an assessment of Kraft's work, see Johnston's review article (1974, 203-207).

[32] Mint buildings that are positively identified usually contain evidence of metal refining and coin blanks, together with bronze bars and discs cut from similar bars. Few official mints have ever been located in the Graeco-Roman world. See Howgego 1995, 26-30. For more on excavations and identification of the mint of Athens, see Lewis 1990, 257-263. For mints in Rome, see Coarelli 1985, 192-5.

[33] The finds of silver-plated Tissaphernes' *drachma* at Tel Dor has led some scholars to believe that there was a mint operating at Dor during the Persian period. In the excavation report of 1967, Meshorer attributed one Tissaphernes' coin excavated in D3 to the mint of Dor (1967, 466, No. 10). A similar coin excavated in D2, however, was attributed to the mint of Sigeum in Troas by von Aulock (1967, No. 7636). A total of ten Tissaphernes' coins have been excavated since the 1960s, and Qedar has recently attributed all ten coins to the mint of Dor (2002, 9-14), basing his analysis on comparison to Tissaphernes' coins minted in Astyra. Any analysis of these coins is beyond the scope of this study.

[34] Tyre, Sidon, and Arwad were the first Phoenician cities to mint coins. See Elayi 1993, 89-90, 240-241, 363-65. For coins of Judea, see Meshorer 1982.

[35] The total number of silver *tetradrachma* unearthed at Tel Dor, including the two hoards, is 135. The coins come from mints throughout the area — Sidon, Tyre, Jaffa, Gaza, Ephesus, and Alexandria (Stern 2000, 256-257). The coin hoards have not been published.

[36] Mørkholm (1981, 5) and Meshorer (1995, 356) have attributed the coins to the mint of Dora. More recently, scholars (Meadow, 3/2/2010) have questioned the validity of ΔΩ as a mintmark and therefore doubted the definite attribution of the coin to the mint of Dora. For the sake of our study, however, we will follow Mørkholm and Meshorer and accept the Ptolemaic silver coins as having been minted at Dora.

[37] Mørkholm 1982, 290-305; Newton 2006, 211-227. Reece (1993, 59) notes, however, that the different standards and denominations of coin finds make it difficult to arrive at any conclusive study of coin finds to assess circulations. He also argues that coin hoards are "bad indicators of

Since Ptolemaic coins were readily available in Dora, it is interesting to assess the need to operate a mint in the city during the last few years of the Ptolemies' rule. However, According to Von Reden although the coinages of the Ptolemaic political sphere mixed very easily through circulation, "their issue often had local purposes."[38] It is therefore tempting to assume that the minting of Ptolemy V coins in Dora was a matter of local royal authority, i.e., a final attempt at maintaining the established Ptolemaic sovereignty over the city. If, however, as Martin argues, the purpose of coinage was that of "a source of revenue"[39] or a means to pool resources for the state, it is reasonable to assume that the Ptolemaic Dora coins had a fundamentally economic reason behind their production. In other words, the city's Egyptian authorities issued Ptolemy V *tetradrachma* to sustain the war efforts during the Fifth Syrian War (202-195 BCE). Coins were in fact issued in other mints throughout Phoenicia during the same years, in an "effort to stave off the Syrian invasion."[40] The Ptolemaic closed currency system prohibited the use of foreign coins in any of the Egyptian territories, making the exchange of foreign coins compulsory. This might also explain the minting of Ptolemy V coins at Dora, since new Ptolemaic coins would be needed to keep up with the foreign exchange.[41] On the other hand, a festival, a ritual, or a royal donation may have provided the occasion for the new coinage.[42] The economic factors involved in the minting of Ptolemy V *tetradrachma* in Dora are, however, particularly important when one considers that the issuing of coins stopped completely after the Seleucid conquest of Dora. In fact, the mint did not issue any coinage for the entire period of Seleucid domination (199-100 BCE), and most of the coins found at Tel Dor from the period were minted in Antioch, Apamea, and Akko-Ptolemais.[43]

It is tempting to view the disappearance of minting on political grounds, i.e., "a gesture of dominance"[44] from the incoming power. It is just as likely, however, that the mint stopped issuing coins because the people who previously ran it were no longer in power, and because the economic factors to which the coins had been a response were no longer in place.[45] Another possibility is that the mint ceased its operation during the entire Seleucid period because the city itself did not have the civic independence to issue coins nor was the Seleucid royal control strong enough to produce coinage in the city. In reality, given the size of the city, the non-issue rather than the issue of coins the normal occurrence.[46]

In contrast to the Ptolemaic royal monopoly of coinage, the Seleucids' attitude of non-interference in money matters created a de facto laissez-faire policy in Phoenicia. While the production of gold and large silver coins was in fact controlled by royal mints, most cities issued their own bronze coins, and under King Antiochus IV (187–175 BCE) as many as nineteen cities, including the Phoenician and Palestinian cities of Tripolis, Byblos, Berytus (renamed Laodicea in Canaan), Sidon, Tyre, and Akko-Ptolemais (renamed Antioch in Ptolemais), were allowed to mint semiautonomous and autonomous bronze coins.[47] Moreover, in the second half of the second century, all Phoenician seaports (Sidon, Tyre, Berytus, and Akko-Ptolemais) produced a new *tetradrachm* on the Ptolemaic standard, with an eagle on the reverse side.[48] As seen from the excavation reports, Dora was flooded with Seleucid coinage from nearby mints and was not in need of issuing its own coins. Finally, toward the latter part of the second century, the city was directly involved in the Seleucid dynastic feuds, becoming the final stronghold of two usurpers — Tryphon (142-139 BCE) who fought against Antioch VII, and Zoilus (104 BCE) who eventually lost Dora to the Hasmoneans — and no minting took place in the city.[49] Understandably, the mint did not operate during the brief reign of Alexander Jannaeus, whose coins were all struck in Judea.[50] On the other hand, since the abundant Seleucid coinage, especially the municipal bronzes, were in many ways the precursors of the Roman coins for their "incongruous mixture of royal portraits and civic design,"[51] it is no surprise that once Pompey annexed Dora to the province of Syria, the mint reopened in Dora, issuing quasi-autonomous coins perhaps as an expression of the city's civic identity at a time when this identity might as well be under threat, or perhaps as an affirmation of Rome's authority.

standard with the issuing of coins being the 'anomalous' state of affairs.
[47] Mørkholm 1961, 63. After the Peace of Apamea (188 BCE), the Seleucid Empire west of the Euphrates comprised three districts: 1) Syria with capital Antioch; 2) Coele Syria and Phoenicia with capital Akko-Ptolemais; and Cilicia with capitol Tarsus. For the first 20 years no silver coins were produced in Coele Syria and Phoenicia. See Mørkholm 1985, 93-95; le Rider 1986, 3-5; Howgego 1995, 52. For the Seleucid monetary policy in Coele Syria and Phoenicia, see Le Rider 1995, 391-404. For a thorough study on money in Ptolemaic Egypt, see von Reden 2007.
[48] Mørkholm 1985, 93-95. The use of the Ptolemaic standard may imply a certain reaction to the gradual withdrawal of Seleucid control. See Howgego 1995, 52.
[49] Tryphon minted coins in Antioch, always with a Macedonian helmet on the reverse type, as a reference to his Macedonian soldiers. See Newell 1915, 71-73.
[50] During the reign of Alexander Jannaeus, the main currency of his kingdom was the autonomous silver *shekel* (and half-*shekel*) of Tyre. He, like his predecessors, failed to mint any silver coinage, but issued instead a huge quantity of bronze *prutot*, inscribed with his royal and priestly titles. According to Jewish coin tradition and in opposition to the surrounding Greek and later Roman types, the coinage eschewed human or animal representations, focusing on symbols, either natural, such as the palm tree, the pomegranate or the star, or man-made, such as the Temple, the Menorah, trumpets or cornucopia. Alexander made changes to Jewish coinage, however, by adding a royal bilingual type, with inscriptions in Hebrew and Greek or Aramaic and Greek. For an in-depth study of Alexander Jannaeus' coinage, see Meshorer 1982, 57-59; Hendin and Shachar 2008, 87-94; for a study on the relations between Alexander Jannaeus and the Hellenistic cities of Israel, see Kasher 1990.
[51] Meadows 2001, 61.

the relative frequency of denominations in circulation or in production" (61) because coins in hoards tend to be of high value.
[38] Von Reden 2007, 11; Le Rider 1995, 391-404. For a thorough study on Ptolemaic and Seleucid coins, see Le Rider and Callataÿ 2006.
[39] Martin 1996, 264.
[40] Mørkholm 1991, 109.
[41] Jenkins 1967, 53-54; Von Reden 2007, 43-4. Ptolemy I had stopped minting coins with Alexander's portrait by c. 310 BC, abandoning the Attic weight of 17.2 gr. and establishing the Ptolemaic *tetradrachm* at 14.3 gr. See also Le Rider 1986, 3-57.
[42] Von Reden 2007, 12.
[43] For a complete list, see Chapter 1.8.
[44] Meadows 2001, 54.
[45] Ibid., 58.
[46] Meadows pointed out (02/28/2010) that the non-issue of coins is the

Date on Coin L	A	B	ΘI	ΔA	BA	NZ	OH	PKH	MP	AAP	BAP	ΘAP	POE	IIP	CZ	EΞC	AOC	EOC
	1	2	19	31	32	57	78	128	130	131	132	139	175	180	207	265	274	275
Historical Date	64/63 BCE	63/62	45/44	33/32	32/31	7/6	14/15 CE	64/65	66/67	67/68	68/69	75/76	111/112	117	143/144	201/202	210/211	211/212
Type																		
Quasi-Autonomous	X	X			X		X	X	X	X	X	X						
Antony and Cleopatra			X?	X														
Augustus						X												
Vespasian											X							
Titus											X							
Trajan													X					
Hadrian														X				
Antoninus Pius															X			
Septimius Severus																X		
Julia Domna																X		X
Geta																X		
Caracalla																	X	
Plautilla																X		

TABLE 1: ROMAN PERIOD ISSUES

Roman minting at Dora resumed a tradition that had ceased for almost 140 years and continued, although with several interruptions, for 275 years. Dora was, in fact, the first city of western Palestine to mint Roman coins of various values from the very first year of Pompey's arrival.[52] Although the coins continued a Greek tradition, there is no doubt that the arrival of Rome caused a civic need for the minting of Dora's own coins. The lack of a king and the presence of Roman authorities fostered the city's civic development, which in turn created a need for currency to be minted locally.[53] Dora's first year minting of quasi-autonomous coinage was therefore done under the auspices of Pompey, who provided the impetus to initiate a new civic era in Dora.[54] In fact, the mint started designating the dates on its coins starting from Year One of the Roman era, although it continued the Ptolemaic tradition of designating the year (ετων) with a symbol resembling the Roman letter L.[55]

As shown on Table 1, the first output of Dora coins is dated L A (Year 1 = 64/3 BCE) (**No. 2, 3, 4, 5, 6**) and was followed by L B (year 2 = 63/2). The dating of the only surviving specimen of the second year (**No. 7**) is not secure, however, as Hill and Meshorer have conflicting views on how to read the date.[56] Several undated coins seem to fit either the first or second-year type, but, again, the dating is not secure.[57]

Minting seems to have ceased for some years, and no coins have been found until the two Antony and Cleopatra issues respectively dated LΘI (year 19) (**No. 8**) and LΛA (year 31) (**No. 9**).[58] However, while coin **No. 9** is clearly datable to 32 BCE in relation to the new Pompeian civic era — a date that is historically feasible for a joint coin of Antony and Cleopatra — the date of coin **No. 8** as 44 BCE is questionable. Cleopatra was physically in Rome in 45 BCE, a guest of Julius Caesar, and a joint portrayal of the Egyptian queen with Antony on coins issued by the mint of Dora in 44 BCE is historically unfeasible. Furthermore, as stated earlier, Cleopatra acquired Dora in 35 BCE, and it is therefore unlikely that the mint of the city would issue a coin with her portrait any time before 35 BCE. Baldus' suggestion is that a different civic era should be considered, i.e., year 19 from the era of Cleopatra's becoming queen (51 BCE), which would give coin No. 3 the absolute date of 33 BCE, a feasible historical date.[59] The date, however, would still not fit with the date of coin **No. 9**, raising the possibility that coin **No. 8** was minted in a different city.[60]

---

[52] Meshorer 1995, 359.

[53] The link between the mint and the Roman military presence will be discussed later in the chapter.

[54] According to Josephus (*Jewish War* 1.7.7) Pompey was able to win over the inhabitants of the East not only with his good will, but also with the building and rebuilding of cities, including Dora, which was annexed to Syria. See Chapter 1.

[55] Avigad 1962, 7.

[56] Hill dated the coin (*BMC, Phoenicia*, No. 24) 68/9 CE; Meshorer (1995, 362) dated it 63/2.

[57] Henceforth all the numbers of Greek dating will be considered 'of the Pompeian era'.

[58] Meshorer 1995, 359.

[59] Baldus 1989, 477. For the date of Cleopatra's acquisition of Dora in 35 BCE, see Josephus, *Antiquities* 14.5.3 and 15.4.1; *The Jewish War* 1.7.7. Van Henten (2005, 119) believes, however, that Josephus' identification of the territories that Antony gave to Cleopatra is not historically accurate.

[60] One possibility raised by *RPC* (I, 661) is the city of Tripolis. Another suggestion made by Meadows (02/28/2010) is the city of Askalon, where Cleopatra minted coins. However, Cleopatra seems to have lost control of Askalon after 38 BCE (Sidonius, *Letters* 8.12.8; cited in Roller 2010, 92), making Baldus' date of 33 BC again difficult to reconcile. The proper dating of coin **No. 9** is, however, beyond the scope of this study.

The rise and consolidation of Augustus' rule prompted the mint to issue coins portraying the emperor in 7 BCE (LNZ = year 57) (**No. 10**); the alleged issue of 14 CE (OH = year 78) is disputed because of the difficulty of reading the date on the coin.[61] A more systematic production of quasi-autonomous coinage of three different denominations was carried on yearly from 65/64 (PKH = year 128) until 68/69 (BΛP = 132) (**No. 11-21**). The largest minting, in 67/68 (MP = 130), was connected to the outbreak of the Jewish War in 67 and corresponds to an increase in minting in other cities that sided with the Romans, perhaps as contributions to the war expenses.[62] The coinage of 68/69 consists of both quasi-autonomous coins (**No. 18**) and coins with portraits of Vespasian (**No. 19-20**) and Titus (**No. 21**) — perhaps issued to celebrate the Flavians' accession to the throne. Coins issued in the year 75 (ΘΛP = 139) (**No. 22-23**) are only autonomous. The mint did not operate under Domitian (81-96 CE), when the neighboring city of Caesarea Maritima seems to have fulfilled Dora's currency needs. Coins of Domitian, struck by King Agrippa II at Caesarea Maritima, were in fact circulating in Dora in large quantities.[63]

Although no minting occurred under Nerva (96-98 CE), the mint of Dora reached its greatest output under Trajan (98-117) in 112 CE (EOΠ = 175) (**No. 24-29**), the only year in which coins were minted. The emperor's monetary policy in Syria might be the basis for Dora's large output and production climax. Dora's mint saw two more years of activity, when it issued coins with the bust of Hadrian in 117 CE (ΠP = 180) (**No. 30-34**), and again with the bust of Antoninus Pius in the year 144 CE (CZ = 207) (**No. 35-37**), after which it was not operative until 202. With the advent of the Severans in 193, a flurry of minting took place throughout the eastern provinces, and the number of mints issuing imperial coinage rose from 150 at the time of Augustus to over 360.[64] Dora seemed to join in celebrating the eastern roots of Septimius Severus' wife and in 202 (year EΞC = 265) the mint issued coins portraying each individual member of the Severan family — Septimius Severus (**No. 38**), Julia Domna (**No. 39**), Caracalla (**No. 40**), Plautilla (**No. 41**), and Geta (**No. 42**). The most likely explanation for such a large representation of the Severan family could be connected to either the marriage of Caracalla and Plautilla, which took place in 202, or the upcoming *decennalia* (i.e., the tenth anniversary) of Septimius' reign in 203.[65] The reopening of the mint after a fifty-eight-year break and the minting of a large number of coins were, however, most likely connected to the economic growth of the city under the Severi.[66] The mint honored Caracalla as sole emperor (**No. 43-47**) in 210/1 (year ΔOC= 274), the year both his father and his brother died, while Julia Domna was portrayed in the issuance of 212 (year EOC = 275), five years before her death (**No. 48-50**). No coins minted in Dora after this date are known to exist, prompting the assumption that the mint ceased to exist with the end of Caracalla's reign. As shown from the Israel Antiquities Authority (IAA) collection, the autonomous types seem to be the largest number of Dora's coins available today, with Trajan's type as the second largest number (**Table** 2).[67]

The issue of minting autonomy in the Greek *poleis* under Roman imperial rule has been much discussed by Roman scholars and numismatists, and it is particularly important at Dora, where 'quasi-autonomous' coins are very common. The lack of imperial portraits on the 'quasi-autonomous' coins has often been taken as an indication that cities could issue coinage without requiring Roman authorization, and that consequently Roman authorities had granted these cities the right to issue coinage without imperial portraiture as a sign of political autonomy. Butcher, however, has successfully argued that the "evidence from cities with 'autonomous' or 'free' status contradicts that theory."[68] While Athens, for instance, always struck coins without imperial portraits, other free cities, such as Apamea in Syria and Amisus in Pontus, only issued coins with imperial portraits.[69] Furthermore, the notion that the minting of coins without imperial portraits was a sign of the autonomy or independence of a city may very well be the imposition of modern post-colonialist concepts on those ancient cities, which in fact may have regarded imperial portraits on their coins as "a mark of prestige honoring the emperor and his family."[70] In Dora, the issue of coins with and without imperial portraits seems to indicate that the city could honor local religious icons, together with, and not in contrast to imperial figures. In fact, the religious iconography of Dora is the most important and constant coin iconography, with Tyche and Zeus Doros present on the majority of Dora's coins either as the obverse type — in the autonomous coins — or as the reverse of the imperial types. Moreover, the mint of Dora issued quasi-autonomous and imperial coins contemporaneously, often with very close visual links between them (Coins **No. 17** and **No. 19**).

From its opening with the arrival of Pompey in 64 BCE to Caracalla's final issues, the mint of Dora produced only bronze coins, and although minted in large numbers, they are not very diversified. In an attempt to assess their value, Meshorer classified them as having three denominations, the largest being the equivalent of a *dupondius*, the medium of an *as*, and the small one the equivalent of a

---

[61] Meshorer (1996, 362) claims that the date is illegible, and could be LΘI (year 19) making it contemporary with coin **No. 8**.
[62] The cities of Caesarea, Nysa-Scythopolis, Hippos and Gerasa fought on the Roman side and saw a larger output of coins in the same year. See Meshorer 2001, 104; Kindler and Stein 1987, 104-111.
[63] A close ally of Rome, King Agrippa II broke from the traditional Jewish iconoclastic zealotry and struck coins in Caesarea with his portrait on the reverse of imperial coins of Nero, Vespasian and Domitian. See Kreitzer 1996, 22. Many of Agrippa's coins minted at Caesarea Maritima have been unearthed at Tel Dor. See Meshorer, 1982.
[64] Jones 1966, 295.
[65] Jones 1963, 331.

[66] See Chapter 4.
[67] Some coins originally attributed to Elagabalus and Aquilia Severa have been re-identified as portraits of Caracalla and Julia Domna by the staff of the Israel Antiquities Authority (Bijovski, 07/19/2010).
[68] Butcher 1988, 30.
[69] Ibid.
[70] ibid.

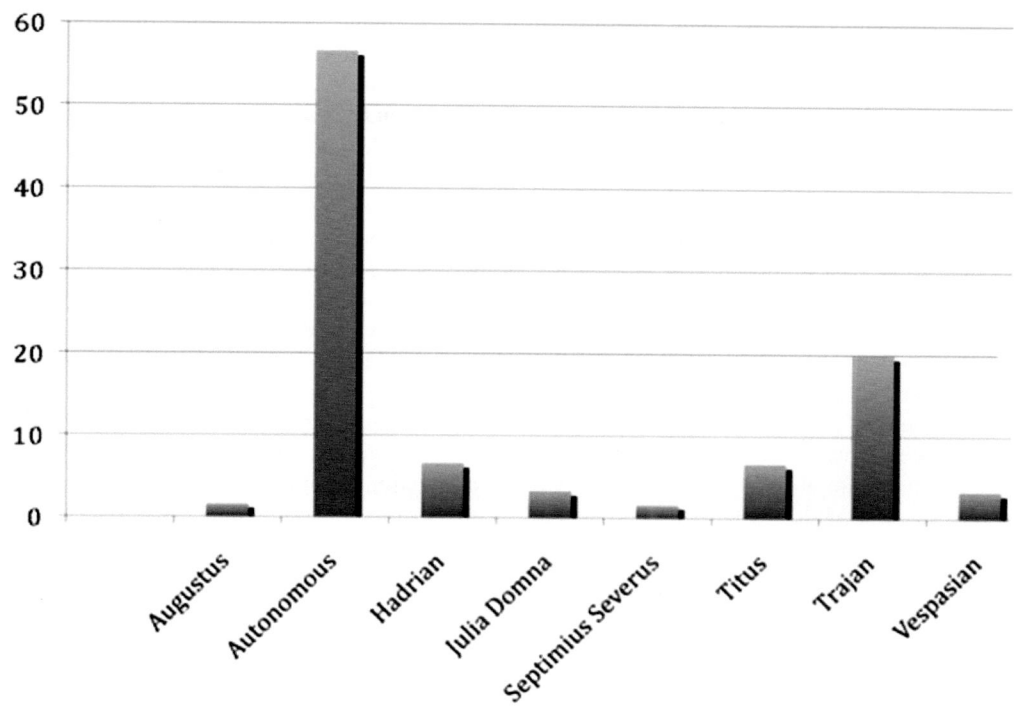

TABLE 2: DENOMINATIONS OF DORA'S IMPERIAL COINS AT THE ISRAEL ANTIQUITIES AUTHORITY

semis.[71] Like most provincial coins, however, Dora's coins lack marks of value, and it is therefore nearly impossible to establish their absolute value against the silver coins of the same period. According to Jones, who pioneered a study of coin values in the 1960s, provincial bronze "flourished in a state of complete metrological anarchy,"[72] and the only estimates of value must rely therefore on the metal, size, and weight of the coin and the image it bears. Analyses of certain cities show, however, that there was control of the weight standard that provides the relative value of the coinage. The standard ratio was in fact one large bronze = two medium bronzes = four small bronzes.[73] Additionally, the designation of 'bronze' is often used to include leaded bronze, copper, and orichalcum.[74] Although the denominational system differed from one province to another, it has long been established that the provincial *dupondius* was generally over-valued against its metal content, approximating one-sixth of a Roman *denarius*, instead of the standard one-eighth of the western-issued coins.[75] Following Meshorer's standardization, it can therefore be assumed that Dora's largest denominations (*dupondii?*) were also valued at the same ratio, although their weight has a broad range, ranging from the 9. 91 gr. for the coins issued by Augustus (**No. 10**) to the 18.46 gr. for the ones issued by Caracalla (**No. 44**). The Roman system of the *as* or *assarion,* as one-half of the value of the *dupondius*, appears to be the standard system of the eastern empire as well, and the denomination is present among the coinage of Dora. Finally, the smallest denomination minted in Dora, the *semis*, would be valued at one-half of the *as*.

More recent studies of provincial coin denominations and the rate of exchange between Roman imperial silver and provincial bronze, however, have questioned the validity of trying to categorize provincial bronzes into Roman denominations, as it is not even clear if or "when Greek denominations were replaced by Roman."[76] According to Butcher, cities in Asia Minor produced civic coins with denominations that were tailored to their own use. He writes,

Although compatibility with Roman usage can be interpreted as a recognized rate of exchange between civic coins and Roman 'monetary units' to a level where

---

[71] Meshorer 1995, 359. Ziegler (1999, 125) has noted that "in the eastern provinces, bronze coins were a substitute for the following denominations: *sestertius, dupondius, as, semis* and *quadrans*, even though their nominal value was not exactly the same as that of the Roman imperial issues." This study will follow Meshorer's three designations.

[72] Jones 1963, 308.

[73] Butcher 1988, 33. In the Antonine period some coin issuing-authorities of the Black Sea region placed the Greek numerals A, B, Γ, and Δ onto their coins, presumably standing for 'one,' 'two,' 'three' and 'four *assaria*' respectively.

[74] Orichalcum is the golden-colored bronze alloy used for the *sestertius* and *dupondius*. It was considered more valuable than copper, which was the metal for the *as*.

[75] Butcher 1988, 33.

[76] Johnston 2007, 243.

Roman *aurei* and *denarii* could circulate empire-wide, denominations were not necessarily identical.[77]

Furthermore, since the coins were intended to circulate into neighboring cities, as is the case with Dora's coins, which have been found in areas throughout Israel, it seems that the city-state could regulate its own compatibility with neighboring cities, while still keeping "compatibility with Roman denominations at least for accounting purposes."[78] As a result, categorizing Dora's coins or any other provincial coins into specific denominations is not a simple task, as the process runs the risk of "forcing unrelated local denominational systems into some *a priori* system."[79] In fact, as recently argued by Johnston, with the exception of the epigraphic evidence presented by Howgego in 1985 on the coins of Chios, "there are virtually no clues as to the denominations in Asia Minor in the first and second century." [80] The most common means to distinguish denominations seem to be tied to the coins' weight and dimensions as well as their designs.[81]

The lack of silver coins from the mint of Dora during the Roman period raises the question of whether this lack was due to political, economic or fiscal reasons. The answer lies in the Roman monetary system itself and with the Roman authorities. After the Third Mithridatic War (74-63 BCE) and the administrative reorganization by Pompey, the only silver coins remaining in circulation were issues by friendly kings and free cities that paid heavy taxation to the Roman authorities.[82] After Augustus' rise to power and the adoption of a new monetary policy to serve the needs of the empire, the traditional eastern *cistophori* became Asia's regional currency, and circulated extensively together with the different denominations of Attic *drachma*[83] During the early empire, Roman authorities continued issuing silver coinage at the same mints that had produced silver coinage under the Seleucids — mostly Antioch, but also at the mints of Damascus, Tyre, Akko-Ptolemais, Laodicea, and Aradus. However, in 5 BCE, Augustus (31 BC–14 BCE) introduced a new silver coin with his image in Antioch, and regular minting of silver ceased in all other cities with the exception of Tyre, which was allowed to continue producing its silver *shekel* until 65 CE.[84] In 98-100 CE,

Trajan, undertaking a series of reforms that entailed a complete withdrawal and re-minting of *tetradrachma* and a depreciation of the *denarius*, re-issued a large quantity of *tetradrachma* bearing his portraits in most cities of Asia, including Tyre, but not in Dora and neighboring Caesarea Maritima.[85] After Trajan, no *tetradrachma* were struck in the Eastern provinces until the reign of Septimius Severus, but under Caracalla and Macrinus debased silver issues were struck at a number of mints throughout the eastern empire, although again not in Dora. Dora's lack of silver coinage during the Roman period is therefore explained in the context of the city's secondary role within the Syrian province. The flow of silver was dictated by regional patterns of trade and by tax obligations to Rome, who ensured "sound silver money in the East."[86] Dora's production of bronze fractions was evidently fulfilling some of its internal and external trade and taxation needs.

3.3 Circulation of Dora Coins throughout Israel

Coin finds are often used to analyze coins in circulation and therefore to arrive at some evidence of economic activity and trade. The assumption is that the accidental loss of coins would to some extent have a pattern similar to that of the coins in circulation at the time.[87] Moreover, there is also some evidence that political divisions affect coin circulation since coins do not usually leave the area of political control to any significant extent, especially in periods of political turmoil.[88] In fact, although it is quite possible that trade takes place in conditions of political fragmentation, it is also quite unlikely that coinage of usurpers would circulate in an area where it would not be accepted as legal currency.[89] Finally, the denomination of a coin can affect its record, and this variable adds significantly to predictions about coin circulation based on the numbers of coins found. Low-value coins, for instance, are more likely to be lost than high-value coins, which are more often recovered by the owner or re-struck by the authorities, making it difficult to assess coin circulation purely on coin finds.

Just as in any other city that minted money, it is likely that some of Dora's coins were placed in circulation by moneychangers or by the mint, which converted minted and circulated money for a profit, waiting for the best offer.[90] Yet, some of Dora's coins were probably issued to pay imminent governmental expenses and were therefore disbursed to the intended recipients soon after minting by the mint, reaching their many destinations in a relatively short time. The remainder stayed in the city a bit longer, providing the small denomination coins necessary to

[77] Butcher 2004, 144.
[78] Butcher 2004, 144. For a recent study on the rate of exchange between Roman imperial silver and provincial bronze, see Johnston 2007, 17-27. The study, however, does not take Dora's coins into consideration.
[79] Johnston 2007, 243. See also *RPC* I, 371-374.
[80] Johnston 2007, 243. Howgego 1985, 56-57.
[81] *RIC* 1, 371.
[82] Harl 1996, 70.
[83] Augustus' first issues of *cistophori* in 28 BCE were minted to celebrate the victory at Actium and were probably obtained by melting the Republican *cistophori* and civic *drachma,* some of which had been struck by Antony at the mint of Ephesus to commemorate the marriage of Antony and Octavia in 40 BCE. See Carson 1978, 77. For more on the *cistophori* of Augustus, see Sutherland 1970. For provincial imperial silver, see Butcher 2004, 146. See also Kleiner et al 1977; *RPC* 1, 7.
[84] The silver *shekels* minted in Tyre were the dominant currency of Palestine from 126 BCE to 65 CE and the only currency acceptable for payments and tributes to the Jerusalem Temple on account of their purity (95% silver). After Nero stopped issuing Tyrian *shekels* in 65 CE, Jewish *shekels* were issued in Jerusalem, possibly on blanks prepared from melted Tyrian *shekels*. Instead of the Greek expression 'Holy Tyre,'

Jerusalem *shekels* were inscribed with 'Holy Jerusalem' and 'Shekel of Israel.' See Meshorer 2001, 73-78.
[85] It is argued that Trajan deliberately overvalued the *tetradrachm* against the *denarius* to restrict the local coins' circulation. See Harl 1996, 105-6.
[86] Harl 1996, 106.
[87] Newton 2006, 215. See also Reece 1993, 57-62; Aitchison 1988, 270-284.
[88] Howgego 1994, 12.
[89] Ibid.
[90] Crump 1985, 428.

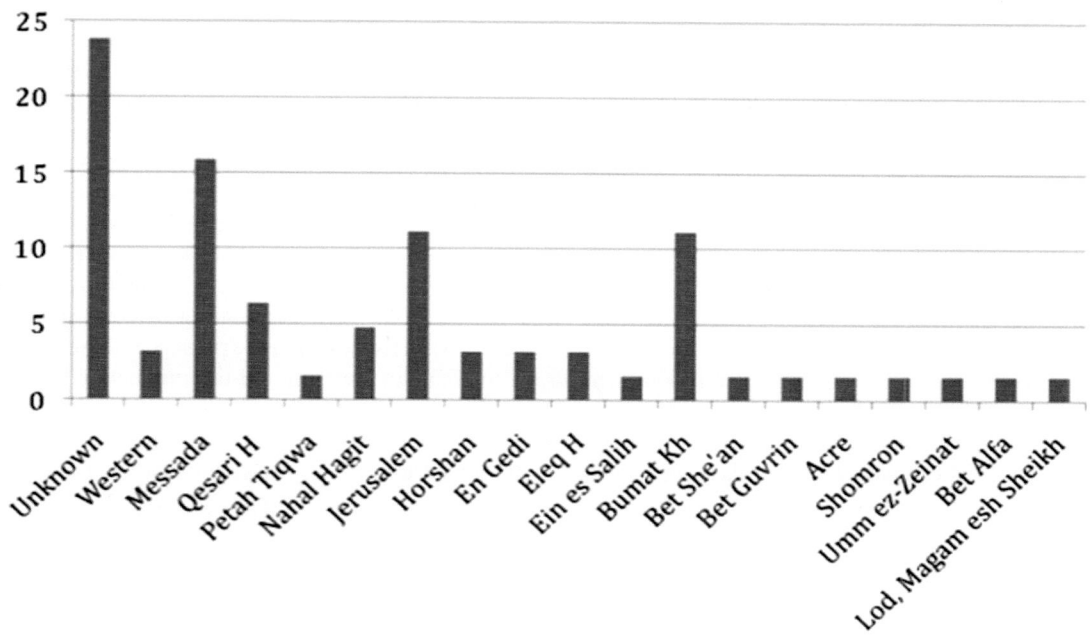

exchange the Roman army imperial gold and silver issues and the provincial silver.[91] Dora's civic coins were in fact mostly of small value and therefore suitable as a medium of exchange rather than as store of wealth.[92] As Butcher argues, "The profit made from exchange of silver and bronze may have been a relatively small part of the total budget for civic finance, but it provided an incentive to keep coins circulating."[93]

While no find spot is available for any of the Ptolemaic *tetradrachma* minted in Dora in 205-202 BCE (**No. 1**),[94] and it is therefore impossible to speculate on the circulation of those coins, nearly fifty percent of Dora's Roman-period coins presently housed at the *IAA* have known origins, making it easy to assess their circulation within Israel.[95] The coins with known origin were found in archaeological contexts in areas throughout Israel, from as far north as Bet Alpha, Bet She'an, and En Hagit, to as far south as Jerusalem, Masada, and at En Gedi. The sites include Roman legionary encampments (Masada, Jerusalem, En Gedi) and their adjoining *vici*, i.e., small civilian settlements with a servicing role to the Roman army (Bet Alpha and Bet She'an), and small towns scattered throughout the country (**Table 3**).

None of the known coins came from hoards, but, rather, they were found singly, implying that they were most likely accidental losses, rather than intentional deposits.[96]It has long been speculated that peripheral eastern coins circulated on a local basis, rarely traveling more than fifty miles from their center of origin,[97] yet Dora's coins have been found in sites more than one hundred miles from Dora (Jerusalem and Masada).

Although it is difficult to exclude the possibility that the coins were lost in the context of market exchanges or that trade and subsequent currency exchange existed between Dora and the places where the coins were found, it is more likely that the movement of Dora's coins is a reflection of the Roman military activity in the area. Freshly minted coins might have been transported from Dora to military encampments in order to pay soldiers, and they, as well as those doing business with the military, in turn passed the coinage along to secondary recipients in the nearby towns. Alternatively, as explained earlier, soldiers came to do business transactions at Dora and received the small denomination coins as change for their Roman silver. Especially pertinent to the first interpretation is the fact that some of the coins minted during the years 67/68 are countermarked with the legion X symbol on the right field of the obverse (**No. 16**).[98] Additionally, a large number of the same year's issues have been found at sites in or around centers where military campaigns took place during the Jewish Wars. After the Zelot revolt

[91] Ziegler 1996, 125.

[92] Bernstein 2008, 29-39.

[93] Butcher 2004, 146.

[94] Mørkholm (1981, 9) claims that there are only nine specimens available and all in private collections.

[95] No coins available from other collections have origination certificates. See Table 2. No attempts have been made, however, to find out whether excavation records from Syria or Jordan have any Dora specimens.

[96] Isolated finds are not always necessarily accidental losses, as is the case of single coins found in post-holes or graves. See Newton 2006, 212. None of the Dora coins, however, has been found in those contexts.

[97] Jones 1963, 295.

[98] Both Roman authorities and the city benefited from Dora's minting. Roman authorities avoided the task of transporting small coins over distances (Howgego 1985, 54-60; Burnett 1993, 145-147), while the city must have found the task both "prestigious and profitable" for its economy (Ziegler 1996, 125).

of 66, which destroyed the Roman garrison in Jerusalem, thousands of Roman soldiers moved into Judaea to restore order. Cestius Gallus, the legate of Syria, brought the legion *XII Fulminata*, while Vespasian landed in Akko-Ptolemais with the legions *X Fretensis* and *V Macedonica*, and was subsequently joined by the *XV Apollinaris* under the command of Titus. With more than 60,000 soldiers, Vespasian conquered most Galilean towns, and by the year 68 Jewish rebellions in the North had been crushed. He then set up his headquarters at Caesarea and proceeded methodically to clear the coast of Jewish rebels, including those in Dora. After Vespasian, hailed emperor by his own troops in 69, moved to Rome, Titus conquered Jerusalem in 70 CE, while the Roman governor of Judaea, Lucius Flavius Silva, conquered Masada with the *Legio X Fretensis* in 72.[99] The Dora coins excavated at Masada comprise the largest number of coins, representing twenty-one percent of the total number of Dora's coins with identified origin (**Table 3**) at the IAA. Moreover, two of the six coins that portray Titus and Vespasian in the collection were found at sites around Jerusalem, where most Roman soldiers were deployed, and are probably accidental losses from the purses of legionaries from the three legions under Titus — *V Macedonica, XII Fulminata*, and *XV Apollinaris.*

The link between Dora's coin production and military campaigns and the subsequent economic needs of the city might also explain the three large single-year issues struck at this mint. Trajan's military campaigns against Arabia and Parthia were in fact planned out of Syria, and the subsequent presence of Roman legionary soldiers was "the most … perceptible aspect of changes in the cities of Syria."[100] As argued by Ziegler, an increase in bronze coin production in certain cities of Asia Minor "frequently coincided with major military campaigns;"[101] and with its issue of 112, Dora, as a city in southern Syria, might have played its part in helping finance the campaign against Parthia in 113, while also profiting from the economic advantage of the military presence in the area. The single-year issue of coins in 117, with portraits of Hadrian, corresponds to Hadrian's accession to power and again provided an opportunity for Dora to profit from minting new coins. Since Hadrian was governor of Syria at the time of Trajan's death and needed to buy the support of the troops in Syria to legitimize his accession,[102] he might have provided an influx of capital in the shape of imperial gold and silver paid to his soldiers, which in turn might have created the necessity for small change in Dora. All the coins depicting Hadrian from the IAA collection were found at Masada, which was most likely in the hands of legionary soldiers from the *X Fretensis*. Finally, although there is no find context for any of Antoninus Pius' Dora coins,

the city's single-year issue of 144 can also be attributed to military affairs. During the Bar Kokhba revolt (132-136 CE) auxiliary forces had to be transferred from Syria into Judaea, including the legions *Legio VI Ferrata* and *III Gallica*.[103] Once the revolt was crushed and the province re-drawn as Syria-Palaestina, these legions remained to maintain order as is attested by the presence of units from Syria in the province between 137 and 139.[104] Although it is not possible to completely assess the effects that "these large masses of soldiers,"[105] had on the province's economy in general, the minting of coins at Dora in 144 was very likely linked to the presence of the many soldiers of the Roman garrison and the interaction between those soldiers and the civic economy of Dora and other cities in the area. But if the issue of coins in Dora during the Roman period was strongly connected to the movement of legionary troops, and if the city's economy benefited from having some kind of economic interaction that created a need to mint coins, the question arises whether there is a way to ascertain the size of Dora's issues, especially since Dora's mint was a small one and secondary to larger mints such as those at Tyre, Caesarea, and especially Antioch.[106]

Some numismatists have argued that an educated guess at the number of coins in circulation in a given period can be obtained from an estimate of the number of coins that a die can make.[107] Assuming that a die is used to extinction, Sellwood's practical experiments in 1963 demonstrated that a single obverse die could strike nearly 10,000 coins.[108] The study was followed by other numismatists, most notably Crawford, who proposed as many as 24,000 coins per obverse die in his analysis of republican coins in 1974,[109] and Walker, who in 1988 also tried to extrapolate calculations from hoard evidence for the years 153-5 CE.[110] These calculations, however, have been considered rather uncertain if not futile by Buttrey, who has argued in several articles that "nothing can be done [other than] create quantitative studies built on imaginary data … to force an answer."[111] Although he accepts, in fact, that

---

[99] Sartre 2005, 125; Millar 1993, 97. See also Josephus, *Jewish War* 2.8.11; 2.13.7, 2.14.4; 2.14.5.
[100] Millar 1993, 97. The campaign against Parthia in 113 CE, however, might be the one campaign for which coins were struck at Dora.
[101] Ziegler 1996, 121.
[102] There is some uncertainty on whether Hadrian was properly adopted by Trajan as his successor since, according to Dio, Trajan's wife Plotina secured Hadrian's adoption after her husband's death. See Scarre 1995, 100.

[103] Eck 1999, 80-81. According to Dio Cassius, "Hadrian sent … the best generals… against the Jews" (*Roman History* 69.13.1-3).
[104] Ibid. See also Cotton 2000.
[105] Millar 1993, 108.
[106] According to Millar (1993, 103-105), Antioch emerged as the de facto secondary Imperial 'capital' during the reign of Trajan, whose eastern expansion forced him to spend a long period of time in the province, setting up his capital in Antioch.
[107] Allen 2004; Esty 1986, 1990.
[108] Sellwood 1963, 229. Sellwood built on the work of Lodovico Brunetti, who analyzed the Brinell hardness of various metals and concluded that the total number of silver coins produced by dies of tempered steel or incandescent bronze could be 1000 for an anvil die and anything between 500 and 800 for a hammer die. See Brunetti 1963, 16.
[109] Crawford 1974, 694-5. His study uses only the C. Annius' *denarii* (No. 366, p. XLVII), which he claims were "struck in considerably lower relief than most Greek coinage and with less attention to technical perfection [making it] reasonable to suppose that dies lasted longer."
[110] Walker 1988, 301-305.
[111] Buttrey 1993, 351. In a later article, Buttrey identifies six general variables which makes it impossible to calculate the number of coins struck by a die: destruction of the die; wear and tear of the die; nature of the flan being struck; organization of the striking; expiration of the information conveyed by the die; and size of the order for coin production. Attempting to calculate coin productions, he argues, damages not only numismatics, but other disciplines as well. See also Buttrey 1994, 341-352.

more dies certainly indicate more coins, he argues that the general assumption that a die was used to extinction is flawed, since it does not take into consideration that production may just have ceased when the demand had been met or when the information conveyed by the die expired.[112] More recently, however, de Callataÿ has argued that "the best results about ancient production can be obtained with original die counts with hoards as a way of control;"[113] he added, however, that master hoards must be used accurately and a large numbers of die-studies must be done.[114] According to Meadows, Sellwood's study is still useful today to ascertain the number of obverse dies used to strike a coinage.[115]

Although die analyses of Dora's coins have yet to be done, and it is therefore impossible to ascertain for certain how many dies the city produced, the "numismatic material [of Dora] is not very varied, nor are there many types."[116] The lack of variation, however, does not necessarily entail low production. In fact, if, as Newton argues, the number of finds of accidental losses is "by far the best predictor of coins in circulation,"[117] then, based on our finds, it is safe to assume that Dora's production of low denomination types was indeed a large one. Moreover, considering that only a fraction of Tel Dor has been excavated, there is still a possibility that more coins as well

as the building complex dedicated to minting coins might be recovered at the site in the future, adding potentially useful evidence to the numismatic history of Dora.

Regardless of the reason for the minting of coins at Dora, and of their importance for the economic well-being of the city as well as the military establishment of the entire province of Syria-Palaestina, the aspects of the Dora coins that are most important to this study are, however, the iconography and the epigraphy of those coins. It is in fact through the Dora coin imagery and legends that it is possible to better understand the reality of the people of the city, their language, their religion, and their cultural self-identification. The next two chapters will therefore confirm the validity of my thesis that the coins of Dora represent the vehicle through which the city built its identity. Indeed, the coins of Dora will be studied as those "markers or signals" that de Saussure compared with words and Polanyi to a "system of symbols,"[118] with a "striking resemblance"[119] to language and writings. Through a thorough analysis of the iconography and the epigraphy of Dora's coins, I will attempt to break the elaborate cultural codes that the people of Dora necessarily understood and that Roman soldiers must have accepted while carrying those coins in their purses.

---

[112] Ibid.
[113] De Callataÿ 1995, 310.
[114] Ibid.
[115] Based on discussion with Professor Meadows on 02/28/2010.
[116] Meshorer 1996, 355.
[117] Newton 2006, 222. Newton also notes (2006, 211), "Coin size and denomination can affect the coin record but these variables did not add significantly to prediction about coins in circulation based only on the numbers of coins found."

[118] Polanyi 1968, 175.
[119] Polanyi 1968, 179.

Chapter 4
The Iconography of Dora's Coins

Many scholars have studied art as a language of meaningful communication and art interpretation as an act of near literary analysis that requires a deep knowledge of the artist's environment. Writing in the 1930s, Panofsky argued that the interpretation of an art object carries three layers of analysis, which corresponds to the object's three layers of meaning. The first layer of meaning is the *primary meaning* - the analysis of the object's content and subject matter in a "pre-iconographical description."[1] The next layer is its *secondary meaning* — the exploration of its form, made of images and allegories, and the third and final layer is the *intrinsic meaning*, constituting the world of "symbolic values" and the object's various connotations within its culture.[2] The "act of interpretation," which is iconographical in the secondary meaning, acquires a "deeper meaning" in the third level, requiring "more than a familiarity with the specific themes or concepts,"[3] which are depicted, and "synthetic intuition,"[4] i.e., a sense of the meaning of the whole object. In 1955, Wittkower added, "Representational meaning cannot be understood unless the objects or event shown by the artist belong to the general human experience of the percipient."[5] In other words, the percipients creates their own meaning of the object based on their personal sensuous construct, so the only visual messages that communicate meaning are those that percipients judge useful or important. This deeper meaning of the work of art is therefore one that is open to subjective interpretation for both Panofsky and Wittkower.

More recently, Tonio Hölscher and Paul Zanker have made important contributions to the debate of "art as a vehicle of communication,"[6] especially with regard to Roman artifacts and their iconological messages. Hölscher's notion is that objects of art must not be seen as reproducing an ancient reality, but rather as ideological statements of the people involved in the production of the objects.[7] Images, he argues, do not represent reality — they "construct" reality.[8] Fundamental to this argument is, of course, Panofsky's idea that in order to reach the intrinsic meaning of the artifact, the viewer must take into account the creator's personal, technical, and cultural history.[9] Wittkower argues, in fact, that the reading of a work of art "depends first on a familiarity with the religious, mythological, literary, and social conditions of the civilization to which the work belongs, and secondly on the particular knowledge of the

verbal or textual tradition which the work illustrates."[10] Moreover, it is also just as important for the viewer to understand why and how the artist chose a particular style to turn an idea into a visual image. As Zanker points out, a work of art does not just reflect the artist's creative spirit, but also the "society's inner life [giving] an insight into people's values and imagination."[11] In the imagery of Imperial Rome, he argues, the use of symbols that had been devoid of "specificity"[12] allowed the artist to create many varieties of combinations, therefore enabling the viewer to make a "broad spectrum of associations."[13] When analyzing the intrinsic meaning of Roman artifacts, it is therefore necessary that modern viewers be as familiar as possible with the symbols portrayed by the artist as both the artist and the contemporaneous viewers were when the artifact was created. Panofsky's analysis of meaning is possible only when the viewer transcends iconography and moves into iconology, reaching "the underlying principles that shape the expression of an age."[14] Images are then understood as signs, and for modern viewers the act of interpreting art becomes the same semiotic act that it was for contemporaneous viewers.[15] Just like a language, Roman imagery is, in the words of Hölscher, a "semantic system [that] functions according to a sort of grammar on the basis of certain specific structures … that evolved over time."[16] Although one cannot, according to Alain Schnapp, "reconstruct the semiotic of Greek sculpture and painting in a very detailed way,"[17] it is possible to appreciate the cognitive dimensions of those artifacts. The inanimate statues of the Greek gods, Schnapp suggests, make the living gods present through their images, linking "the visible [the statue] and the invisible [the god]."[18] Consequently, carving a stone to make a god or a hero was more than "a mere process of imitation,"[19] requiring the artist to create images that would convey the essence of divinity. The same interpretation can obviously be extended to other ancient artifacts, since all objects are part of a signifying system created from the interweaving of the visual object with literature, history, culture, and politics — all fields that must be taken into consideration when analyzing any art form. When analyzing Greek vases, for instance, Lissarrague emphasizes, "The objects were not made to illustrate Athenian life but … [to] convey the visual way of thinking and experiencing through which

---

[1] Panofsky 1939, 14.
[2] Ibid., 5-9. The operations, he writes, may appear unrelated, but they "merge with each other into one organic and indivisible process" (17).
[3] Ibid., 14.
[4] Ibid., 15.
[5] Wittkower 1955, 113.
[6] Hedlund 2008, 22.
[7] Hölscher 2000, 147-149.
[8] Hölscher 1987, 13; see also Hölscher 2000, 159.
[9] Panofsky 1939, 16.

[10] Wittkower 1955, 117.
[11] Zanker 1988, 3.
[12] Zanker 1988, 177.
[13] Ibid. 180.
[14] Hasenmueller 1978, 297.
[15] Hasenmueller 1978, 296.
[16] Hölscher 2004, 2.
[17] Schnapp 1994, 43.
[18] Ibid. See also Elsner 1996, 515-531.
[19] Schnapp 1994, 42.

many aspects of this society were aestheticized, as though the painters held a mirror to the Athenians themselves."[20]

It is easy to understand that by applying the imagery-as-a-language approach to the analysis of ancient coin iconography, it is possible to arrive at the intrinsic meaning of coins iconography. But in order to assess what kind of association viewers of ancient coins made with the symbols depicted on coins, the symbols' emic signification must first be assessed in terms of their internal elements and their functioning rather than in terms of contemporary existing external scheme.[21] As discussed earlier, culture, whether viewed emically or etically, has no existence independent of its reification.[22] In order to arrive at the intrinsic meaning of Dora's coin imagery, one must understand the reified semiotic code that was intelligible to the people of Dora as a cultural group. Of course, Dora's coins also had a practical purpose, but as Durand and Lissarrague have written, an object, however useful it may be, is inseparable from both the practical reality and the social imaginary in which it is found.[23]

4.2 Coin Imagery and its Function

The use of symbols to create a pictorial language found applications in the iconography of ancient coins, where symbols were often combined in multiple ways to illustrate complex realities in the very limited space of a small token. From patron deities and their attributes, to geographical features, to local agricultural products, to military and political events, ancient Greek coin-types displayed pictorial designs that evolved just like a language. Greek coin imagery used symbols that seldom became "static," but changed when they became insignificant, i.e., when they no longer had a message to deliver.[24] When there was a need to preserve "acceptability," however, there was also an impetus toward conservatism in the design, as was the case of the Athena/owl and the Alexander the Great types. Both symbols, for example, remained the same for a long time to make sure the messages of the new rulers were acceptable.[25]

Greek coin imagery and symbols found application in Roman republican coins, which developed from the tradition of Greek coinage, but the use of symbols reached its greatest relevance in the Roman imperial period.[26] In fact, the imagery of Roman imperial coins had such a rich pictorial language that the debate over the function

of the coin-types has been ongoing for nearly a century. Consequently, no study of any coin iconography can be complete without briefly addressing the debate.

As early as 1917, Mattingly wrote that Roman imperial coins should not be considered "only as currency, but as a convenient means of political advertisement and propaganda."[27] The idea that authorities used coins to shape public opinions remained undisputed until the early fifties, when A. H. M. Jones questioned whether coins had messages that could be conveyed or understood at all.[28] Jones' view prompted immediate reactions, most notably by Sutherland, who wrote, "Imperial coin types were, beyond doubt, the result of official interest by whomsoever exerted authority; and this in turn suggests … that they possessed an intentional propaganda-value."[29] Other numismatists, however, came to Jones' support, pointing to the lack of literary sources that refer to coin imagery, the lack of reference to the notion of coins used as propaganda, and the lack of evidence that coin imagery was understood at all.[30] Some scholars stated a third viewpoint, positing that coin-types "were intended to appeal, not to the public, but to the man whose portrait as a rule occupied the obverse of the coins: they were a public tribute to a great individual."[31] On the same note, in the interpretation of Wallace-Hadrill, "one of the most significant features of the idiom of the imperial age is its tendency to engross the whole potential of the coin for making value-laden statements for the benefit of the emperor."[32] More recently, Meadows and Williams have added to the debate by viewing the imagery of Roman coins as "small-scale but widely-circulating monuments … intended to promote ideas of continuity and tradition."[33] Imagery on coins, they argue, has the same characteristics of any other monument that was built for the purpose of rendering someone or something immortal.[34] Finally, other numismatists suggest that coin images functioned as a form of modern-day publicity, or brands.[35] Although a definitive answer concerning how to interpret the function of coin iconography might remain elusive, it seems likely that the imagery of ancient coins was created with some intentions, and that those intentions must have been familiar not only

---

[20] Lissarrague 2001, 9. Furthermore, Lissarrague (2007, 151-164) suggests that Attic vase representation on shields preceded Aeschylus in creating a link between sign and warrior; the centaur, for example, symbolizes the warrior's savagery.
[21] The emic vs. etic signification of artifacts was discussed in Chapter 2.
[22] Hall 2003, 25.
[23] Durand and Lissarrague 1980, 89: "Si technique soit-il, un objet est inséparable à la fois de la réalité pratique et de l'imaginaire social dans lesquels il trouve place."
[24] Kraay 1976, 4-5. Examples of coins changing symbols are those commonly associated with tyrants, as was the case of Rhegium in 462 BCE and in successive issues.
[25] Meadows, interview (11/3/2010).
[26] *RIC* Vol. I, 3.

[27] Mattingly 1917, 69.
[28] Jones (1956, 15) writes, "If a modern analogy is to be sought for the varying types and legends of Roman imperial coins, it is perhaps to be found… in the postage stamps of many modern countries."
[29] Sutherland 1959, 22.
[30] Hedlund 2008, 30. For an in-depth study on the controversy of coins used as propaganda, see Buttrey 1972, 101-109; Wallace-Hadrill 1986, 67-69; and Crawford 1983, 50-59.
[31] Levick 1982, 107.
[32] Wallace-Hadrill 1986, 76.
[33] Meadows and Williams 2001, 43. The fact that the Latin word *monumentum* has the same root as *moneta* and *moneo* (to remind/suggest) implies, according to the authors, that a *monumentum* served as a means of bringing something or someone to people's mind. So, anything done to preserve the memory is a *monumentum* (ibid., 41).
[34] Indeed, Horace supports this concept of achieving immortalization through *monumenta*, when he writes that he "has made "a monument more lasting than bronze (*monumentum aere perennius*) and that he will achieve immortality (*Non omnis moriar*) through his poetry (Horace, *Odes* III. 30,1,6).
[35] Levick 1982, 106; Hekster 2003, 24.

to the authorities who issued the coins, but also to at least part of the population.

The recurring use of the same symbols to create certain images, indicating that those symbols were common knowledge and that people using the coins had an emic perspective of those symbols, was also common in provincial coins. However, according to Levick, while some provincial coins were echoes of Rome and "Rome oriented,"[36] most provincial coins "spoke with different voices, and those voices all differed sharply from that of Rome."[37] In fact, although provincial cities and dependent monarchs under Roman rule were not obliged to portray the ruling emperor, they were nevertheless required to get permission to issue coinage.[38] Accordingly, as Levick puts it, "city and royal coinage could be manipulated for Roman purposes," becoming a form of flattery toward the Roman authorities, or stressing their Roman connections.[39] Since most of the coins from Dora were issued during the Roman period, one must assume then that the mint of Dora selected its images with the Roman authorities in mind, as well as its own citizens. The question arises, however, of how the citizens of Dora could be confident that the figure on their coin was that of the emperor, unless some kind of guarantee had been given to the die maker by a Roman authority. On the other hand, the earliest coins attributed to the city portray Ptolemy V, so recognition of the young Hellenistic king on the city's coins must have been effortless, since it followed an older Hellenistic tradition.

4.3 Royal Figures

The portrayal of Ptolemy V in the Ptolemaic minting of coinage at Dora had deep roots in the Hellenistic tradition of depicting royal portraits on coins. The practice had first appeared in Lycia and in Persia, where as early as the late fifth century BCE coins of local rulers had portrayed realistic-looking heads identified by names.[40] Although this practice was in contrast to Greek custom, which primarily depicted deities and their attributes or sacred animals on coin types,[41] the arrival of Alexander's coinage was a significant event in the development of Hellenistic coin portraiture. Alexander's depiction of Herakles, which became more common than the omnipresent Athenian owl, was taken as a portrait of Alexander himself, and

formed a public perception of the king as having a "heroic and divine nature."[42] Some scholars argue that there is no way to know that Alexander declared the image of Herakles as being his own portrait. However, after the official promulgation that the king was to be considered a god, following the visit to the oracle of Zeus Ammon at Siwa, the symbolism on his coins underwent changes, indicating that the representations were "intended as portraits of Alexander."[43] Moreover, Alexander's eastern subjects readily accepted Alexander as Herakles, adapting the image to their own cultural and religious needs.[44] After Alexander's death, his image as Herakles became even more powerful than in his life, making him "the archetype of the divine ruler-hero."[45] From then on, it seems that later Hellenistic and Roman rulers wanted to be portrayed in the very same fashion. In fact, Alexander's coins "stand at the beginning of a long … series of Hellenistic royal portraits,"[46] whose legacy continued well into the Roman world. The first successor to put his own image in place of Alexander's was Ptolemy I soon after his coronation in Alexandria, and the tradition continued under nearly all Ptolemaic successors not only in Alexandria, but also in Gaza, Joppa, Dora, Ptolemais-Ake, Tyre, and Sidon. Ptolemaic coins from the different mints travelled freely across the kingdom's internal boundaries, including Dora, where coins of Ptolemy I and his successors have been unearthed in relatively large numbers.[47]

As stated earlier, the city of Dora minted only one Ptolemaic coin type in 205 BCE, with the portrait of Ptolemy V. (**No. 1**), and its royal coin depiction presents nothing new or specific to Dora, but follows a tradition of elegant idealism that had been used by other Hellenistic mints.[48] Although it is difficult, therefore, to consider Ptolemy V's portrait a faithful official likeness of the young monarch, the portrait does indeed show some age-specific traits.[49] The king's youth is in fact emphasized, and his portrayal shows a young face with broad forehead, a large eye, a straight nose, and the thin pointy chin of a young person. The portrait is somewhat different from those of the young king's predecessors, whose portraits show "dramatic and dynamic"[50] heads with "unnaturally wide" eyes opened

---

[36] Levick (1999, 47) claims that most likely "the governor and/or the procurators" were responsible for choosing the type, as is the case of the *aes* of Lugdunum from 64 onward.

[37] Sutherland 1986, 89.

[38] *RPC* Vol 1: 2-3. The authors acknowledge the argument that "the recording of imperial or governors' permission is merely a form of imperial or gubernatorial flattery and irrelevant to the realities of the production of coinage." However, they claim that "permission was a requirement," and that it may have been the cause for the cessation of minting in the western cities (18-19).

[39] Levick 1999, 47.

[40] The ruling dynasty of Xanthos seems to have been one of the earliest to represent itself on coins. See Keen 1998, 138.

[41] Among the most common examples are: Athena and the owl in Athens; the Pegasos in Corinth and in her colonies in *Magna Graecia* (Italy and Sicily); the wheat ear in Metapontum; a boy riding a dolphin in Taras; a rose in Rhodes; a nymph carried off by a naked satyr on the island of Thasos; horses in Larissa; the nymph Arethusa and chariot of Syracuse; and the hare of Messana.

[42] Pollitt 1986, 26.

[43] Pollitt (1986, 26) refers to "the bulging forehead, the narrow mouth with almost pouting lips, even some of the aspiring gaze" as features that are typical of Alexander's portraits.

[44] According to Seltman (1955, 205), "The Phoenician was to see in the obverse type his own god Melqarth … and the Babylonian might recall his own god Gilgamesh, the lion-slayer." Cf. Pollitt 1986, 26. For an in-depth study of Alexander's cult within the context of Hellenistic politics, see Stewart 1994, 419-437.

[45] Pollitt 1986, 26.

[46] Ibid.

[47] Brown 1995, 21; Stern 2000, 256-7.

[48] In discussing the depictions of royal portraits on gems, Plantzos (1999, 42-58) notes the difficulty in distinguishing the identifiable portraits from the generic depictions influenced by the idealized image of Alexander. The same is of course true of Hellenistic coin portraits, which would keep "the individual features of the king himself to a greater or lesser degree of realism, but also allow for the recognizable Alexander traits to be employed" (1999, 60).

[49] Stanwick 2002, 56.

[50] Brown 1999, 13.

to the "illumination of divine inspiration."[51] Unlike the *frühhellenistische pathetische Stil* (early Hellenistic 'pathetic' style) that Cahn attributes to earlier Ptolemies, Ptolemy V's Dora portrait is linear, simple, and somewhat static.[52] Finally, while the earlier Ptolemies' curly and abundant hair reached over the neck and the ear, giving "a profile [that] is made up of opposing curves that swing counter to one another, alive with energy,"[53] Ptolemy V's hair in this portrait is neatly arranged under the royal diadem, and barely reaching the ear, perhaps a sign of his young age. Further traits of youth are shown in the delicate features of the face and the rather small shoulder. Although Ptolemy V's coins are not absolute evidence of a numismatic workshop at Dora during the Ptolemaic period, they are nevertheless a "remarkable intimate archive,"[54] of a royal workshop that produced imagery that the people of Dora understood. Ptolemy V's coin type was certainly familiar to Dora's citizens, who had already used Alexander's and other Ptolemaic coinage for over a century. The young king's image was then a sign in a clearly understandable language, and allowed the people of Dora to share the broad overview of other cities with contemporaneous Hellenistic coins in the same style. The commonality of Dora's Ptolemy V coin type with other Ptolemaic coin types is further testimony to the cultural integration of Dora's citizens with the citizens of other Hellenistic cities as far away as Alexandria.

4.4 Imperial Figures

By the end of Augustus' reign, Roman portraiture had two established Roman stylistic traditions on which to draw — verism and a sort of Greek classicism that emphasized the ideal aspects of the emperor's appearance. Despite stylistic evolution through time, these two concepts remained fundamental to the way emperors were depicted on statuary and on coins in terms of both their physical appearance and their divinely inspired power.[55] As discussed in the Chapter 3, Dora's mint portrayed several emperors on its coinage, starting with Augustus in 6 BCE and ending with Caracalla in 211 CE.[56] Since Dora was, as stated earlier, a Hellenistic city with a hybrid population, it is therefore important to address both the deliberate promotion of imperial images by a Roman authority and their creation by a people that was projecting deeply rooted Hellenistic beliefs on those images. An emic approach to the imperial coin iconography must be taken therefore to investigate how the people of Dora perceived their coins, and what meaning the imperial depiction had for them.

FIG. 4.1. PORTRAIT OF AUGUSTUS. BRITISH MUSEUM, INV. 1812,0615.1

Not all of Augustus' coins bore an obverse portrait type, but most coins from mints outside of Rome bore his portraits, and it is therefore not surprising to find Augustus depicted on coins struck in Dora (**No. 10**).[57] The portrait, which is facing right and shows an ageless Augustus, follows the same essential physiognomy and hair treatment of the *Prima Porta* statue (**Fig. 4.1**), the principal Augustan portrait type that saw a return to the classical language of Polykleitos.[58] Dora's coin portrait seems compatible with the desired portrayals of the *gravitas* of Augustus, but one must wonder how the image reached the mint of Dora and whether the people of Dora were supposed to recognize Augustus by his appearance on coins alone.[59]

It has long been suggested that imperial portraits were erected in provincial cities, and that local artists reproduced the latest official statue of the emperor in local shops for local consumption.[60] Although there were different combinations of scale and statue type in different places, the head type was changed very little – the provinces reproduced whatever imperial image was sent to them.[61] It

---

[51] Ibid.

[52] Cahn 1948, 118. For more on the Hellenistic coins of Alexander's successors, and the use of royal portraits, see Carpenter 1941; Babelon 1950; H.W. Smith 1950; Westermark 1961; Kraay 1976; Mørkholm 1991.

[53] Brown 1999, 16.

[54] Brown 1999, 54.

[55] King 1999, 130.

[56] As stated in Chapter 3, the mint of Dora issued two earlier coin types with royal portraits, allegedly depicting Antony and Cleopatra. Since the identity of the images still needs verification, the iconography of those coins will not be addressed in this study. See Bijovsky *et al.* 2013, 148.

[57] *RIC* Vol. 1, 12.

[58] Hölscher 2004, 10. Augustus' portrait echoes Polykleitos' *Doryphoros*.

[59] Hölscher 2004, 47.

[60] Ando 2000, 230.

[61] Zanker 1983, 23.

may be assumed, then, that the coin depiction of Augustus was modeled on a version of the *Prima Porta* portrait that must have been introduced in all eastern provinces and in Dora itself.[62] The Dora portrait is very similar to those on other provincial coins, demonstrating that in fact a uniform concept of the emperor's appearance prevailed throughout the area.[63] Just like other provincial mints then, the mint of Dora reproduced official copies of Augustus' portrait on its coins not because ordered to do so, but in the eagerness to demonstrate loyalty to the Roman overlords. As Rose clarifies, "Emperors did not set up portraits of themselves; provincial cities set up portraits of the emperor in gratitude for or in anticipation of imperial benefactions."[64]

The image of Augustus, which is paired with Tyche (**No. 10**), fits within the social and cultural life of Dora and must have evoked feelings of authority and majesty familiar to the people of Dora, reflecting an existing language that they understood. The cult for Augustus had in fact spread rapidly in the East because it could easily be linked with the myth of kings, heroes and gods of the Hellenistic tradition. Augustus' portraits on Dora's coins are then evidence of the divinely sanctioned ruler that had already existed in the provinces.[65]

Whether imperial cults in the East were simply political or public honors bestowed on the emperor rather than religious or private in nature has long been discussed. Scholars who deny the religious aspect of imperial cults have argued that the meanings attached to imperial rituals were only superficial, since they did not engage the private life of the citizens the way other deities did.[66] However, some anthropologists who study religion as a system of symbols see imperial rituals as "religious symbols [that] formulate a basic congruence between a particular style of life and a specific metaphysic."[67] In other words, as Harland puts it, imperial rituals were important for all levels of society because "they played a very important role in sustaining the interplay between social experiences … and the cosmic framework."[68] In the eastern provinces, people used their traditional symbolic system to depict their emperor "in the familiar terms of divine power,"[69] and Augustus, as well as the emperors that followed, was "set on a straightforward, equal footing with the Olympian gods."[70] Municipal and civic authorities, including those in Dora, replaced the portraits of their deities with portraits of Augustus on their coins because they were responding to a new "fundamental shift in civic perspective caused by new political circumstances."[71] Augustus' image on Dora's coins, which have Tyche depicted on the reverse, was then part of a symbolic system that placed the emperor on a par with Tyche in the social imaginary of the people. The Roman emperor was visualized as an "inspired ruler," driven by divine forces.[72] Dora did not depict the emperor on its coins as an act of political loyalty to Rome, although that aspect may also be true, but rather as an expression of the religious views held by the people of the city/ community. The Roman authorities, in turn, did not impose the minting of coins with imperial portraits to legitimize their hold on the *polis* – they simply benefited from an existing framework of beliefs.

Although none of the remaining Julio-Claudian emperors appear on Dora's issues of 14 CE, 64 CE, and 65 CE, imperial portraits reappeared on Dora's coins, after a hiatus of 76 years, in the 69 CE issue with the portraits of Vespasian and Titus. Following the death of Nero and the civil war, Vespasian was proclaimed emperor by his troops in the East, and by the time he entered Rome in 70 CE coins with his image and that of his son had been minted in 49 cities in the East.[73] Although Vespasian rejected an official cult in Rome, he had "set no restrictions on the heroization and deification accorded him as a matter of course in the East,"[74] and it is important therefore to consider Dora's issues of Vespasian and Titus coins (No. **19** and **21**) within these wider socio-political and religious contexts. Through the minting of imperial coins, eastern cities expressed their devotion to the new emperors, while also incorporating the new emperors into their existing religious beliefs. In that sense, imperial cult may have played a part in Vespasian's quick acceptance and the legitimacy of his new role. Vespasian and Titus are both depicted on Dora's coins with Tyche on the reverse, linking the imperial images to that of the divine protectress of the city just as with Augustus' coins.[75] Vespasian's portrait sculptures, which some scholars tend to divide in two types according to the emperor's apparent aging and whether they are idealizing or realistic portraits, always show a middle-aged man, with a stocky figure and the commanding gaze of a military man.[76] Vespasian was

---

[62] From the very beginning of the empire, a laureate portrait of each new emperor was sent to the provincial cities. The portrait, known as the *laureata imago* was carried by white-clad officials and attended by a column of soldiers. As it approached, the people of the city received it with lights and incense, and they celebrated its arrival at a popular festival. See Swift 1923, 297-8. For a study on the dating of the *Prima Porta* statue, see Müller 1941.

[63] Zanker 1988, 301-2; Rose 1997a

[64] Rose 1997b, 109. See also Boschung 1993; Burnett and Walker 1981.

[65] Zanker 1988, 301-302. The imperial cult established itself quickly also because August himself allowed the inhabitants of Asia Minor and the Greek East to set up sanctuaries to Roma and to deified Julius Caesar in Ephesus and Nicaea, while also authorizing cult centers for himself at Pergamum and Nicomedia. See Mitchell 1995, 100-117.

[66] Nilsson 1948, 177-178; 1961, 384-394. For a thorough study of Roman imperial cults in Asia Minor, see Price 1984.

[67] Geertz 1988, 90.

[68] Harland 2003, 104.

[69] Price 1984, 248.

[70] Smith 1987, 136. Although Smith's study is based on the Sebasteion of Aphrodisias, where he finds a "visual conception of the divine emperors," one can only assume that the same is true of other cities of the Greek East.

[71] Heuchert 2005, 44.

[72] Zanker 1983a, 21.

[73] Levick 1999, 142. During the civil war of 68-69, there was a complete decentralization in the minting of coinage because each general minted in his own province in order to pay his troops. Although Galba and Vitellius issued some coinage from the mint of Rome, most issues were provincial issues. At the beginning of Vespasian's rule, issues were minted from several western and eastern mints, including the provinces of Judea and Asia Minor. By 76, however, Vespasian had centralized nearly all minting in Rome. See Huot 1996; *RPC* Vol 2: *From Vespasian to Domitian*.

[74] Fishwick 1965, 155; Mitchell 1995, 100-117.

[75] Tyche's role on the religious life of Dora and in the social imaginary of Dora's people will be addressed later in the chapter.

[76] Pollini 1984, 550. Bergmann and Zanker (1981, 317- 412) eliminate

FIG. 4.2. VESPASIAN, BRITISH MUSEUM, LONDON.
INV. 1850,0304.35

FIG. 4.3 TITUS, BRITISH MUSEUM, LONDON.
INV. 1892,0121.3

sixty when he became emperor, and in his portraits he looks his age – heavy-set and bald, with a broad, deeply lined forehead, and deep creases around his mouth and neck (**Fig. 4.2**). His portraits, which distance him from the luxurious depictions of his predecessor, reflect simpler tastes, making a political statement about a new era. His tight-lipped mouth, hooked nose, and protruding chin give him the look of a battle-hardened man, and the sort of frown which the Roman writer Suetonius said he had at all times.[77] These iconographical traits, which are paralleled in most of Vespasian's numismatic appearances, are also visible on Dora's coins (**No. 19-20**), where the emperor is depicted laureate and facing right, with an aquiline nose, narrowed eyes, thin lips, and a strong, broad chin. The broad forehead, usually a sign of a receding hairline, might be an indication of the emperor's age. Vespasian's older son, Titus, is also depicted on Dora's 69 issues (**No. 21**), when he was still his father's subordinate in Palestina. The image on the coin presents a rather robust Caesar, laureate and facing right. The fuller face and large neck, with a large fat ring around it, and the narrow forehead give the impression of a younger man when compared with

his father's coin portrait. However, the prominent chin, the aquiline nose, the short-cropped hair, and the overall robust appearance recall his father's physiognomy (**Fig. 4.3**). Portraits on the coins of Vespasian and his son reveal how they thought of themselves and how they wanted to be seen. The images, however, owe their features and significance to the sculptors who made the dies, most likely working from sculpted models that moved from city to city. With their imperial images, the coins of Dora thus participate in the successful integration of the new rulers within the city's socio-political and religious realms. Vespasian and Titus became an integral part of the city's belief system, and were paired with Tyche in the city's effort to safeguard its welfare. From the Flavian emperors on, citizens of the East and most likely of Dora, began taking oaths by invoking the *Genius* or τὺχη , i.e., the divine spirit of the living emperor.[78]

Trajan's portrait on Dora's coins is the most easily recognizable and parallels the many coins that were struck throughout the eastern part of the empire during his reign. Contrary to the iconography of Trajan's official mints

[78] Polotsky 1962, 260. The author cites the Greek papyri from the *Cave of the Letters*, where the Jewish woman Babatha declares her rights to a property with "an oath by the τὺχη of the Lord Caesar."

that portray him as a "mature, small-jawed emperor with prominent forehead ridge," most eastern coins depict him as a very idealized and youthful emperor, with small eyes, large jaw, and smooth forehead (**Fig. 4.4**). [79] In fact, the bust on Dora's issues is laureate, facing right and undraped, and while his hair, with its locks that hang over the forehead, seems to imitate Augustus' hair, the square cranial shape of the head appears to recall Trajan's statue. The imperial portraits are on the obverse of four reverse types, minted in the same year, respectively portraying Zeus Doros (**No. 24 and 28**),[80] the bust of Tyche (**No. 26**), Tyche standing on a ship's prow (**No. 25**), and a galley (**No. 27 and 29**). As with the imperial issues of the previous rulers, the reverse draws from the local civic world, reflecting enduring communal symbols of self-identity.

Trajan's coinage was the most prolific of Roman emperors whose coins were minted at Dora, and his coinage has more types than previous emperors. An analysis of this sudden increase in the number and types of coins in 112 CE can therefore help elucidate the political discourse between Roman imperialism and the citizens of Dora during Trajan's reign. According to Kevin Butcher, proliferation of coinage and types in the Roman East was "an integral part of an imperial social management strategy" that "accommodated and manipulated" cities.[81] Roman authorities not only allowed local mints to issue local coinage with local types, but also encouraged them to do so. Trajan's imperial cult was no doubt well integrated into the collective consciousness of many eastern cities, and in Dora, perhaps more so than with the previous emperors; his image became part of the pantheon of the city; it is paired not only with Tyche, but also with the male god Zeus Doros. The depiction of the galley, the symbol of Dora's Phoenician past, on one of Trajan's reverse types reflects another of the city's relevant elements of self-identification.[82]

The depiction of imperial images continued in Dora with Hadrian's portrait in the issues of 117 CE, on the obverse of the same reverse types that were used by Trajan, such as Zeus Doros (**No. 30 and 34**), the bust of Tyche (**No. 31**), Tyche standing on a ship's prow (**No. 32**) and a galley (**No. 33**). The obverse image depicts the bust of Hadrian draped, laureate, and facing right with his hair and beard shorter than is usually depicted in such portraits. The thin face and sharp chin parallel the imagery of the coins of his first to third consulate. It has often been assumed that Hadrian's extensive travel throughout the various provinces affected the output and the typology of his statues, which in turn affected the coin iconography.[83] Max Wegner cited Hadrian's visits to provincial towns to establish a portrait

FIG. 4.4 TRAJAN, BRITISH MUSEUM. LONDON. 1805,0703.93

chronology and typology, dividing the extant corpus of Hadrian's portraits into six basic types.[84] There are, of course, quite a few variants within each of Wegner's types and not all scholars agree with Wegner's classification, but Dora's coin portrait seems to resemble Wegner's Type V of an armored imperial bust (*Typus Panzerbüste Imperatori 32*), which depicts Hadrian shortly after his accession to the throne when he was in his early forties. Wegner's Type V is believed to be the most widespread and authoritative type throughout the empire (**Fig. 4. 5**).[85] In fact, Dora's coin portraits, done in 117, the year of Hadrian's accession and while he was still in the East, depict him as a rather young-looking man, and it is quite possible that a statue of Hadrian was in Dora immediately after his accession to power.

[79] Riccardi 2000, 128.

[80] The bearded figure, usually referred to as 'Doros,' will be covered later in this chapter. Henceforth, we will refer to him as Zeus Doros.

[81] Butcher 2005, 153.

[82] The iconography of nautical elements on Dora's coins will be addressed later in the chapter.

[83] Kleiner (1992, 238) notes, "There are more surviving statues of Hadrian … because statues of him were erected in cities throughout the empire in anticipation of or in appreciation of his visits."

[84] Wegner (1956, 54) writes, *Das besonders zahlreiche Vorkommen von Bildnissen des Hadrian aus den Provinzen wird durch diese Reisen erklärt, und es liegt nun nahe, zu erwägen, welche provinzialen Bildnisse sich mit dem jeweiligen Aufenthalt des Herrschers in einer bestimmten Provinz in Verbindung bringen lassen, und ferner zu prüfen, ob sich daraus nennenswerte zeitliche Anhaltspunkte für Datierung der Bildnisse ergeben* (The remarkably high number of Hadrian's portraits from the provinces may be explained by these trips, wherefore we may then attempt to draw individual connections between particular provincial portraits and the emperor's respective residences, and also examine whether we can arrive at any noteworthy clues by which we may establish a chronology for dating the portraits (translated by Nicholai Ostrau).

[85] Wegner 1956, 20-24. The Type *Panzerbüste Imperatori* 32 includes the statue of Fig. 4.6 at the Capitoline Museum.

FIG. 4. 5. HADRIAN. MUSEI CAPITOLINI. ROME MC 817

FIG. 4.6. ANTONINUS PIUS. BRITISH MUSEUM. LONDON.
INV. 1850,0116.1

Much has been discussed about Hadrian's journeys through Syria-Palestina and, although scholars agree on an imperial visit in 129, a debate exists as to whether he visited the province in 117, upon his accession in Antioch on August 11.[86] Prior to becoming emperor, however, Hadrian had traveled with Trajan to Syria as *comes Augusti* and *legatus Augusti pro praetore*, and was appointed governor of Syria in 114.[87] As a governor of the province, it can be assumed that Hadrian traveled from one city to another, and although there is no indication that the emperor visited Dora itself, it is very likely that the people of Dora might have had more exposure to him than to other emperors.[88] Indeed, it is altogether possible that a statue of Hadrian could have already been erected in Dora before becoming emperor, allowing the engraver to make the die immediately after his accession.[89] The smooth transition of power between Trajan and Hadrian, and the fact that the legend on the coins still continues to use the name TRAIANUS and the same reverse iconography as Trajan's coins (**No. 30-34**), must have made it easy for the people of Dora to integrate Hadrian in the city's pantheon. In the religious imagery of the people of Dora, Hadrian's cult was more than a living

emperor's cult, as it was necessarily tied to the cult of a deified Trajan.

The iconography of Zeus Doros and Tyche continues on the reverses of Antoninus Pius in the single-year issues of coins **No. 35, 36,** and **37** in 143 CE, illustrating a continuation not only in the city's religious imagery but the legacy of the preceding emperors. Antoninus Pius, who was in fact adopted by Hadrian, governed the province "with great wisdom and integrity; insomuch as to have exceeded in repute all his predecessors."[90] Dora's coins show the bust of the emperor, laureate and draped, facing right, and always in the proximity of a star. In this portrait he is depicted as having a high round forehead, with thick curly hair falling over it. The generous nose (**No. 36**), and the long chin covered with a curly beard that also covers his cheeks give him a paternalistic aspect, proper for a man his age. Since the portrait is seen from the rear, one has the impression that his gaze is fixed upward, giving him the expression of calmness and equanimity that is typical of his portraiture. Antoninus Pius came to the throne at the age of 52, and his imperial portraits show his face from about the time of his accession.[91] In the early portraits, he appears young for his age (Fig. **4.6**), much as he is depicted on Dora's coins, but the look changed during the twenty

[86] Among those who believed that the emperor traveled from Antioch to Palestina is W. D. Gray (1923), who based his assertion on works by J. Dürr (1881). The discovery of a bronze head and torso of a statue of Hadrian found at Tel Shalem, a Roman fort 5 km south of Beit Shean, Israel, in 1975, could confirm Hadrian's presence in Palestina. For more on the statue, see Dewsnap 1997.

[87] Opper 2008, 47.

[88] See Opper 2008, 55.

[89] Opper 2008, 59.

[90] Stevenson 1964, 55.

[91] Alexander 1934, 28.

FIG. 4.7. SEPTIMIUS SEVERUS. BRITISH MUSEUM, LONDON. INV. 0703.104

FIG. 4.8. SEPTIMIUS CLASPING HANDS WITH HIS SON CARACALLA, WHILE TYCHE FORTUNA PRESIDES OVER THE SCENE. ARCH OF SEPTIMIUS SEVERUS. LEPTIS MAGNA.

years of his reign, revealing a much older countenance on some coins minted when he was in his late sixties.

There was no minting in Dora under the reigns of the remaining Antonines, but the rise of Septimius Severus (193-211 CE) provided an impetus for new issues that portrayed the emperor as well as members of his family from 202 CE to 211. Furthermore, in a break with Dora's coin types of previous emperors, the Severan coins portrayed family members on the obverse as well as the reverse of coins. The obverse of Septimius Severus' coin (**No. 38**) made in 202 CE, depicts the emperor facing right, laureate and draped; the tightly curled and short hair is in the manner of the so-called Serapis type portrait of the emperor, thought to have been commissioned after 200 CE, after Septimius Severus' journey into Egypt in 199/200 (**Fig. 4.7**.[92] However, the curly beard, which covers the side of his face and hangs off his chin in two long, corkscrew curls, seems to be a recollection of Marcus Aurelius' beard rather than of Serapis'.[93] In a change from the coins

of Septimius' predecessors, the coin's reverse does not depict Zeus Doros or Tyche, Dora's traditional religious icons, but the emperor's young sons, standing facing each other and clasping their right hands in a symbolic act of joining the right hands (*dextrarum junctio*). Caracalla and Geta, aged 14 and 11, are portrayed as young boys, with Caracalla on the right, slightly taller and in frontal view in a welcoming gesture toward the younger brother, seen in profile from the back.[94] The imperial family was in the Near East between 197-202, and Caracalla and Geta were respectively raised to the rank of "Augustus," i.e., co-ruler(s) with their father, and "Caesar" in 198 to celebrate the victory over the Parthians.[95] The depiction on Dora's coin does not, however, show any difference in rank between the brothers – the pose and the direct gaze into each other's face in fact suggest an equal standing. The *dextrarum junctio* depiction on Dora's coin, which recalls the scene in the relief of the arch at Leptis Magna in which Septimius and Caracalla clasp hands, must be seen in terms of family harmony and as a clear propagandistic message, asserting the continuance of the Severan dynasty (**Fig. 4.8**) [96] The coin also seems to suggest a connection to the *Concordia Augustorum* coinage of Marcus Aurelius

---

[92] Fejefer 2008, 408. Vermeule 1962, 65.

[93] Raeder (1992, 179-80) sees the style as having its roots in the portraiture of the Hadrianic period. In 194, Septimius claimed to have been adopted by Marcus Aurelius in an attempt to legitimize his reign.

[94] Reekmans 1958, 69. See also Walter 1979, 273.

[95] Ghedini 1984, 8.

[96] Walter 1979, 273. For a study of the iconography of the *dextrarum junctio*, see Reekmans 1958. For the significance of the arch of Leptis Magna, see Townsend 1938. The Arch, which has a *terminus post quem* of 202 CE, might be contemporaneous with the coins of Dora.

Courtesy: Numismatica Ars Classica

FIG. 4.9. AUREUS, 161 CE.
OBV: LAUREATE HEAD OF LUCIUS VERUS, R. IMP(ERATOR) CAES(AR) L(VCIVS) AVREL(IVS) VERVS AVG(VSTVS).
REV: LUCIUS VERUS AND MARCUS AURELIUS STANDING, FACING EACH OTHER, SHAKING HANDS. CONCORDIAE
AVGVSTOR(UM) TR(IBVNICIA) P(OTESTATE). EX: CO(N)S(VL) II. RIC VOL. 3, P. 251, NO. 456.

and Lucius Verus, in which the two emperors are clasping hands (**Fig. 4.9**), attesting that Septimius Severus, in his attempt to establish his own legacy, looked forward to his sons' future role as emperors, but that he also looked backward to Marcus Aurelius' legacy to legitimize his own standing.[97] Most importantly, however, Septimius Severus' coin from Dora shows that under Septimius Severus the city had reached a closer connection with the emperor, his politics, and his campaigns than with the previous Roman rulers–a connection that allowed the mint to issue imperial/imperial types, indicating that Dora's status assumed that of a "mini-Rome."[98]

Despite the closer association of the city to the imperial family, the mint of Dora did not lose its central connection to the more traditional city symbols, and busts of Doros and Tyche as well as the Phoenician galley reappear on Dora's 202 CE coins with other members of the Severan family. In fact, the issues of that year include a portrait of the empress Julia Domna (**No. 39**) with the bust of Tyche on its reverse. The empress is depicted facing right and with her hair extending to the level of her chin and gathered behind in a broad, flat chignon that covers most of the back of her head (**Fig. 4.10**).[99] The long face, small mouth, high cheekbones, and long nose of the coin depiction seem to have been her real features as is shown by other portraits. Later coins of the empress, minted at Dora in 212 CE shortly after her husband's death and

FIG. 4.10. JULIA DOMNA, MUSEI CAPITOLINI, ROME.

---

[97] The depiction of the *dextrarum junctio* by members of the imperial family dates from the reign of Vespasian, where Titus and Domitian are represented together, joining right hands in the presence of Pietas in 80 CE. Later, after 161 CE, Marcus Aurelius and Lucius Verus are represented the same way in the presence of Concordia. See Walters 1979, 273.
[98] Howgego 2005, 15.
[99] Scrinari 1953-55, 117. Julia Domna's portraits have been separated into two groups on the basis of changes in her hairstyle; in the first group, dated between 196 CE and 211 CE, her hair extends to about the level of the chin, and in the second, dated between 211 CE and 217 CE, her hair hangs farther down the neck. See also Hiesinger 1969, 73. For a thorough classification of Julia Domna's portraits, see Meischner 1967.

FIG. 4.11. JULIA DOMNA. STAATLICHE ANTIKENSAMMLUNGEN UND GLYPTOTHEK. MUNICH.

FIG. 4.12. YOUNG GETA.
STAATLICHE ANTIKENSAMMLUNGEN UND GLYPTOTHEK, MUNICH.

during Caracalla's reign, portray her on the obverse of the Phoenician galley found on previous Dora coins (**No. 48**), Tyche standing (**No. 49**), and a bust of Tyche (**No. 50**). These later portraits depict Julia Domna thinner and aging, perhaps due to her advanced age and personal trials, but still show the profound charm of her personality.[100] The coiffures of the female figures on the coins are different. While on the earlier coin, Julia wears the hairstyle typical at the end of the second century, echoing the styles of Faustina the Younger, in the later coins Julia Domna's hairstyle appears heavier, like a helmet or a wig. Coins **No. 48-50** portray her facing right, and with her hair flowing down the side of her head in long waves that end at the neck and curl upward in a twisted bun on the back of her neck (**Fig. 4.11**).. This later hairstyle is the one most associated with Julia Domna's portraits, especially those from the later years of Septimius Severus' principate until her death in 217 CE.[101]

In the same year that Dora's mint struck Septimius Severus' and Julia Domna's coins (202 CE), it also issued coins depicting their young sons Geta (**No. 42**) and Caracalla (**No. 40**), and the latter's new wife Plautilla (**No. 41**). The realistic portrait of Geta's bareheaded and draped bust captures a rather slim thirteen-year-old Caesar seen from behind and facing right. The short hair, together with the small chin and long skinny nose of the depiction, gives the figure the sense of fragility appropriate to his young age. (Fig. **4.12**). The bust of Caracalla on coin **No. 40** shows the older brother, also from behind and facing right, with a laureate head that indicates his rank of Augustus.[102] Although only a few years older than Geta, Caracalla definitely looks older than his brother on this coin – more so than he did on the *Concordia* depiction on coin **No. 38**, where the brothers look equal in size and age. The fine features of the beardless young boy on coin **No. 40** recall the statue that portrays the young emperor in 198 CE, (**Fig. 4.13**), and seem far from the strong-jowled man with a protruding, wrinkled forehead, which would be typical of Caracalla's later portraiture.[103] The reverse of coin **No. 40** contrasts with previous depictions of Tyche that represent her as a bust or standing on the prow of a galley, as it shows Tyche standing inside a tetrastyle temple.[104]

---

[100] In her role of *mater castrorum* (mother of the camp) and, after 209, *mater Augustorum* (mother of the *Augusti*), Julia Domna wielded great political influence. After the death of Septimius Severus (February 211) and Geta (December 211) and under the reign of Caracalla, her political role increased, as shown by her new title *mater patriae et senatus*. See Ghedini 1984, 14. For a study of her portraits, see Scrinari 1953-55.

[101] Wessel 1946-7, 62. Scrinari 1953-55, 125; Bartman 2001, 15-16.

[102] Caracalla was raised to the rank of Augustus in 198. See Ghedini 1984, 8.

[103] Wood 1986, 28. See also Nodelman 1965, 185-203; Pollini 2005, 55-78.

[104] The architecture of the temple will be discussed later in this chapter.

FIG. 4.13. YOUNG CARACALLA
PALAZZO MASSIMO DELLE TERME, ROME.

FIG. 4.14. YOUNG PLAUTILLA
PALAZZO MASSIMO DELLE TERME, ROME

Finally, the portrait of Plautilla on coin **No. 41** depicts the very young, unfortunate wife of Caracalla. The daughter of the immensely wealthy and powerful Praetorian Prefect Plautianus, she was married to Caracalla in 202 CE, acquiring the title of Augusta the same year (**Fig. 4.14**).[105] Although the young empress was in power for less than three years and was subject to *damnatio memoriae* after her death in 211 CE, there are several numismatic representations of her, with five distinct portrait types, differentiated on the basis of coiffure and physiognomy.[106] On Dora's coin (**No. 41**), perhaps one of Plautilla's earliest since it was issued in the same year as her wedding, the young empress appears to be in her teens, wearing her hair parted in the center and arranged in a series of braids drawn into a large bun that sits high at the back of her head.[107] Her hair, arranged neatly in the back (*Melonenfrisur*), gives the young empress, according to Scrinari, a decidedly Roman look in opposition to Julia Domna's long, unkempt barbarian hairstyle.[108]

The city honored Caracalla as the sole emperor in 212 CE with an obverse portrait set on four different reverse types respectively portraying Tyche standing inside a temple (**No. 43** and **46**), Caracalla on horseback (**No. 44**), Zeus Doros (**No. 45**), and a galley (**No. 47**). On all four types, the obverses portray a bust of the emperor who is laureate and facing right, with tightly curled hair and a short, but full beard. The portrait shows all the traits, which according to Richter, characterize most of Caracalla's portraits — "the thick neck, turned rather sharply to the left; the protruding muscles of the forehead with wrinkled brows and the two oblique swellings above the eyes, which impart a frowning, somewhat sinister expression to the face; the thick, plebeian nose with an oblique furrow across the bridge; the mobile mouth with curving lips; and the cleft chin" (**Figs. 4.15** and **4.16**).[109] The assertiveness of Caracalla's expression on these and other coins was meant to emphasize the emperor's strength as a military commander, highlighting his need to maintain the support of the armies throughout his reign.[110] The reverse of coin **No. 44** shows Caracalla on horseback, holding the reins

---

[105] After the death of her father, Plautilla was exiled to the island of Lipari and killed after the death of Septimius Severus in 211. See Ghedini 1984, 10.

[106] Varner 2004, 164. See also Scrinari 1953-55, 128-129.

[107] Plautilla's numismatic portraits display at least eleven different types — a much higher number than the five different types of Julia Domna who reigned for twenty-four years. See Nodelman 1982, 105. For a thorough study on the coin representation of the Severan women, see Scrinari 1953-55.

[108] Scrinari 1953-55, 128.

[109] Richter 1940, 139.

[110] Parker 1966, 90. After Geta's murder, Caracalla even increased the soldiers' normal pay by a half to win their support (Speidel 1992, 19). Additionally, he envisioned himself as a military leader in the fashion of Alexander, and the title Alexander was in fact used on the commemorative coins for the occasion of his journey to Philoppopolis in Thrace in 214 CE. See Vagi 2000, 279.

FIG. 4.15. CARACALLA. BRITISH MUSEUM, LONDON
INV. 1805,0703.102

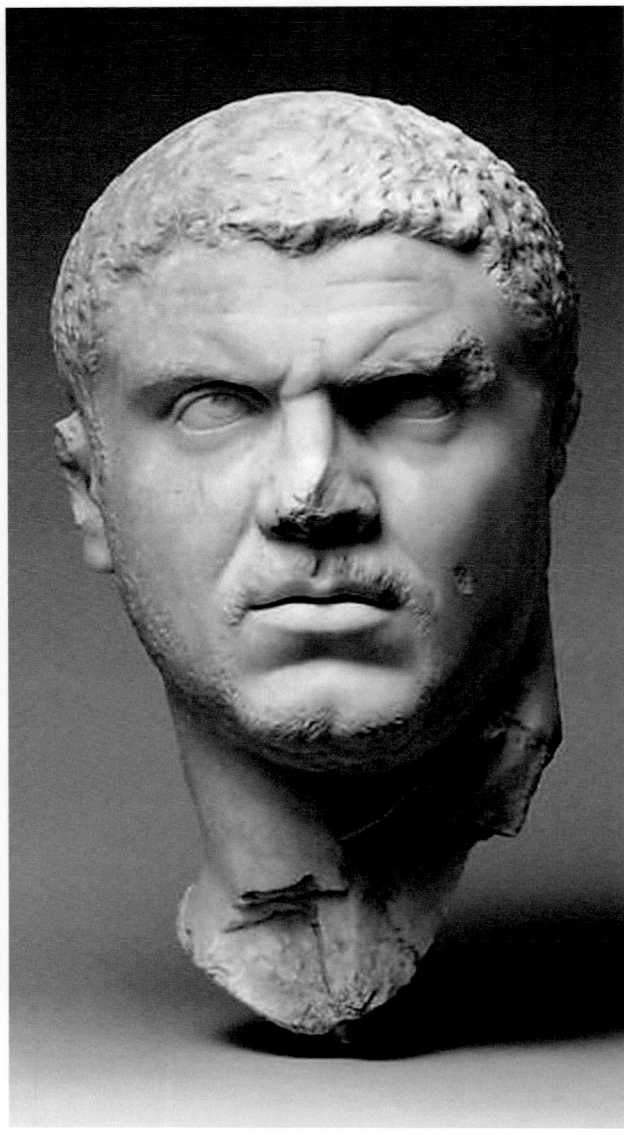

FIG. 4. 16. CARACALLA, NEW YORK METROPOLITAN, NEW YORK.
NO. 40.11.1A

with his left hand, while his raised right arm is bent at the elbow and his hand holds a spear. The horse has its ears pricked up and is rearing back, causing the rider to tilt his body slightly backward. Although the scene could easily appear to fit the trampling enemy warfare type initiated by Domitian,[111] it does not show the emperor holding a shield, i.e., in military attire, nor is there an enemy lying below the horse. The depiction is in fact a closer match to the iconography of the Greek hero relief and connected to images of deities on horseback widespread throughout the Aegean and Asia Minor.[112] The spear in Caracalla's

hand is a symbol of power enshrined in Roman beliefs and the typical weapon of mounted portraits of emperors.[113] Additionally, it is easy to understand the significance of the iconography of Caracalla riding a horse like a Greek hero, since, according to literary sources, Caracalla claimed to have seen Achilles darting around in his armor or heard the hero riding horses. In fact, Cassius Dio, a contemporary of the emperor, wrote that when Caracalla crossed the Hellespont in 214 CE, he visited Achilles' tomb and honored the hero with sacrifices, setting up a bronze statue in his honor.[114]

[111] Tuck (2005, 221-245) ascribes to Domitian the origin of the Roman imperial hunting imagery as an attempt to redefine *virtus* in the Hellenistic tradition of 'bravery and military strength'.
[112] The rider is often called "Thracian" because he appears on reliefs, mostly found in Thrace, its neighboring territories, and other places with a strong Thracian presence. The rider motif, however, was commonplace in the Greek world on both sides of the Aegean. Will (1955, 78-9) writes, "Avant de devenir le motif le plus banal de l'iconographie thrace de l'Empire, l'image du Heros cavalier était déjà banale dans le monde grec sur les deux rives de l'Égée" (before becoming the most banal motif of the Thracian iconography of the Empire, the image of the rider-hero was already commonplace in the Greek world on both sides of the Aegean (my translation), concluding (105, 116) that there were no rider-gods in Thrace and Moesia, but only gods depicted on horseback. More recently, Petsas (1978, 192-204) interprets certain rider reliefs in Macedonia as

"prototypes" of the Thracian rider. Finally, a recent study by G. Horsley (1999, 43) on the detail of the "Rider God" on the stelai at the Burdur Museum in Turkey concludes that the rider gods are predominantly images of Herakles and the indigenous god Kakasbos. The main collections of riders are described in *LIMC* Vol 1, 1992, pp. 1018-1081, pls. 673-719. For an in-depth study of the inscriptions on these reliefs, see also Dimitrova 2002, 209-229.
[113] Henig 1970, 255. See also Toynbee 1962, 157-8.
[114] Dio Cassius, *Roman History* 78.16.7. Caracalla's visit to Achilles'

The Severan coins at Dora, with their obverses depicting the entire imperial family and with imperial portraits on the reverses, seem to bring the city closer to imperial Rome. Coins, however, just like the festivals that celebrated the imperial cults that were often represented on coins, never lost their "central meaning as an expression of the city's special relationship with its gods and its autonomy as a *polis*."[115] As previously stated, imperial portraits of all emperors, the Severans as well as the previous emperors, reinforce the fact that imperial cult and its rituals fit within the social, cultural and religious life of the city. Even when the city authorities depicted imperial portraits — the most obvious symbol of Rome's power — on their bronze coins, those emperors coexisted with Dora's religious iconography. As Harl suggests, "These coins and ceremonies upheld the religious symbols of the *polis* and its autonomy rather than the universal majesty of the Roman emperor."[116] It is therefore of great importance for our study of Dora's cultural identity to explore Tyche and Zeus Doros, the two divinities that are represented alone on the obverse of the autonomous coinage, and on the reverse of most imperial coins almost as the supporting cast of the emperors.

4.5 Religious Iconography

Much of the religious expression and iconography on Dora's coins focuses around two figures — the easily identifiable Tyche whose depictions appear in different settings— and the portraits of a less identifiable male figure who is reminiscent of both Zeus and Poseidon and who has been given the conventional name of 'Doros,' eponymous founder of the city.[117] Although the Dioskouroi's caps appear on at least one coin above the prow of a galley (**No. 2**) and a winged Nike, standing on a galley appears on another coin, the frequency with which Tyche and Doros appear on both the obverse and the reverse of coins from Dora can leave no doubt that the citizens of the city were primarily devoted to these two deities. The two gods' cults must have been celebrated in regular civic festivals, providing the most important and lasting source of images for the city's coinage. Religions are primarily, according to Woolf, "means of making sense of the world, of mankind and of each individual worshipper's place in it."[118] But considering the many changes that took place in this port city throughout its history, one must wonder what the main characteristics of the *polis* religion model of Dora's were and how Tyche and Zeus Doros aided its citizens in the "explanations of and remedies for common misfortunes.[119]

The term "*polis* religion" was first used by Sourvinou-Inwood to describe a religious system in which "full participation was reserved for citizens, that is, those who made up the community … [since] the *polis* anchored, legitimated and mediated all religious activity."[120] The religion of the *polis* was thus homologous with the social and political structures of that *polis*, and priests, selected from the civic élite, controlled and presided over public cults, reinforcing the homology. The spread of the city-state throughout Greece, the Mediterranean areas, and the Hellenistic and Roman empires led to the consequent diffusion of the *polis* religion, which Gordon calls a "civic compromise," i.e., "a close nexus between sacrifice, benefaction and domination by elite."[121] Gordon's account of public cult and elite domination explains how cults that were not organized by the authorities were deemed private and defined negatively, and how syncretism in the naming and representations of deities were always subject to political interpretations.[122] It also explains how Tyche and Zeus Doros survived the vicissitudes of Dora's history — they were the official deities of a *polis*-centered cult that was sponsored by the political authorities of the city.

The importance of Tyche in the Greek world was already established in literature of the Archaic Period. According to Pausanias, Homer is the first to mention Tyche in his poems, but she is mentioned in several other sources.[123] As the daughter of Oceanus, Tyche ruled the religious beliefs of sailors and was revered as the protector of seamen, thus also acquiring an association with chance and luck. However, she was not a goddess in her own right until the mid-fourth century BCE, when it seems that some temples were built for her.[124] Following the conquest of Alexander the Great, "an atmosphere of syncretism settled throughout the Hellenistic world, particularly in Asia Minor … where the gods of each cult merge with one another, blending diverse elements so as to present a configuration of Greek and Oriental ideas."[125] Tyche, the capricious daughter of Oceanus, fused with other strong preexisting female goddesses of the areas to form the Tyche that is detectable in Hellenistic art in a number of forms. Although sculptures of Tyche did exist in earlier periods, representations of Tyche became most popular in the fourth century BCE, in

---

tomb is also described by Herodian in *History of the Empire* 4.8.3-5 (*Ab Excessu Divi Marci*). For more on the emperor's imitation of Greek heroes, see Zeitlin 2001.

[115] Klose 2004, 131.

[116] Harl 1987, 66.

[117] Since there are no certain literary or archeological sources that indicate that the male figure on Dora's coins is Doros, son of Poseidon, the name Zeus Doros will be used in this work and the figure will be discussed later in this chapter. Hill started the numismatic convention of using the name 'Doros' to identify the figure in 1910; the conventional name is also used in *RPC* Vol 1, 660-1.

[118] Woolf 1997, 74.

[119] Ibid.

[120] Sourvinou-Inwood 1990, 295 and 297.

[121] Gordon 1990, 235.

[122] Wolf 1997, 75.

[123] Pausanias, *Description of Greece* 4.30.4. In the *Homeric Hymn to Demeter*, in fact, Persephone tells her mother, "All we were playing in a lovely meadow, Leukippe … and Melobosis and Tykhe and Okyrhoe, fair as a flower" (5.420).

[124] According to Hesiod's *Theogony*, Tyche is one of the daughters of Tethys and Okeanos, "A race apart of daughters … They are Peitho … Kalypso, Eudora and Tykhe" (346). Pindar describes her in *Olympian Ode* 12. 1, "Daughter of Zeus Eleutherios, Tykhe our savior goddess, I pray your guardian care for Himera, and prosper her city's strength. For your hand steers the ships of ocean on their flying course, and rules on land the march of savage wars, and the assemblies of wise counselors." In Agamemnon, Aeschylus concludes that she is a savior goddess (664), but Euripides has Odysseus argue that Tyche's attributes are less than those of a divinity (*Cyclops* 707). Smith (2003, 18 January) notes Lycurgus' reference to a Temple of Tyche, repaired as part of the city's renewal.

[125] McMinn 1956, 202 and 204. According to Pausanias, *Description of Greece* (4.30.6), the Tyche that Boupalos made at Smyrna was the first to have a cornucopia. See Fullerton 1990, 85.

the version of the Tyche of Antioch by Eutychides, which represents the personification of a city as a female wearing a city wall crown (**Fig. 4.17**).[126]

Modern scholars believe that all ancient religions were complex belief systems that developed as the result of an accumulation of successive layers of religious contacts.[127] Within the complex reality of Dora's maritime environment and culture, it is therefore easy to understand the Hellenistic Tyche of Dora as a syncretistic cult, whose origins were deeply rooted in the pre-existing Ashtart/ Astarte, the Iron Age Phoenician goddess of fertility, sexuality and war.[128] Additionally, according to Albright, Ashtart was herself the incarnation of the earlier Bronze Age Canaanite Asherah, whose "original character was of the sea."[129] The syncretism of Asherah/Ashtart and Ashtoreth, wife of Ba'al, the storm god, is documented in the Hebrew Bible where "Solomon followed Ashtoreth, god of Sidon."[130]

During the political, social and economic instability of the Hellenistic and early Roman periods at Dora and in other Phoenician cities, Astarte/Asherah/Ashtoreth received new civic attributes; she became Tyche, protectress of cities, yet linked to the sea through her father Oceanus.[131] Rooted in cult-rituals that stemmed from the sea, the significance of Tyche/Astarte/Ashtoreth increased greatly in port cities, until she was perceived as a superior force protecting not just the cities but also each individual life. Tyche in fact protected individuals in the Greek sense of a *daimonion,* or a Roman *genius*, resembling the Abrahamic מלאך אלוהים (*mal'akh elohim)*, the guardian angel of Semitic religions.[132] At the same time, Tyche's cult as a

FIG. 4. 17. TYCHE OF ANTIOCH BY EUTHYCHIDES (ROMAN COPY) MUSEO VATICANO, ROME. INV. 2672

[126] Some lost fourth century representations of Tyche are the statues by Xenophon of Athens, and at least two by Praxiteles that served as cult statues in the Sanctuary of Tyche at Megara. Pollitt (1986, 2) cites Pausanias (I.43.6) for the Megara statue and Pliny (Natural History 36.23) for the Athens statue. For other pre-Hellenistic examples, see Dohrn 1960, 41-42. For more representations of Tyche, see Fullerton 1990, 85-102.

[127] Woolf 1997, 76.

[128] Scholars have long recognized a one-to-one correspondence between the Greek goddess Aphrodite and the Phoenician goddess Ashtart (Astarte). For more on the syncretism between Aphrodite and Ashtart, see Budin 2004. For the Hellenistic and Roman evidence of Ashtart/Astarte as the most important deity of the Phoenician cities of Sidon and Tyre, see Seyrig 1963, 19-28. While according to Langdon (1930, 28) Ashtoreth is the Canaanite goddess of fate borrowed from Babylonia, Dever (2005, 176-208) suggests that Asherah was the consort of El and of Yahweh in ancient Israel. Whether Asherah and Ashtoreth are variations of the same underlying deity's name is still being debated on the basis of linguistic differences, as both versions are found in literature of Semitic nations (Smith 2002, xxx-xxxiii).

[129] Albright (1942, 74-75) notes, "The same Babylonian ideogram is employed in the Amarna Tablets to write the names of both Astarte and Asherah; in contemporary Egypt Anath and Astarte are even fused into one deity 'Antart,' while in later Syria their cult was replaced by that of a composite deity 'Anat-Ashtart,' Aramaic 'Attar'atta' (Atargatis). Astarte was goddess of the evening star, and originally she must have been identical with a male figure, 'Ashtar,' god of the morning star, known to us from South Arabia, Moab, Ugarit and Roman Syria."

[130] 1 *Kings* 11:5.

[131] A Hellenistic clay figurine of Tyche with a crown of city walls was found in a cave on Mount Carmel, opposite Tel Dor. See Stern 2000, 244.

[132] Pollitt 1986, 2. A powerful *daimonion* was nearly as powerful as Tyche herself, causing people to take official oaths by invoking the Tyche/daimonion of kings or rulers deemed to have favorable fortunes. For an in-depth study of the Roman genius, see MacCormack 1974.

city-goddess expanded via the *polis* institution, and was encouraged by the authorities that viewed the cult as a means to unite subjects of various ethnic origins into one uniform framework.[133] With the arrival of the Romans, the syncretic tendency of Tyche showed itself more clearly as she merged with Fortuna, acquiring some of her characteristics. As previously stated, the process of Romanization of Dora, much like Hellenization, was also a process of hybridization, with both cultural symbols acquiring hybrid significations emically associated with both the local and the Roman cultures.[134] The Hellenic Astarte/Tyche represented on the obverse of the

[133] The *polis* mediated the participation of individuals in the cult activities of a god, allowing even a non-citizen to participate as a *xenos* with the help of a citizen, the *proxenos* who acted as an intermediary. See Sourvinou-Inwood 1990, 296.

[134] Hall 2003b, 44.

autonomous coins was then easily identified with Tyche/ Fortuna represented on the reverse of Dora's imperial coins.

As the patron goddess of Hellenistic and Roman Dora, Tyche is depicted on the obverse of the autonomous coins, sharing her role only with Zeus Doros and on the reverse of imperial coins. The portraits show her as a young woman, wearing a crown over the himation of the type of the Tyche of Antioch, and facing either right (**No. 2**) or left (**No. 18**).[135] Her large eyes, full cheeks and lips, and dangling earrings of coin **No. 2** are the signifiers of her function as the mother-goddess who can inspire faith and trust in her devotees. The turreted head alone is a popular symbol on Dora's coins as a personification of the city. Her crown, shaped in the form of the city walls, symbolizes the *polis* itself and the goddess's function as protectress of the *polis*.[136] In her early full-length images, she is only once portrayed in a non-marine environment, holding a palm branch in her right hand and a caduceus in her left hand (**No. 3**) in the type found in **Fig. 4.19**. As the daughter of Oceanus, she is portrayed in a maritime environment on the reverse of more than half of all coins minted at Dora. These full-length images always depict her wearing a long, pleated chiton with short sleeves and a peplos that folds at the upper extremity to form first a narrow and then a wider shawl that covers her head.[137] In each of these representations, Tyche has a cornucopia resting on her left arm while holding either a rudder with her right hand (**No. 4 and 9**), in the type of the statuette at the British Museum (**Fig. 4.18**) or a standard (**No. 11**) as in the Tyche of Dura (**Fig. 4.19**). The weight of the figure seems to be based on the right leg, with the foot resting on a tiller (**No. 21**), a prow (**No. 30**) or an aphlaston (**No. 31**). While the standard extends the meaning of Tyche as a power over the city's fate, the cornucopia, her oldest attribute, illustrates her power to bestow prosperity.[138] Finally, Tyche's portrayals as a sea-goddess express the city's obvious connection to the sea, the main source of livelihood, economic prosperity, and political success for Dora. Additionally, the type with the representation of Tyche inside the temple on the reverse of Caracalla's coin (**No. 40, 42, 46**) denotes complete syncretism with the goddess Fortuna, to whom Caracalla was devoted.[139]

In her maritime depictions, Tyche links the city of Dora to the entire coastal region of Phoenicia and Syria as the common source of cultural identity. As Butcher puts it, "Tyche may be seen as an expression of the spirit of the city itself, of its citizens, or of both…. The city goddess is the commonest and clearest expression of civic identity on the coinage of those cities."[140] Tyche's Dora type portraits

FIG. 4.18. TYCHE WITH CORNUCOPIA AND RUDDER. BRITISH MUSEUM. LONDON. INV. 1975,0201.2

are in fact represented on the coins of nearly all cities of the Phoenician coast, such as Tyre, Tripolis, Byblos, Ashkelon, and as far north as Antiochia ad Orontem (**Figs. 4.20 - 4.25**). On the coin of Sidon (**Fig. 4. 26**) she appears in a jugate portrait with Zeus, while in the Roman period she often appears inside a wreath supported by the Roman eagle as at Caesarea (**Fig. 4.27**), demonstrating total syncretism with Roman Fortuna. Tyche's standing type images are also common throughout the area (**Figs. 4. 28-31**), although not as common as the bust type. The coins of Tiberias, Gadara and Hippos-Susita — cities near the Sea of Galilee — also show marine symbols together with the city-goddess. Finally, the Tyche-inside-the-temple types depicted on Caracalla's coins are also common in many other cities, including Aelia Capitolina (Jerusalem) and Berytus (**Fig. 4.32-33**).

---

[135] *LIMC* 1997, I: Antiocheia, 840–851.

[136] *LIMC* 1997, VIII: Tyche/Fortuna No. 123. *RPC,* 1992, 794.

[137] *LIMC* 1997, VIII: 125-135; also the types No. 39-92.

[138] Edward 1990, 533.

[139] Fortuna appears on the Arch in Leptis Magna (Fig. **4.8**), between Septimius Severus and Caracalla, almost as a guarantor of the Severan dynasty. See Parra 1978, 807-828. For the Fortuna/Tyche type represented at Leptis Magna, see *LIMC* VIII 1997, 115-141.

[140] Butcher 2004, 231

FIG. 4. 19. RELIEF OF TYCHE OF DURA. PHOTO COURTESY OF YALE UNIVERSITY ART GALLERY. NEW HAVEN.

FIG. 4.20. TYCHE OF ARADOS, 152 BCE. BMC 97

FIG. 4.22. TYCHE OF TRIPOLIS. 22-21 BCE. BMC 206.

FIG. 4. 21. TYCHE OF TYRE. 117-118 CE. BMC 344.

FIG. 4.23. TYCHE OF BYBLOS. 1ST C. BCE. BMC 12

FIG. 4.24. TYCHE OF ASHKELON. 76-77 CE. ROSENBERG 30

FIG. 4.28. TYCHE OF ASHKELON, 138-161 CE, RPC 6384

FIG. 4.25. TYCHE OF ANTIOCH AD ORONTEM, 127-8 CE. BMC 105

FIG. 4.29. TYCHE OF TIBERIAS, 177-192 CE, RPC 6313

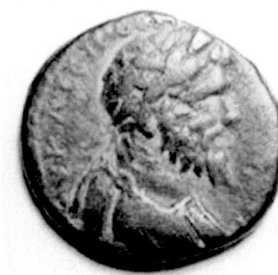

FIG. 4.26. TYCHE OF SIDON, 78-7 BCE. LINDGREN 2324.

FIG. 4.30. TYCHE OF GAZA. 197 CE. MIONNET 169

FIG. 4.27. TYCHE OF CAESAREA, 248 CE.

FIG. 4.31. TYCHE OF MARCIANOPOLIS 197 CE MOUSHMOV 394

FIG. 4.32. TYCHE OF AELIA CAPITOLINA, 161-169 CE. RPC 6413.

FIG. 4.33. TYCHE OF BERYTUS, 161-169 CE. RPC 6756

FIG. 4.34. ZEUS/JUPITER
BRITISH MUSEUM, LONDON 1805,0703.50.

While Tyche/Fortuna is depicted on Dora's coins with characteristics that make the image unequivocally clear — the turreted crown, the cornucopia, the rudder, etc. — the male figure on Dora's coin portraits is not as easily identifiable. The head shows the usual markings of an archaic type mature god who recalls the features of both Zeus (**Figs. 4.34 - 36**)[141] and Poseidon (**Figs. 4.37 - 39**),[142] with long hair hanging freely and a thick long beard. None of these two gods' attributes — an eagle, a bolt of lightning, or a scepter for Zeus; a trident or a dolphin for Poseidon — are present on Dora's coins, making it difficult to identify the male figure from the features alone. In the earliest studies of Dora's coins, Seguin (1674) and Eckhel (1794) refer to him as head of Jupiter, "*caput Iovis.*"[143] Rouvier (1901) also notes that the figure is the laureate head of Jupiter, "*tète laurée de Zeus,*" following de Saulcy's (1874) same description as "*tète laurée de Jupiter.*"[144] In his *Catalogue of Greek Coins of Phoenicia* (1910), Hill names the figure 'Doros,' starting a convention that was followed by Rosenberg (1975) and Meshorer (1986) and still continues in *Roman Provincial Coinage*.[145] Given, however, the near identical representation of the male figure on Dora's coins with figures on coins that either

---

[141] "Zeus" in *LIMC* 1997, VIII, 283, No. 154b, 157, 160.

[142] "Poseidon" in *LIMC* 1994, VI, 356-357, No. 42, 50, 54.

[143] While describing the obverse of Trajan's coins, Seguin (1684, 309) writes, "*In aversa autem parte caput Iovis laureatum.*" Eckhel (1794, 3: 362-363) identifies the figure as "*Typus: caput Iovis.*"

[144] Rouvier 1901, 125-131. de Saulcy 1874, 142-148; 405.

[145] *RIC* Vol 1, 660-1. Hill (1910, 1: xxiv) notes that according to Stephanus of Byzantium, Doros, the son of Poseidon, was the eponymous founder of the city, making it "probable that this hero is intended by the Poseidon-like deity represented on some of the coins." See also Rosenberg 1975, 31-37 and Meshorer 1986, 59-62.

FIG. 4.35. ZEUS/AMMON.
BRITISH MUSEUM. LONDON. INV.1856,1226.1744

FIG. 4.36. ZEUS/JUPITER
BRITISH MUSEUM. LONDON. INV. 1818,1114.1

FIG. 4.37. POSEIDON, LIMC NO. 42, P.357

clearly identify Zeus by legends (**Figs. 4.40-4.41**) or have attributes identifiable as Zeus's own, this study identifies Dora's male figure as Zeus Doros, i.e., Zeus from Dora.[146]

The fact that the features of Dora's male god do not clearly separate Zeus from Poseidon, by giving him specific attributes, is further evidence that the Hellenistic gods of Dora absorbed several native deities into their own nature. Just like Tyche, Zeus Doros is a syncretic figure with roots in two preexisting deities – Hadad, the Bronze Age Semitic storm god who reigned on a lofty mountain in the north and Dagan, creator and weather god of the Syrian hinterland and northern Mesopotamia, who became Dagon in the Philistine Pantheon.[147] The two gods later merged

FIG. 4.38 POSEIDON, LIMC NO. 50   FIG. 4.39. POSEIDON, LIMC NO. 54

FIG. 4. 40. ZEUS STRATEGOS, AMASTRIS (BITHYNIA, 101 CE).
RPC 4899. OBV: ΖΕΥΣ ΣΤΡΑΤΗΓΟΣ

---

[146] Motta 2011, 79-92. Hill's suggestion that the figure on Dora's coins was intended as Doros, son of Poseidon was mostly based on literary sources that had originated from Stephanus' Ethinica. Eckhel (1794, 362) had cited Stephanus' *Ethnica*, that "*Dora, maritima et longae vetustatis ... condita a Doro, Neptuni filio*" (Dora on the sea and of ancient beauty ... founded by Doros, son of Neptune). As discussed in my article, however, Stephanus was primarily a grammarian interested in the formation of ethnic adjectives, and might have imposed Doros on Dora in an attempt to give the city a founder father and therefore justify its name.
[147] Albright 1920, 319; Singer 1992, 436; Feliu and Watson 2003, 241 and

FIG. 4.41. ZEUS STRATEGOS, AMASTRIS (BITHYNIA, 101 CE) RPC 4897
OBV: ΖΕΥΣ ΣΤΡΑΤΗΓΟΣ

into Ba'al Hammon, the Iron Age Phoenician storm god who, like the Greek Zeus, regulated people's lives with his dominant environmental force and who eventually became the great adversary of Yahweh, god of the Hebrews.[148] However, it is impossible to ignore that with the arrival of Hellenism in Dora, Hadad/Dagon/Ba'al also acquired some of the Greek characteristics of Poseidon, god of the sea. Unlike Tyche, Zeus Doros was never portrayed in any maritime environment in Dora, but like Poseidon, he was always depicted as a bearded adult, with think curly hair covering the back of his neck[149] The visual distinction between Zeus and Poseidon is of course not clearly defined, demonstrating the oneness of land and sea, and man and nature in the imagination of Dora's religious conscience – a oneness which might be difficult for modern religion to grasp, but that was an important aspect of ancient religions; it is in fact not a good idea, as Singer states, "to approach ancient religions and syncretistic schemes with an overly strict and systematic logic."[150]

Aside from portraits on one Roman glass pendant, and on a fragment of one clay bowl,[151] the only representations of Zeus Doros found in Dora are coin portraits that depict his bust, always laureate and facing right on either the obverse of autonomous coins (**No. 3, 11, 14, 17, 23**) or the reverse of the imperial coins starting with Trajan (**No. 24, 28**), and continuing with Hadrian (**No. 30, 34**), Antoninus Pius (**No. 35**), Geta (**No. 42**), and Caracalla (**No. 45**). In his first appearance, on the obverse of coin **No. 3** (year 63/62 BCE), he is portrayed as an adult male with a full head of curly hair, a beard composed of wild wavy locks, and a thick neck. His vigorous, strong features seem those of a young man. The reverse of the coin portrays Tyche in her sea goddess role, denoting the gods' parallel and joint rule over the harbor city. Zeus Doros' obverse portraits are repeated with minor changes on autonomous coins from 62 BCE to 75 CE, but his appearance changes on

the reverse of imperial coins, where he looks older and more authoritative. On Dora's final imperial coins, on the reverse of young Geta's (**No. 42**) and Caracalla's (**No. 45**) coins, his hair is long enough to cover the back of his neck.

While the portrayals of Tyche and Zeus Doros place the harbor city of Dora within its Phoenician and Greek religious contexts, the depiction of Tyche inside her temple might provide an opportunity for a look at the physical setting of the cult, and therefore a chance to analyze the architecture of the city. After all, a temple with its permanent setting is more specific to the city environment than a mobile statue of either a god or an emperor. Since Dora's die-makers depicted temples on two of Caracalla's coin types (No. 40 and 46), one must wonder whether those images reproduced the architecture of actual buildings in Dora, and whether the Roman process of "logoization" of monuments, which attempted to determine social memory through coin minting, was taking place in Dora.[152]

4.6 Architecture on Dora's Coins

While architectural coin types were sporadic in the Hellenistic world before 30 BCE, they became regular issues of Roman rulers, who used architectural type coins to celebrate new buildings or commemorate old ones in cities throughout the empire.[153] However, the debate about whether these coin depictions were reliable representations of real architectural structures or just artistic interpretations has been going on for some time. In 1836 the *Royal Institute of British Architects* claimed that the "authority for the restoration of many ancient buildings,"[154] could be derived from coins, while in 1856 the *Edinburgh Review* had a different view, claiming that the representation of structures on coins should not be considered important, since the building might as well be "a conventional type rather than a strict resemblance of the reality."[155] Finally, Donaldson's *Architectura Numismatica*, published in 1859 "to persuade the writer in the *Edinburgh Review* that his remark was hasty,"[156] provided the first and most systematic study of architecture from ancient coins. More recently, numismatists have addressed the same debate, and they are divided among those who believe that architectural type coins make "a contribution …[to] our knowledge of ancient architecture,"[157] and those who question the authenticity of the structures depicted on coins. According to Burnett, for instance, it is impossible to prove that the die engraver was reproducing a real building, since he might have been more concerned with "a particular event or idea that might also happen to be commemorated in a particular monument, rather than to depict the monument itself."[158] Furthermore,

---

304. See also Montalbano 1951, 396-7; Wyatt 1980, 377.
[148] Green 2003, 175.
[149] Keel and Uehlinger 2001, 174.
[150] Singer 1992, 442.
[151] The identification of Zeus Doros on the glass pendant is not secure, but the bearded old man's features do in fact resemble those on Dora's coins. According to Stern, such pendants, worn at the end of a chain, followed the Persian and Hellenistic traditions of warding off evil spirits and they replaced the image of the Egyptian god Bes during Roman times. See Stern 2000, 316. For the image of Zeus Doros on the clay fragment, see Stern 2000, pl. IV.

[152] Burnett 1987, 48.
[153] Price and Trell 1977, 57 and 66.
[154] Donaldson 1859, 1.
[155] Donaldson 1859, ix.
[156] Ibid., 2.
[157] Price and Trell 1977, 15.
[158] Burnett 1999, 140. He later points out that another problem with architectural type coins is the large number of counterfeit coins, since forgery was a common activity during the Renaissance because of the strong interest in classical architecture. His claim is based on M. Baldanza, *Instruttione sopra le medaglie degli imperatori antichi*

the engraver might have portrayed a structure that had been commissioned but was never constructed.[159] Finally, after citing many examples of architectural coin depictions that "fail to confirm numismatic testimony with regards to architectural details," Drew-Bear concludes, "Numismatic representations must be treated with great caution, for clearly such depictions attain their full value as evidence only when they can be compared with the results of actual excavation of the monuments which they portray." [160] Architecture-type coins were, however, very common in eastern cities under the Roman Empire, and although these architectural coin depictions often required the adoption of certain conventions to represent the cult statue, they were normally "meant to be identifiable as illustrations of specific edifices."[161]

The city of Dora produced two architecture type coins with the depiction of a temple, in two separate issues — one in 202 CE on the reverse of young Caracalla (**No. 40**) and the other in 212 CE on the reverse of Caracalla as the sole emperor (**No. 43** and **46**). On all such coins the temple contains a shrine of Tyche inside, indicating that the illustrations depict the same building. However, while coin **No. 40** shows the goddess standing within an arched aedicula, which can be seen behind a tetrastyle portico on a low podium, coins **No. 43** and **46** show the statue standing inside the tetrastyle temple, with the portico columns forming an arch above her. Further differences among the three coins are the illustrations of Tyche herself, who is facing left and holding the cornucopia with her left hand on coin **No. 40**, and facing right and holding the cornucopia nestled in her left arm on coins **No. 43** and **46**. She holds the standard with her right hand in all depictions, but on coin **No. 40**, her arm seems to be wrapped around the pole of the standard.

While the most important concern of the artist seems to be not the temple as a structure *per se*, but as a place that housed Tyche's shrine, it is likely that the temple depicted on the coins represents an actual structure that existed in Dora. The on-going archaeological excavations at Tel Dor have in fact verified the existence of "a southern temple [that] stood upon a well-constructed, rectangular podium adjacent to the temenos ... the foundation of which cut into the bedrock in the sea."[162] Nothing remains of the temple or even the podium fill, but a retaining wall that separated the temple from the rest of the city and cut into the earlier Roman city provides much information. The analysis of settlement data around the wall has established that the temple was founded in the second century CE. Since the Severi were able to sustain a large program of construction in nearly every city of the empire,[163] it is very

feasible that the temple depicted on the Severan coins was built during their reign, and perhaps dedicated in 202 CE. As demonstrated by the large coin issues of the Severi, between the end of the second and the beginning of the third centuries, Dora experienced strong economic growth and physical expansion.[164] Consequently, the building of a new temple dedicated to Tyche would be part of this growth. The actual temple would have been, according to Meshorer, "a tetrastyle temple with a distyle façade where the goddess was standing."[165]

While it seems obvious that coins **No. 40, 43,** and **46** would depict the same temple based on the fact that the shrines house Tyche and there would only be one temple dedicated to the same goddess, it is difficult to determine that the images do actually portray the same building. One can assume, therefore, that the differences between the images are due to the image on the later coins (**No. 43** and **46**) being an artistic rendition of the actual temple depicted on coin **No. 40** or to all images being artistic renditions of the temple. The cult image shown on both coins in the middle of the temple, in an opening between the columns of the façade, is an obvious artistic rendition to help the viewers recognize the temple, since the statue was enclosed by the cella wall and could not be seen from the outside.[166] Another factor in the analysis of the real structure is the architrave above the columns forming a central arch, or an arcuated lintel — a shape that few scholars accept as a real feature of any temple.[167] The current excavation reports do not, however, warrant any more specific observations.

The depiction of Tyche's temple on the Severan coins demonstrates not only the "primacy of religion in the expression of identity,"[168] but also the city's response to its process of Romanization. Monuments and temples were a "natural part of the visual language of Romans ... [and] an important aspect of their cultural outlook."[169] Romans celebrated the building of monuments by fixing their images on coins in a logoization process akin to the present day nation-building process that removes images from their contexts, makes them reproducible, and implants them in people's minds as seeds of national fellowship.[170] By putting Tyche's temple on its coins, Dora carried out the well-established Roman tradition of using the image of a monument as an expression of imperial power, attempting a sort of political community building of its own. But while Dora's architectural iconography can be connected to a Romanization process, the city was also asserting its own identity through nautical coin depictions. Images of galleys, prows, aphlasta, and rudders on Dora's

---

romani. See Burnett 1990, 79. The authenticity of the two architectural type specimens is, however, well established.

[159] Ibid. 141. He points to the example of a coin minted in 44 BCE by P. Sepulius Macer and depicting the temple of *Clementia Caesaris* — a temple that was commissioned but never actually built.

[160] Drew-Bear 1974, 63.

[161] Ibid., 28.

[162] Stern 2000, 285; 379.

[163] Sear 1983, 231-254. For an in-depth study of Roman urban renewal,

see also MacDonald 1986.

[164] Stern 2000, 285. The remains of a second, larger, temple were excavated on the northern part of Tel Dor. See Berg 1986.

[165] Meshorer 1995, 360.

[166] Drew-Bear 1974, 28-29; Burnett 1999, 147.

[167] Burnett 1999, 147.

[168] Howgego 2004, 4.

[169] Burnett 1999, 155.

[170] Anderson (1991, 182) originally ascribed the process of nationalism as "logoization" to the controllers of the printed press, but later added other institutions of power – census, maps, and museums – through which modern states try to control their citizens.

Roman coins are in fact essential to Dora's own identity as a Phoenician port city.

4.7 Nautical/Marine Symbols

As discussed earlier, Dor was a Phoenician trading emporium with an important fleet that was used by the Assyrians in their attempt to conquer Egypt and by the Persians in their strategy against the Greeks.[171] During Dora's Hellenistic and Roman periods the importance of the port continued, providing the city with its most significant economic resources. Maritime imagery on the city's coins is therefore one of the most prevalent features of Dora's coinage, and the depiction of nautical symbols is a logical, common occurrence. In fact, the depiction of the prow of a galley appears on the very first issues of Dora's coins (63 BCE), on the reverse of Tyche's bust, either turning left and with the Dioskouroi's caps above it (**No. 2**), turning right with nothing above (**No. 3**), or in the proximity of Tyche. Since Castor and Pollux were also Argonauts (and thus connected with the early heroism of sailing), it is easy to understand the depiction of the Dioskouroi's pointed caps (*piloi*) above the prow, the part of the ship that is most exposed to the dangers of the wind and water. The twin brothers are, according to Homer, the "deliverers ... of swift-going ships when stormy gales rage over the ruthless sea ... [giving] ... the shipmen rest from their pain and labor."[172]

While the prow of the galley is a recognized emblem of naval power, the acrostolion, the ornamental curved extension of the prow depicted on coin **No. 2**, and the aphlaston of the stern on coin **No. 24**, may be more important signifiers of naval might, perhaps connecting Dora to the naval victories of Pompey, whose arrival provided the impetus to initiate the new civic era that supported the minting of coins.[173] Since both the acrostolion and the aphlaston were torn from the enemy's ship after a naval victory and exhibited as trophies, their depictions on Greek coins had a long tradition going back to the fourth century BCE; such imagery on its coins thus connects Dora's history to its Greek past.[174] The aphlaston reappears alone on Dora's coins of Trajan (**No. 24**) and Caracalla (**No. 45**). It is usually in the proximity of Zeus Doros, whose realm was evidently connected to the water, and appears as an important symbol of Roman naval victories.[175] Unlike the acrostolion, which was an ornament, the aphlaston was in fact a significant part of the structure of the stern, "a semaphore or signal-post, consisting of a group of curving slats or boards of varied heights on which were hung the pennants or *taenia*, signals of the captain who thus controlled the maneuvering of the fleet from his position aft by the rudder."[176] The two other nautical implements, the rudder and the tiller, which were regularly depicted on Dora's coins in proximity to Tyche (**No. 4** and **No. 9**), are to be considered Tyche's attributes rather than maritime symbols connected to the city as a port. Both devices are essential parts of the steering apparatus of a ship,[177] and as such, they symbolize Tyche's control over the 'steering' of the city rather than an attribute of the city itself.[178]

Galleys with oars, sailing to the left, are depicted on many small-denominations issued throughout Dora's minting history, on the autonomous issues (**No. 13, 15** and **16**) and on the reverse of imperial portraits — Trajan (**No. 27, 29**), Hadrian (**No. 33**), Plautilla (**No. 41**), Caracalla (**No. 47**) and Julia Domna (**No. 48**). The depiction of galleys on Dora's coins is not, however, something unique to Dora's mint, following instead a tradition that was prevalent throughout the Mediterranean and especially in the Phoenician cities of Aradus, Byblos and Sidon from the fifth century BCE on.[179] The galleys depicted on Dora's coins are in fact long, narrow Phoenician vessels powered by banks of oarsmen, with upper decks that cover the top row of oarsmen, corbel-shaped bows and sterns, and large rams, usually made of metal, for attacking and sinking enemy vessels.[180] Since a mast and sails are never depicted, one must assume that the galleys depicted on Dora's coins were meant to represent military vessels, which worked solely under oars during battles. According to Casson, because the maneuvering of sails would be a hindrance, sailing gear was usually stowed away before going into action, or left ashore.[181] There is little variation in the depictions of the galleys on the different coins of Dora. The oars on the ships seem to be working directly from ports pierced in the hull,[182] but the addition of a railing indicates that a possible third row of rowers, the *thranites*, is working the oars from it.[183] In fact, one of the coins of Julia Domna (**No. 48**) might depict heads of men above the deck, indicating that the galley is carrying a platform for fighting men, since boarding, rather than ramming, was the more common naval tactic in later Roman times.[184]

A final maritime, if not nautical, feature found on Dora's coins, is the murex shell depicted on coin **No. 14**, to the right of Tyche's image. The depiction of the murex might offer a direct link between Dora and Tyre, where this shell

---

[171] For more on the Greek-Persian wars, see Green 1996.
[172] *Homeric Hymns* 33. 5-15. For a list of the Dioskouroi images, see Hermary 1986, LIMC III: 567–93; Gury 1986, in LIMC III: 608-635. On the *piloi* caps, see Smith 1997, 15 and Plate II. In the article Smith notes that the Spartan twins were often portrayed "wearing fitted caps."
[173] See Chapter 3.
[174] The aphlaston was first seen on coins commemorating Syracuse's naval battle over Athens. See Brett 1938, 24.
[175] A large number of Roman coins of the first century have images of aphlasta, always commemorating naval victories. For a complete list see, Brett 1938, 30-32.
[176] Brett 1938, 32.
[177] Mott 1991, 12.
[178] Tsetskhladze 1993, 246.
[179] Lloyd 1975, 46.
[180] Basch (1969, 152; 231-2) claims that triremes were invented in the seventh century at Sidon and that Greek triremes did not exist before the sixth century. His theory has been challenged, however. Lloyd (1975, 45-61) believes that Greek triremes were built in Corinth during the seventh century and that they were the prototypes for Phoenician triremes. Casson (1995, 81) suggests, "Greek naval architects created the trireme by adding an outrigger above the gunwale and projecting laterally beyond it to accommodate a third line." The argument is not relevant to this study; the galley depicted on Dora's coin is accepted as Phoenician.
[181] Casson 1967, 43; 1995, 77-97. See also Gardiner 1995; Casson 1991.
[182] Casson 1971, 143.
[183] Ibid., 95.
[184] Ibid., 103. See also Lendon 2006.

was used as a mintmark.[185] However, the shell on coin **No. 14** probably links Dora to its own dye industry. The purple dye was produced from the hypobranchial gland of several species of marine snail, the most common of them being the murex. According to Pliny, in order to extract the gland, the large shells were broken and the smaller ones were crushed.[186] The broken and crushed shells and the large installations with traces of the purple dye that have been found at Tel Dor are evidence that a textile-dyeing industry existed at Dora.[187] Since Tyre was, however, the more important center for the industry along the Mediterranean Sea, it seems that Tyrian experts might have extended their industry to other cities, including Dora.[188] The murex shell on coin **No. 14** might indeed be a symbol of a commercial agreement between the two cities.

Although we have no archaeological knowledge of a shipbuilding industry in Dora during its Hellenistic and Roman periods, we have literary sources that document its possible existence in earlier times. According to Herodotus, both the Assyrians and the Persians used tributary cities of the seacoast for shipbuilding and shipping to transfer luxury goods and raw materials from abroad and to transport their armies during wartime.[189] Since Dor was a tributary city to Eshmunazar, King of Sidon during the period 465-451 BCE, it is possible that the city supplied shipbuilding and craftsmen during the intense naval construction that followed the destruction of the Phoenician ships by the Athenians.[190] The iconography of nautical elements on Dora's coins is thus further documentation of the city's history as a Phoenician coastal city, as it puts the city in the context of the historical, political, and economic structure of the Levant. The coins with nautical themes demonstrate that the natural harbor and the sea contributed to the city's social, military, and economic fabric. Literary sources also describe the land of Dor as a land "rich of wheat"[191] showing that the city had affinity with agricultural as well as maritime activities. But while the depiction of galleys connects Dora to its Phoenician past, the symbols of wheat and grapes/vines depicted separately on a few of Dora's autonomous coins connect the city to its Greek and Hellenistic, and perhaps also Jewish identity. Since we presently associate wheat and grapes with the 'bread and wine' symbolism of religious iconography, it is natural to ask whether those two symbols depicted on the reverse of Tyche's coins had any religious significance in Dora or

FIG. 4.42. SILVER STATER FROM METAPONTUM (550 BCE). BMC 238.3.

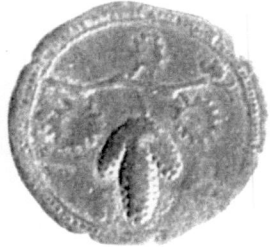

FIG. 4.43. TRIOBOL FROM SERDAIOI (520 BCE). BMC 395.

whether they were only the signifiers of Dora's agricultural activities.[192]

4.8 Agricultural Symbols

Coin depictions of wheat/barley and vine/grapes, which with olives form what Colin Renfrew calls the "Mediterranean triad"[193] of agriculture, go back to the Archaic Greeks of Southern Italy. In fact, a large single ear of barley first appeared on the coins of Metapontum in 550 BCE **(Fig. 4.42)**, and a vine-branch with grapes on the coins of Serdaioi in 520 BCE **(Fig. 4.43)**.[194] The symbols were adopted throughout the Mediterranean and were used on coins of different cities. But while elsewhere the depictions of wheat/barley and vine/grapes had strong connections respectively with Demeter and Dionysos, the same symbols appear on Dora's first-year coins on the reverse of Tyche (**No. 5** and **No. 6**). One can assume therefore that the symbols are not related to any specific religious ritual, but are instead the "live symbols" that, according to Goodenough, were carried from one religion or culture to another, retaining their original values and establishing the sort of continuity that he calls the "lingua franca of symbolism."[195]

---

[185] Jensen 1963, 111.

[186] Pliny, *Natural History*, 9.60.126-135. See Karmon and Spanier 1988, 184.

[187] Stern and Sharon 1986, 208; Lanigan 1990, 45-57.

[188] Jidejian 1969, 143-159.

[189] According to Herodotus, *The Persian Wars* 6.48, Darius ordered "tributary cities of the sea-coast to build warship and horse transport." See Littman 2001, 170; Chapter I.2.

[190] The naval Battle of the Eurymedon took place in 466 BCE on the Eurymedon River in Pamphylia in Asia Minor, and was fought between the Athenian-led Delian League and Persia. The Athenians destroyed 200 Phoenician ships. See Littman 2001, 170.

[191] The text is taken from the Sarcophagus of Eshmunazar II, King of Sidon, in the Achaemenid Persian period, first quarter of fifth century BCE. See Caubet 2007.

[192] Goodenough 1988, 183.

[193] Renfrew 1972, 280.

[194] Kraay 1976, Plate 81, No. 228 and No. 229; Plate 79, No. 228 and No. 229.

[195] Goodenough 1953 (4), 36-37. His study of Graeco-Roman symbols in Judaism established a continuity of symbolic values that goes back to Mesopotamia and Egypt. He separates "dead symbols" used purely as ornaments from "live symbols" that retain their intrinsic value.

The iconography of the reverse of coin **No. 5** presents an ear of wheat with spikelets only on the top and two leaves that start from the stem and fold out, one on each side, giving the impression of a three-flower bouquet. The image seems to be neither a purely religious symbol associated with Demeter, goddess of wheat, nor a dead symbol that merely decorated the coin.[196] The images must have been placed on the coin of Dora to evoke emotions and ideas that went beyond a specific identifiable god or goddess, but that reached deeply into the subconscious imagination of the citizens. At some point in its Phoenician history, in fact, Dora must have experienced the grain deficit typical of most Phoenician cities whose territory never spread beyond the coastal range.[197] Consequently, the depictions of wheat on Tyche's coins are not simply a celebration of the fertility of the land in its Greek Demeter-agricultural sense of growth and regeneration, but the expression of a Phoenician city's hope for an increase in its trading market and agricultural resources. Perhaps, since the arrival of Pompey started a new era in Dora, the wheat image on the first-year coins signifies the city's hope that this new era would guarantee a good wheat supply and plenty of bread for the community.

Similarly, the depiction of a cluster of grapes, still attached to the stem, on the reverse of coin **No. 6** might suggest Dionysos, god of wine, grapes, and fertility.[198] Again, however, the symbol is paired with Tyche, and seems to have no "denotative, precise meaning,"[199] linking it to any specific god or ritual. Grapes and wine must have been a familiar sight to people at Dora, just as throughout the Mediterranean world, so the symbol might also have a "connotative"[200] meaning that reached deeply into people's emotions rather than their minds. Although we have no archaeological evidence that wine was produced in Dora at any time during its history, existing local soil and climate conditions would have favored viticulture, and it is therefore altogether possible that grape growing was one of the city's farming activities. Literary sources also show that the Phoenician inhabitants of Dor were already trading wine in the twelfth century BCE.[201]

Unlike the depictions of wheat and grapes in the iconography associated with Demeter or Dionysos, the archetypal expressions of the human experience of biological life and death of the Graeco-Roman world,[202] the iconography on Dora's coins seems to have a less god-centered nature. The wheat and grapes on Dora's coins are the symbols of year around food reserves that were consumed and traded by a mercantile society that produced and traded those goods. As such, they are part of what Goodenough calls "the symbols of life urges," [203] i.e., the symbols of food and eating – symbols that operated on the "bio-psycho-social"[204] reality of the people who used the coins and who had an emic perspective of those symbols. And yet, the idea that the wheat and grapes of Dora's coins were profane with no sacred connotations for the people of Dora cannot be excluded.[205] These "live symbols"[206] were sacred in the cultures of early Mesopotamia, Asia Minor, Syria, Egypt, and Judea, eventually crossing from Judaism into Christianity and becoming the most important sacramental symbols of Christianity — bread and wine.[207] As seen earlier in the chapter, the *polis* religion of Dora was a large melting pot of religious syncretism with different currents of influence deriving from the city's multicultural identity. The absence of the Graeco-Roman deities associated with wheat and grapes on Dora's coins does not therefore exclude religious significance, but places the coin iconography in a broader geographical area than the Graeco-Roman world, connecting Dora to its pre-Greek roots.

As seen so far, the iconography of Dora's coins is not an exact reproduction of any specific reality, but it can be argued to represent an ideological statement of the people involved in the production of the coins.[208] As argued by Hölscher, images do not reproduce reality, but they "construct reality,"[209] and the images on Dora's coins offer "an insight into people's values and imagination."[210] As stated by Panofsky, analysis of the meaning of any image is possible only when we transcend iconography and move into iconology, i.e., reach "the underlying principles which reveal the basic attitude of a nation, a period, a class, a religious or philosophical persuasion."[211] By applying the imagery-as-a-language approach to the analysis of Dora's coin iconography, the semiotic act that understands images as signs has been performed and an attempt has been made at reaching those "underlying principles."[212]

---

[196] Ibid.

[197] Elayi 1980, 16. According to 1 *Kings* 5:23, Hiram, king of Tyre, traded Phoenician luxury goods and technical assistance with Solomon for agricultural products that were in deficit in Phoenicia. See also Aubet 2001, 76-79.

[198] Burckhardt (1988, 211) notes that with its immense celebrations connected to wine and fertility, the cult of Dionysos "must have overtaken all others in size and splendor."

[199] Goodenough 1953, 4: 36-37.

[200] Ibid.; for Goodenough, connotative is "a meaning in a language designed to speak to the mind, but having more immediate relation to the emotions."

[201] From the *Journey of Wen-Amon to Phoenicia*, we know that Beder, prince of Dor, offered a jug of wine to Wen-Amon, Superior of the Forecourt of the House of Amon. See Aubet 2001, 356 (Appendix I).

[202] Henrichs 1984, 210.

[203] The other two basic kinds of symbols are the symbols of hunting and fighting and the symbols of sex. See Goodenough 1953, 50.

[204] Knappett 2005, 35. The images partake of human characteristics, defined as biological animacy, psychological agency, and social personhood. See Chapter 2, p. 41.

[205] For the lack of clear boundaries between sacred and profane in the ancient world, I am indebted to Jodi Magness who graciously discussed the topic with me.

[206] Goodenough 1953, 4: 36-7.

[207] It was during the Graeco-Roman period that Jews seemed to have adopted rituals that used bread and wine. Wheat was, however, an important part of the Temple services. See Goldberg 1987, 67-68. The use of grapes and vines on Jewish coins suggests that drinking wine was an integral part of Jewish life. See Goodenough 1953, I.279.

[208] Hölscher 2004, 147-149.

[209] Hölscher 1987, 13; See also Hölscher 2004, 159.

[210] Zanker 1988, 3.

[211] Panofsky 1939, 15.

[212] Ibid.

Chapter 5
Epigraphic Analysis of Dora's Coins

5.1. Coin Legends as Inscriptions

Although legends on ancient coins are customarily considered part of the discipline of numismatics and not epigraphic studies, the boundaries between the two disciplines are not always defined. As inscriptions, i.e., "writing ... stamped on a durable surface,"[1] coin legends represent, in fact, a body of philological and epigraphic evidence that can give access to different strata of language use in its historical context. Harris points out that in order to understand the place of writing and literacy in the ancient world, it is necessary to be concerned with the multiple functions of writing as well as the variety of media used, and coin legends on Greek coins are indeed an important function of Greek writing.[2] Inscriptions on coins go back to the end of the sixth century BCE, when about forty city-states all over the Greek world were using writing to identify their coinage with the city name or an abbreviation of the name written on their coins. By the end of the year 500 BCE, approximately 500 city-states, including those of the Western Greek world, were producing coins with rather sophisticated written messages.[3] Just like any other examples of early texts, coin inscriptions are an indication of some degree of literacy and an example of the various purposes of early writing that, although not widespread, appeared in public and semi-public life in the course of the sixth century BCE and helped the spread of the written word.[4] Additionally, coin inscriptions mark an important step in the acceptance of written texts as a sign of authority. Since monetary exchange, unlike the bartering of pre-moneyed societies, involved a third party —an authority whose power could legitimize the production and circulation of money,[5] the words inscribed on a coin by the minting authority, although meaningless to many, guaranteed that that coin was legitimate and had its intended value in the process of the exchange. Consequently, the relationship between economics and verbal symbolization began in the ancient Greek mints where coin makers became aware of the relationship between the writing on their coins and the concept to which the writing was referring. In fact, the first inscribed coin has the words *Phaneos eimi sema* on it, implying that the coin engraver personified the token so that it would speak for itself, calling itself a *sema* (a sign) and thus become a semiotic sign.[6] The growing consciousness of this new use of writing on coins was the beginning of numismatic semiology, i.e., "the science of signs that is monetary theory."[7]

With the analysis of the social connections between language and commerce, which, according to Marx, developed simultaneously as a "first historical act," coin inscriptions took a central stage, being the most logical intersection between linguistics and economics.[8] As Derrida has written,

Before metaphor – an effect of language – could find its metaphor in an economic effect, a more general analogy had to organize the exchanges between the two regions ... and coin [inscriptions] imposed themselves with remarkable insistence in signifying the metaphorical process.[9]

Indeed, while the iconography of ancient coins, with its evolving language of images, illustrated the complex realities of the city's cultural milieu,[10] the writing on the coin, i.e., its inscription, gave the coin its value as 'money,' allowing it to function as a medium of exchange. As noted by Saussure, coin inscriptions appeal to economics because linguistics, just like economics, concerns "a system for equating things of different orders."[11] Words can in fact "be compared and exchanged with something dissimilar, ... or compared with another word," and coins of a marked value "can be compared with a similar value of the same system or exchanged for a fixed quantity of a different thing."[12] The monetary value of a coin is then guaranteed only by its inscription, since its "value will vary according to the amount stamped upon it and according to its use inside or outside a political boundary."[13]

---

[1] Bodel 2001, 2.
[2] Harris 1989, 26-9. The author lists groups of functions—legal, economic, religious, civic, commemorations of various kinds, transmission of literature, and letter writing. For a catalogue of all possible epigraphical uses, see Guarducci 1967.
[3] Kraay 1976, 1-10. According to Jeffery (1990, 65) legends on coins "became part of the city's issuing badge, whereby the coin is recognizable to the rest of the Greek world." Additionally, since the earliest bronze Roman coins were the work of Neapolitan Greeks, the name *ROMANO* first appeared in Greek in the fourth century. See Crawford 1985, 29; Burnett 1978, 121.
[4] Harris 1989, 52. In her discussion on the origins of visual art, J. P. Small (2003, 2) claims that artists throughout antiquity illustrated oral stories rather than texts because of the lack of textual sources.
[5] Ingham 2000, 3.

[6] According to Shell (1978, 66), the coin carried the message 'I am the sign of Phanos' and was minted perhaps at Ephesus around 600 BCE. See also von Reden 1995.
[7] Shell 1978, 67.
[8] Fromm 2004, 155. In *A Critique of The German Ideology* (1932), Marx and Engels wrote, "The first premise of all human existence, and therefore of all history, the premise namely that men must be in a position to live in order to be able to 'make history'. The 'first historical act' is thus the production of the means to satisfy these needs, the production of material life itself."

[9] Derrida 1982, 216.
[10] Kraay 1976, 4-5.
[11] Saussure 1998, 217-218.
[12] Ibid., 115.
[13] Ibid., 118. When talking about 'value' of money, it is important to distinguish between fiduciary vs. intrinsic value. According to Meadows (11/4/2010), Saussure's value must be referring to the fiduciary value of coinage.

Saussure's theory that coin inscriptions express the coin value in linguistic forms can easily be applied to ancient coins. As discussed earlier, in fact, inscriptions became a recurring labeling technique of Greek rulers and city officials who stamped the mass-produced coins with letters in order to legitimize the circulation and guarantee certain standards. Although there is no basis for thinking that everyone who used ancient coins could read what was inscribed on them, inscriptions eventually became a standard practice on both Greek and Roman coins, perhaps "for the convenience of the authorities rather than of the ordinary citizen."[14] But regardless of whether the writing benefited the authorities or the ordinary citizen, or most likely both, the practice implies that the function of the written word had expanded into the monetary system, becoming a way to codify the coins' "historical and geographical specificity," and to turn a piece of metal from a token into a *sema*.[15] Additionally, once minting became standard for many cities, coin inscriptions strengthened the common identity of a people. In fact, since large productions of low-denomination types allowed coins to penetrate the daily lives of soldiers and ordinary citizens, the common language inscribed on coins, with its conservative form and content, strengthened the sense of belonging to a common place and of sharing the same values and cultural identity.[16] As with other cities in eastern provinces, Dora's coin inscriptions identify either the city or the people by name, contributing to a better understanding of the city's history during the four hundred year span in which the mint operated in Dora.

5.2 Dating Dora's Coins within their Regional Context

The most ancient recorded method for dating ancient coins was by inscribing the name of the eponymous ruler or magistrate of the issuing city or kingdom on them. After the age of Alexander, however, the Seleucids introduced the custom of putting dates in the form of numerals and started to compute from the beginning of their rule in 312 BCE, while in Egypt the Ptolomies dated their money by the reigning years of the kings. In the second and first centuries BCE, the practice of dating coins with numbers became standard in parts of Asia Minor and Syria, and it continued during the imperial period.[17] Most cities marked their civic eras from events that occurred in the city, and their dating was therefore local; other cities computed their coin dating from occurrences in the history of the district or the province, as was the case with the city of Dora. Letters of the Greek alphabet were used to represent the dates, as shown in the chart below.[18]

1 A	2 B	3 Γ	4 Δ	5 E	6 S, ς	7 Z	8 H	9 ∪
10 I	20 K	30 Λ	40 M	50 N	60 ∈	70 O	80 Π	90 Ϙ
100 P	200 Σ	300 T	400 Y	500 Φ	600 X	700 Ψ	800 Ω	900 Ꝫ'

Additionally, the numerals were sometimes preceded by the word *ETOYC* (year), except on Egyptian coinage, in both Ptolemaic and Roman issues, where the word became a symbol resembling the Roman letter L. The mint of Dora also adopted the symbol L to designate the word ετων (year).

The inscription of Dora's Ptolemaic issue of 202 BCE follows the Hellenistic pattern of putting the king's name in a place of honor, written in full length and in the genitive case (No. 1). The young king's name and title, ΠΤΟΛΕΜΑΙΟΥ ΒΑΣΙΛΕΩΣ (King Ptolemy), appears on the reverse, inscribed on the edge, with each word on one side of the standing eagle, forming a decorative circular pattern interrupted by the head of the eagle. There is nothing new about the inscription, as the formulaic naming had been used by all other Ptolemaic kings in Egypt, but the writing is a testament to the Ptolemies' widespread use of the written word in the Greek world and evidence that a sizeable Greek-speaking bureaucracy was managing Dora's economy.19 As discussed in Chapter 3, the arrival of Pompey in Syria in 64 BCE initiated Dora's new minting era. The mint began dating coins with year one (A), and it seems that the same Greek-speaking bureaucracy continued to be in charge of the city. In keeping with the Ptolemaic tradition, in fact, letters of the Greek alphabet designate the dates, which were preceded by the ετων symbol L (No. 2) on the early coin issues. The symbol seems to disappear on the later imperial issues, however, either because the letters of the date took too much space on the coin (No. 17), or because the dating practice was already standardized enough to not need the symbol to designate the year. Moreover, Titus' issues of 68/9 CE (No. 21), in addition to dating the coins according to the Pompeian era (L ΒΛΡ), add a reference to a 'new year' (*ETOY NEOY IEP*), seemingly referring to his father's first year as emperor. According to Meshorer, however, a similar inscription, found on coins of Antioch from 68/9, continued until the reign of Trajan, making the reference to Vespasian's first-year reign difficult to explain.20

5.3 City Titles on Dora's Coins

While the study of ancient coins as a medium of exchange universalizes the role of coins-as-money, eliminating the need to consider the materiality of coins in space and time, the epigraphic study of coins, just as with the iconographic, reflects an analysis that does the opposite, as it goes from the global (or universal) to the local, grounding the coins in

---

[14] Harris 1989, 56. The issue of numismatic propaganda was addressed in Chapter 3, independently of the issue of inscriptions and literacy.
[15] Gilbert 2005, 366.
[16] Helleiner 1998, 1999. See also Kent 1993, 9.
[17] Head 1887, l: xxviii; see also Kraay 1976.
[18] Ifrah 1985, 261-274. The Hebrew alphabet numeration system is very similar to the Greek system, and its origin goes back to the beginning of the first century BCE. A document showing the use of the Greek numeration system (a papyrus from Elephantine) has been dated to 311 BCE. The Hebrew system was first used on coins of Alexander Jannaeus in 78 BCE (Ifrah 1985, 267).

[19] The extensive use of the written word and of paperwork in the management of the Ptolemaic kingdom was unprecedented in other parts of the Greek world. See Harris 1989, 122.
[20] Meshorer 1995, 365.

both their geographical and historical contexts.[21] Nothing grounds coins in history and geography more than the city's name inscribed on them, and it is from the inscriptions of the city's name on Dora's coins, for example, that the coins come to be identified with the city. Likewise, from the inscription of the name, the process by which the city title changed according to the status accorded it by imperial Rome becomes clear.

The name of Dora first appeared on coins in its abbreviated form ΔΩ (PA) on the Ptolemaic *tetradrachm* (**No. 1**). The two-letter monogram ΔΩ, placed in the left field, was used to define the mint, much like the ΣΙ found on the coins from Sidon, giving the coins their specific geographical context.[22] As explained earlier, however, the king's name was the central focus of the inscription, with the city's monogram having only a secondary role, almost that of a control mark. The arrival of the Romans in 64 BCE and the beginning of the new era changed the focus of Dora's coin inscriptions, however, and the city's name began to take the prominent position. On the autonomous coins the name always appears on the reverse in various abbreviations and places — as ΔΩ above the prow and below the Dioskouroi's caps (**No. 2**), or with one letter on each side of a bunch of grapes (**No. 6**). More common, however, is ΔΩΡΙΤΩΝ, the genitive plural form of the name of the inhabitants — sometimes abbreviated in ΔΩΡΙΤ and placed above a galley (**No. 13**); or fully inscribed in one continuous line on the edge of the right field (**No. 12**).

When looking at the genitive noun ΔΩΟΡΙΤΩΝ in its grammatical sense, as equivalent to a genitive of possession of the noun ΔΩΡΙΤΕΣ, i.e., the inhabitants of Dora, one can try to understand the nature of the relationship between the city, as represented by its coins, and the people. [23] The force of a genitive is in the indication of ownership of one notion to the other, and although a single word cannot give us the exact nature of the relationship between the two notions — whether the first notion is the coins, the minting, or the city, the use of *ΔΩΡΙΤΩΝ* indicates that the focus of the inscription had shifted explicitly from the city of Dora to the people of Dora, and that the people of Dora had taken group ownership of either their minting or their coins or both.[24] One could even assume, for instance, that the change could be a sign of the political upgrade of Dora's elite. According to Weiss,

In some cities, this elite identifies on coins by individual names, in others, where that was not the custom, it appears

indirectly as the group upholding both the traditional and the new values, concerned for the city's well-being and its appropriate self-representation.[25]

The inscriptions on Dora's coins, then, clearly demonstrate that the city's new era had instilled in its people civic pride, political optimism, and a consciousness of their need for self-representation.

Under the reign of Trajan, Dora acquired a new title – ΔΩΡ(Α) ΙΕΡ(Α) ΑСΥΛ(ΟС) ΑΥΤΟ(ΝΟΜΟС) ΝΑΥΑΡΧΙС (holy Dora; inviolable; autonomous; mistress of the fleet) – and the coins of 111/112 CE, the largest issue in the history of the mint, reflect the new status. From then on the title appears either in full ΔΩΡ(Α) ΙΕΡ(Α) ΑСΥΛ(ΟС) ΑΥΤΟ(ΝΟΜΟС) ΝΑΥΑΡΧΙС (No. 24), or in shortened forms as ΔΩΡΑ ΝΑΥΑ (No. 41) or more often as ΔΩΡΑ ΙΕΡΑ (No. 27, 47) on all the largest coin types of each issue until the reign of Caracalla, while ΔΩΡΙΤΟΝ appears less frequently and on the lower denomination coins.

With the acquisition of the prestigious title, the focus of the inscription seems to shift again from the people to the city, and the reason for that shift may not lie necessarily in Dora, but in the geopolitical context of the surrounding area. Trajan's acquisition of Arabia in 106/107 CE had involved the reshaping of the provincial structure in Syria Palestina and the construction of the Via Nova Traiana, which went from Philadelphia (Amman) to Aila (Aqaba), a Roman port on the Red Sea.[26] However, neither the annexation of the new province nor the construction of the Via Traiana Nova was made public until 112 CE, when the Arabia-type coins were issued either at Antioch or Bostra.[27] As explained earlier, Dora's minting of 111/112 took place in the context of Trajan's larger imperial strategy, and one must therefore assume that the granting of the city's new title, ΔΩΡ(Α) ΙΕΡ(Α) ΑСΥΛ(ΟС) ΑΥΤΟ(ΝΟΜΟС) ΝΑΥΑΡΧΙС was not a fortuitous coincidence, but part of a strategic plan that benefited both the city and the Roman strategists.

According to Maurice Sartre, eastern cities contended with each other for titles and status because the titles brought "substantial material assistance and sometimes perhaps confirmation of a civic status that had been at risk."[28] Especially with Syrian cities, the titles were in fact

---

[21] Gilbert 2005, 373.

[22] Mørkholm 1981, 5.

[23] Although the noun '*ΔΟΡΙΤΕΣ*' has never been used before, I am using it here as the possible root of the genitive form *ΔΩΡΙΤΟΝ*. My appreciation goes to Emanuele Fadda for the suggestion that *ΔΩΡΙΤΕΣ* may be the nominative of the people of Dora.

[24] With only one word available it is difficult to define for sure that *ΔΩΡΙΤΟΝ* is a genitive of possession. If the implied word is minting, for instance, the genitive *ΔΩΡΙΤΟΝ* could also be interpreted as a genitive of appurtenance, i.e., an adnominal genitive that functions as a nominative; the phrase then would be equivalent to 'the people of Dora minted.' For more on the interpretation of genitive structures, see Baron et al 2005, 32- 38. For adnominal genitive forms, see Petersen 1925,128-160.

[25] Weiss 2005, 68.

[26] The intervention in the Nabataean kingdom and its reduction to a Roman province was celebrated on Roman coins as *ADQUISITIO ARABIA* (*BMC* Imp. III No. 474-477) and not as *ARABIA CAPTA*, the common expression of conquered provinces, e.g., Vespasian's *JUDEA CAPTA*, etc. Following the acquisition of the Nabataean kingdom, in fact, the Nabataean soldiers were immediately integrated into the Roman army, appearing as *Cohortes Ulpiae Petraeorum* already in 106 CE. See Migliorati 2003, 107-177; Graf 1994, 265-311.

[27] Bowersock 1983, 83. Among the speculations on why Trajan suppressed news of his annexation of Arabia for five years is the suggestion that 1) he wanted to wait until the *Via Nova Traiana* was completed; 2) the five-year waiting time was part of an imperial grand strategy to prepare the attack on Parthia. For more on the Arabia type coins, see also Metcalf 1975, 104. For more on Trajan and the Arabia province, see Freeman 1996, 109; Migliorati 2003, 107-177; Cotton 1997, 206-7.

[28] Sartre 2005, 184.

considered so prestigious that upon receiving the imperial gift, cities would regard themselves as 're-founded,' highlighting the importance of the event in their history.[29] The titles of 'inviolable,' 'autonomous,' and 'holy,' granted to Dora by Trajan in 112, always went together and must have had a very important meaning for the city receiving it.[30]

The designation *ACYΛOS* – 'inviolable,' i.e., free from violence and legal pursuit — was a complex title, since the Roman understanding of *asylia* was different from the Greek one. According to Rigsby, in fact, the Greek concept of *asylia* was a religious gesture intended to increase the honor of the god and the city.[31] By having been granted 'inviolability of places,' the city obtained a promise that its citizens would be protected from reprisals and violence.[32] The Romans, on the other hand, shifted their understanding of *asylia* away from the religious expression of honorific devotion to the god and moved it toward the 'juridical concept of right of asylum' for persecuted citizens seeking refuge and immunity of sacred space from civil law.[33] Additionally, many cities of the East became free and independent (*liberae et immunes)* for being on Rome's side during wars, acquiring the status of *asylos,* which gave the right not to extradite a person who sought asylum in them.[34] However, given the fact that all temples were always inviolable and that cities always had the right to remain neutral in war, Rigsby suggested that the granting of *asylia* to a Greek city was a purely honorary title that "never brought a recipient anything but honor ... [and that] for most of its history no more than honor was intended by grantor or recipient."[35]

There is no way to know for sure whether the new title bestowed by Trajan on Dora was honorary or whether it brought any material benefits to the city. According to Meyer, however, there are many inscriptional indications of material benefits tied to grants of *asylia* — fiscal exemptions, financial rewards for construction of temples, harbor zones that could bring dues into the zone of

asylia, etc.[36] Given that the largest issue of coins in Dora corresponds to the granting of the new title, it is possible to conclude that the city reaped some financial benefits from Trajan's titulature. As explained in Chapter 3, in fact, the presence, or the expectation of the presence, of large troop units in an area always played a considerable part in the production of new bronze coinage in nearby cities because of the demand for small change.[37] Dora's new coin production, which followed a 44 year hiatus, must have given the city a chance to enrich its coffers with imperial gold and silver in exchange for the bronze coinage displaying the new title, which was then both prestigious and profitable.

The designation AYTONOMOC, i.e., the right to live according to its own laws, was a common designation of cities throughout the Eastern province and seems to be empty of any specific meaning.[38] During the Hellenistic and Roman periods, *autonomia* in the strict sense of self-government was, in fact, an essential and even indispensable feature of the *polis*.[39] Moreover, the title of autonomy never came alone since it was often conferred together with *IEPA*, the standard designation of holiness, and with the *ACYΛOC* discussed earlier. Dora, as mentioned above, was granted all three titles simultaneously in addition to NAYAPXIC.

Unlike the three previous titles, however, the final designation found on the coin inscriptions, NAYAPXIC, i.e., mistress of the fleet, seems to have more significance in the history of Dora itself. The title, obviously connected to Dora's port activities, was bestowed to four other coastal cities: Sidon, Tripolis, Tyre and Laodicea. Since maritime power was crucial to the logistics of Rome's military campaigns, these interconnected port cities must have played an essential role in Trajan's logistical preparation for the Parthian campaign, receiving the new titles together. According to Bennet, in 111 CE Trajan sent his young cousin Hadrian "to the eastern provinces, perhaps as governor of Syria, on what might have been a commission connected with making logistical preparation for a potential campaign." [40] By the time of Trajan's arrival in Antioch in January 114, legions had been drawn from all southeastern provinces, making it legitimate to infer, therefore, that the various ports of Syria had been involved in the transfer of troops.[41] Like the other four

---

[29] Apamea, for instance, renamed itself Claudia Apamea following the earthquake of 47 CE because, according to Tacitus (*Ann.* 12.58), "Tributumque Apamensibus terrae motu convulsis in quinquennium remissum"(the tribute was cancelled for five years also for the inhabitants of Apamea who had been shaken by the earthquake — my translation).

[30] Sartre 2005, 185.

[31] Rigsby 1996, 19.

[32] Ibid.

[33] Ibid. 14.

[34] The *Lex Antonia de Termessibus* of 71 BCE, for example, regarded the inhabitants of Termessus Maior in Pisidia (a city that sided with Rome during the Mithridatic War), as "*leiberi, amicei socieque populi romani.*" See *CIL* 1 (2): 589. According to Hardy (1911, 94-101), the Roman separated cities into *civitates foederatae* (Athens, Rhodes, Amisus, Tyre, etc.) and *civitates liberae* (Chios, Smyrna, Eruthrae, Cyzicus, Magnesia, Laodicea, Ephesus, Termessus, and Alexandria Troas, etc.), with both types enjoying a certain degree of sovereignty. As noted by Tacitus, however, this *libertas* could be taken away anytime: "*Reddita Rhodiis libertas, adempta saepe aut firmata, prout bellis externis meruerant aut domi seditione deliquerant*" (*Ann.* XII. 58). Broughton (1929, 13) points out that many cities in Africa also acquired the same privileges after the Second Punic War for abandoning Carthage. For more on the *Lex Antonia de Termessibus,* see also Mattingly 1997, 68-78.

[35] Rigby 1996, 22. On immunity of sacred space in Greece see also Alcock and Osborne 1998.

[36] Meyer 1999, 462.

[37] Ziegler 1996, 125. The connection between the minting of 112/113 at Dora and the Parthian War was discussed in Chapter 3. Additional support is given by Butcher (2004, 36): "Much of Trajan's Syrian coinage has been connected with his Parthian war, AD 114-117, and there are good grounds to assume that various cities did issue coins in connection with this campaign."

[38] Sartre 2005, 185.

[39] Gauthier 1993, 212. See also Gauthier 1987-9, 187-202.

[40] Bennett 1997, 187.

[41] Migliorati (2009, 133) reconstructs Trajan's journeys through literary and epigraphic texts. According to Dio Cassius (*Roman History* 68. 17. 2-3), the emperor left Rome on October 27th, 113 CE, traveling through the Peloponnesus to reach Athens and by sea to reach Ephesus, Aphrodisias, and Patara; he arrived at Antiochia on 7th January 114 CE. Between 113 and 116 CE, he was honored with the epithet *Stephanophoros* at the Temple of Apollo Didyma. For more on Trajan's stay in Antiochia, see

Phoenician coastal cities, then, Dora's true power lay in its proximity to the sea and the titulature *IEPA, ACYΛOC, AYTONOMOC, NAYAPXIC* was then a further mark in determining the city's identity. Dora never received the title of *Colonia* from later emperors. When Septimius Severus separated Phoenicia from the Syrian province, he seemed to favor Tyre, which was made a *Colonia* in 197 CE, marking a period when, according to Millar, "the Near East became Roman."42 Although Dora seemed to flourish under the Severi, it never acquired the coveted rank of *Colonia* that would have allowed the inhabitants of the city to become Roman citizens.43

5.4. Imperial Titulature on Dora's Coins

As seen in Chapter 4, visual images of Roman emperors and their families were impressed on Dora's coins as a representation of imperial power, but the inscriptions on the obverse of those coins were also an important concomitant feature of imperial representation. Imperial titulature on coins was in fact intended to be informative, at least for those who could read, about the various aspects of that power, i.e., the various roles that the emperor fulfilled, his specific virtues and qualities, his legitimacy to power, etc.44 The first imperial titulature to appear on Dora's coinage is on the obverses of Vespasian's and Titus' coins on the issues of 68/69 CE. The father, already hailed emperor by his troops, was named *AYTOKPATΩP OYEΣΠAΣIANOΣ* on his coins (**No. 19** and **20**) and the son *T. ΦΛAYI OYEΣΠ KAIΣ* (No. 21).45 In the struggle for emperorship that followed Nero's assassination in 68, the Flavian titulature of their first-year coins express the hope of legitimizing their right to the throne. Hence, the father's title *AYTOKPATΩP*, with its military connotations, is etymologically connected to the idea of power that is unrestrained and *sui iuris*, while the son's power is confirmed by the use of the father's name, *ΦΛAYI OYEΣΠ (AΣIANOΣ)* (son of Flavius Vespasian).

Trajan's titulature is the longest, demonstrating the list of achievements and consequent titles that the Senate had bestowed on him. His full title *AYTOKP(ATΩR),*

KAICAP, TPAIANOC, CEB(AΣTOΣ) ΓEPM(ANIKOΣ) and *ΔAK(IKOΣ)* (**No. 24**) is a direct translation of the Latin *IMPERATOR CAESAR TRAIAN AUGUST*, with *GERMANICUS* and *DACICUS* celebrating his military campaigns in Germany and Dacia.46 Trajan's adopted son and successor, Hadrian, makes reference to his predecessor by adding *TRAI(ANOC)* to the otherwise standard titulature: *AYTO(KPATΩP), TRAI(ANOC) AΔPIANΩ(C) KAIC(AP)* (*IMPERATOR TRAIANUS HADRIANUS CAESAR*) (**No. 28**), legitimizing his right to the throne, while Antoninus Pius' title *AYT(OKPATΩP) KAI(CAP) ANTΩNEINOC CEB(ASTOC) EY(TYXΩΣ)* — *IMPERATOR CAESAR ANTONINUS AUGUSTUS FELICITER* draws from the now standard inscriptions of imperial titulature, with the addition of the adverb *FELICITER*, as a good luck wish.47

In accordance with the Severan policy of showing family unity in the attempt to build their family legacy, Septimius Severus' first issues inscribe the name of the emperor on the obverse and of the young sons on the reverse (**No. 38**). Around Septimius' portrait is in fact *AYT(OKPATOP) KAI(CAP) Λ(OKIOC) CEΠ(TIMIOΣ) CEOYHPOC CEB(AΣTOC) EY(TYXΣ) (IMPERATOR; CAESAR; LUCIUS; SEPTIMIUS; SEVERUS; AUGUSTUS; FELICITER)*, and on the reverse is *AYT(OKPATOP) K(AICAP) M(APKOC) AYP(EΛIOC) ANT(ONINΘΣ) KAI(CAP) [and] Π(ΘBΛIOΣ) (Σ)EΠ(TIMIΘΣ) ΓET(A) KAI(CAP) (IMPERATOR; CAESAR; MARCUS AURELIUS ANTONINUS; CAESAR [and] PUBLIUS SEPTIMIUS GETA; CAESAR)*, mentioning the boys' names and recently acquired titles of Caesars. Each member of the family is also honored with individual coins and inscriptions: the wife Julia, *IYOΛ(IA) ΔOMNA CEB (JULIA DOMNA AUGUSTA)* (**No. 39**); the sons, Caracalla, *AYT K M AYP ANTΩ CEB (IMPERATOR; CAESAR MARCUS AURELIUS ANTONINUS AUGUSTUS* (**N. 40**) and Geta, *Π CEΠ ΓETA K (PUBLIUS SEPTIMIUS GETA CAESAR)*(**No. 42**); and Caracalla's wife Plautilla, *ΠΛA YTIΛΛ (PLAUTILLA* (**No. 41**). As sole emperor, Caracalla only adds *CEB (AUGUSTUS)* after his name (**No. 43-47**), the actual title of the emperors as a living institution.

Contrary to coins minted in Rome, none of the imperial coin inscriptions of Dora and other provinces make reference to any emperor's consulships or his role as *Pontifex Maximus* or *Pater Patriae*.48 According to Buraselis, it is possible that a *polis* had some freedom in asserting its loyalty to the emperor. He writes, "the possession of these titles on a local level was not simply the imprint of the imperial power-nexus on provincial societies – the people of a *polis* were

---

also Downey 1961.

42 Millar 1993, 124

43 A Roman *colonia* was originally a military outpost established in conquered territory. The term was eventually used to name new cities founded to house Roman citizens, or as the title of a pre-existing city to denote the highest political status reached within the Roman Empire. Kindler (1980, 81-83) notes that the number of cities in the Syria-Palestina province with the title was limited: four in Phoenicia (Berytus, Akko Ptolemais, Sidon, Tyre), four in Syria-Palestina (Aelia Capitolina, Caesarea, Neapolis, Sebaste) and five in Syria (Antiochia, Damascus, Emisa, Heliopolis, Laodicea).

44 J. De Jong 2007, 311. The titles on the coin inscriptions often listed the role that the public expected the emperor to fulfill. As Manders (2007, 283) notes, an emperor could simultaneously be, "a citizen, a general, a consul at various stages in his life, a husband and father, a son, a founder or consolidator of a dynasty, a companion of the gods, specially favored by them and even virtually assimilated to them on occasion." As suggested by T. J. Smith (8/15/2010), "The letters of the titulature may have symbolized the same 'power' even to those who could not read."

45 The Greek title *AYTOKPATΩP* used by Vespasian *(OYEΣΠAΣIANOΣ)* is the direct translation of the Latin *IMPERATOR*, an honorific title bestowed on a general who fulfilled specific requirements as ratified by the Roman Senate. See Sayles, 139.

46 Trajan's full titulature *AYTOKP(ATΩR), KAICAP, TPAIANOC, CEB(AΣTOΣ) ΓEPM(ANIKOΣ)* and *ΔAK(IKOΣ)* (Commander in Chief; Trajan; August; conqueror of Germania and Dacia) was also found inscribed on a slab of marble excavated at Tel Dor in 1980. Gera and Cotton 1995, 501.

47 For the translation of Hadrian's and Antoninus Pius' titulature, see footnote above.

48 The *Pontifex Maximus* was 'the greatest' or chairman of the college of the *pontifices*, 'priests,' responsible for the Roman state religion, while *Pater Patriae*, i.e., father of the fatherland was an honorific title granted by the senate.

also allowed some sense (better: illusion) of autonomy in keeping the formal right to confer titles testifying loyalty to the Roman rulers (*Sebastoi*)."[49]

5.5 Language and Identity

Language use on Dora's coins is also an important issue related to ethnicity and cultural identity, as language is one of the most important areas in which cultural groups define themselves against others. The identification of a language with a people has its roots in the ideology of Herder and eighteenth century German romanticism, but recent post-colonial theories of acculturation and studies on contacts between languages have questioned the validity of national languages.[50] In fact, modern scholars of bilingualism and multiculturalism claim that the notions of both identity and language use are dynamic notions that depend upon time and place.[51] In situations of cultural contacts and hybridization, language — both code and content — is a matter of internal and external interpretations of self-identity. When speakers of a group negotiate their sense of self-identity within and across different languages, although one language may be dominant, one single language can no longer be considered a symbol of group identity. As Woolard and Schieffelin specify,

Communities not only evaluate but may appropriate some part of the linguistic resources of groups with whom they are in contact and in tension, refiguring and incorporating linguistic structures in ways that reveal linguistic and social ideologies.[52]

In communities where more than one language is used, the use of a variety of languages can then be an indication of political allegiances or of the social, intellectual or moral values attached to one or the other language, and consequently, of the formations of new group identities. The traditional "equation of one language/one people" and "the insistence on the moral significance of the mother tongue" is restrictive to modern linguistic anthropology that examines multilingualism and language ideologies.[53]

Although more applicable to modern societies, studies of cultural conceptions of language can also be valid in the study of ancient population contacts and hybridization, and of the Greek vs. Roman notion of identity. Language had an important place in Greek self-identification in the Archaic, Classical and Hellenistic periods; in fact, although the Greeks had borrowed from the more ancient cultures

of Phoenicia and Egypt in arts and science, in the area of language they remained exclusive, using the language not only as a tool for self-identification, but also to evaluate the non-Greek behavior of others.[54] During the Roman period, however, Latin was of course the official language of the army and of Roman law, even in the Greek-speaking Roman provinces, and Latin must have been used to some extent.

It is common today to speak about the Graeco-Roman Empire, and to stress the "interconnections"[55] between the two cultures. These interconnections were not due to the Greek acceptance of Rome, however, but to Rome's ability to successfully use the Greek "educational and cognitive structures."[56] In fact, it was the Romans, especially the upper-class Romans, who were using both languages skillfully and treating Greek as "the literary language par excellence."[57] As Rutherford notes,

Bilingualism is what enabled the Romans to govern the provinces, and the lack of any interest in language was a sign of how successfully they persuaded local élites to function in Greek or Latin.[58]

Contrariwise, the Greeks, especially the educated élites, resisted Latin because it was thought to contaminate the purity of their language;[59] additionally, speaking Greek was, as mentioned earlier, also a matter of establishing their Greek identity in their relationship with Rome. However, not all Greek-speaking cities were immune to the need to use Latin, and several cities provide inscriptional evidence of bilingualism, especially in their coin legends.[60]

The city of Dora provides no inscriptional evidence in Latin, and the city's coin legends are exclusively in Greek, making one assume that Greek was the only language ever used. Since Dora's society was an aggregate of cultural systems, it seems feasible to infer, however, that the people of Dora were accustomed to negotiating their sense of self within and across languages, even when Greek was the most used language of the city.[61] After the arrival of the Romans, Latin must have been frequently heard in the context of the city administration, and the Greek-speaking

---

[49] Buraselis 2001, 106. Although the author's study deals with the city of Kos there is reason to believe that most Hellenistic Roman cities functioned in similar ways.

[50] See Irvine 1989, 248-67; 2000, 35-84. Spolsky 1999, 181-192.

[51] Peirce (1995, 9-13) claims that many studies on multilingualism have failed to examine how relations of power affect interaction between the different language speakers.

[52] Woolard and Schieffelin 1994, 62. Earlier in the article, the authors write, "The nationalistic ideology of language structures state politics, challenges multilingual states, and underpins ethnic struggles to such an extent that the absence of a national language can cast doubt on the legitimacy of claims to nationhood" (1994, 60).

[53] Ibid., 61.

[54] Swain 1998, 17-8; following Hall 1989, 3; Baslez 1984, 183-201.

[55] Swain 1998, 9.

[56] Ibid.

[57] Adams 2003, 550. In one of his epigrams, Martial (Ep. 10.76.6) makes reference to the bilingualism of a Roman poet who is very poor but "skilled in each language" (*lingua doctus utraque*); Horace (Ode 3.8.5) makes a similar reference in one of his odes, when he addresses Maecenas as "speaking the prose of both languages"(*docte sermones utriusque linguae*).

[58] Rutherford 2003, 245.

[59] Swain 1998, 41.

[60] Burrell 2004, 65. Kushnir-Stein (2008, 161) notes that Caesarea was the main base for Vespasian's military operations, and Latin was used exclusively on the city coins starting with Vespasian. Latin was also used exclusively on the coins of Tyre after the city was granted the title of *COLONIA TYRE METROPOLIS* by Septimius Severus in 194 CE. Tripolis and Sidon used both Latin and Greek legends on their coins. See Kadman 1957, 57.

[61] No Latin inscriptions have been excavated thus far at Tel Dor; the only inscriptions are in Phoenician and Greek. See Gera and Cotton 1991; Naveh 1987, 1995; Di Segni 1993, 1994.

élite must have used Latin as a sign of collaboration with the imperial power and in order to adopt the *Romanitas* that allowed them to be part of the local administration. [62] However, contrary to what happened in neighboring port cities, where either Latin or both languages were used in the written form, Greek remained the only language of coin inscriptions in Dora during the various minting periods.[63] It is therefore feasible to conclude that Dora's ties to Rome were not as close as those of the neighboring cities, and that the Roman presence was not therefore a strong one.

Additionally, considering the analogies between economics and language discussed earlier and considering that coin inscriptions are the intersection between linguistics and economics, we can conclude that Greek was used exclusively on Dora's coins because the political economy of the city dictated the use of Greek. Greek inscriptions allowed Dora's low-denomination coins to penetrate deeply into the daily lives of soldiers and ordinary citizens whose language was Greek, eliminating language barriers and changing each little coin into a *semeion* of local business transactions. The Greek language of Dora's coins is not only a testimony to the Greek identity of Dora, but it is a testimony to the Greek language's role as the "integrative language"[64] of the eastern Roman Empire, where identity, especially Greek identity, was largely constructed through the use of the Greek language.

---

[62] Swain 1998, 41. As discussed in Chapter 2, Roman assimilation was a slow process wherein the local élite imitated Roman officials present in the city by being part of the local administration and political life in a Roman fashion, including being able to communicate in the Latin language, and by acquiring Roman juridical rights.

[63] Kadman 1957, 57. Tripolis and Sidon used both Latin and Greek legends on their coins.

[64] Whitmarsh 2007, 273. The author sees the use of the Greek language by Roman exiles living in the eastern part of the empire as "a schematic opposition between Greek and Roman in terms of philosophical liberation and oppressive power" (284).

Chapter 6
Drawing Some Conclusions

6.1. Brief Comparative Study

The analysis of Dora's coins, and the approach used here, might also be applicable to the study of coins as markers of cultural identity in other cities of the Roman Empire. For example, the coins of nearby Caesarea Marina — a city with a clear Jewish presence — offers an insight into the hybrid culture of a city that was both capital of Judaea, having been founded by Herod the Great in 25 BCE, and a Roman administrative center that was granted the status of *Colonia* by Vespasian.[1] By briefly looking at Roman coins from Caesarea, it can then be established not only that Dora's coins represent Dora's unique culture, but also that coins are indeed important vehicles through which meaning was constructed in cities throughout the Roman Empire.

6.2. Caesarea Maritima

Caesarea Maritima was founded by Herod the Great in the late first century BCE and named in honor of Herod's Roman supporter, Augustus.[2] According to Josephus, the city was built in an extravagant manner, with Herod erecting Greek style temples "not out of his own inclination, but by the command and injunction of others, in order to please Caesar and the Romans."[3] Josephus equated Caesarea's port to Piraeus in size and called it the most impressive architectural structure. Caesarea was constructed according to the traditional urban planning of a Roman city but it did incorporate a preexisting small Hellenistic harbor, Strato's Tower, which had fallen into disrepair.[4] After Herod's death in 4 BCE, Rome acquired direct political control over Judea, and the envoy of the emperor (*Legatus Augusti Pro Pretore*) took residence in the city, making Caesarea the provincial capital. During the first Jewish war (66-69CE), Caesarea became the Roman military staging area, and in 69 CE Vespasian, who was first acclaimed emperor there, granted the city the title of *COLONIA*.[5] In 70 CE, following Titus' victory over Jerusalem and the large celebration that took place in the city, Caesarea was bestowed the title of *CPRIMA AUGUSTA CAESAREA*. Through the first and second centuries and into the third, the city continued to enjoy the benefits from its status as Roman provincial capital and main entrepôt for Palestine, acquiring the final title of 'mother city of Syria and Palestine' (*METROPOLIS SYRIAE PALAESTINAE)* under Severus Alexander in 230 CE.

Like neighboring Dora, Caesarea had the privilege of minting its own coins, with the right restricted to bronze coins only. Since the identification of pre-Neronian coins minted at Caesarea has been problematic and mostly conjectural, the earliest Roman coins definitely attributed to the mint of Caesarea are those minted in the fourteenth year of Nero's reign (67-68 CE),[6] and with the exception of Nerva and the short-reigning emperors of 192 CE and 235-44 CE, all emperors from Domitian to Volusian (251-253CE) are depicted on Caesarea's coins.[7] As stated earlier, Roman minting started at Dora with Pompey's arrival (64-63 BCE), continuing with several interruptions until the reign of Caracalla (210-11 CE). With the exception of a coin type seemingly portraying Augustus (6 BCE), all coins from Dora are autonomous until the portraits of Vespasian and Titus. For the sake of this study, the numismatic analysis will focus on the early Flavian coins of Caesarea, specifically the coins minted in 70 CE.

6.3. Caesarea and the Flavian Mint

Both Dora and Caesarea minted coins with portraits of Vespasian and Titus, while other cities in the area — Ptolemais, Scythopolis, Aradus, Sidon and Tripolis — seem to have ceased any minting until the reign of Domitian.[8] As discussed earlier, Dora's coins portray Vespasian and Titus in 69 CE with Tyche in a supporting role (**No. 19-21**), demonstrating that the city engaged in the successful integration of the new rulers in the city's socio-political realm. However, the minting that took place in Caesarea at the end of the Jewish revolt was quite different indicating the important status that Caesarea held in the Roman sphere under the Flavians. In fact, Caesarea struck the ΙΟΥΔΑΙΑΣ ΕΑΛΩΚΥΙΑΣ type coins, starting from 70 CE, as a counterpart of the *JUDEA CAPTA* coins struck in Rome.[9] Most of the reverses of these coins celebrated the triumph of the Flavians over Judea, showing a standing Nike, with her right foot on a helmet, inscribing a shield attached to a palm tree (**Fig. 6.1**). On at least one specimen, the triumph is balanced by the public shaming of the defeated province, portrayed as a captive man crouching with his arms tied behind his back.[10]

---

[1] Raban and Holum 1996, 231.
[2] Levine 1975, 11.
[3] Josephus *Jewish Antiquities* 15.9.6. For a thorough interpretation of Josephus' ambiguity towards Herod's non-Jewish buildings at Caesarea, see Levine 1975, 11-14.
[4] Strato was the name of two kings of Sidon, one of whom was honored by the Athenians, as shown by epigraphic studies from the Agora. Tod 1947, 101.
[5] For discussion on the meaning of *Colonia*, see chapter 5.3.

[6] Kadman 1957, 29.
[7] Kadman 1957, 35.
[8] Kadman 1957, 34.
[9] The inscription ΙΟΥΔΑΙΑΣ ΕΑΛΩΚΥΙΑΣ is the Greek equivalent of the Latin *JUDEA CAPTA* (captured Judea) that was used on Roman coins after the defeat of Judea. De Saulcy 1874, 79; Hill 1914, ci; Kadman 1957, 35. RPC 2310.
[10] RPC 317-318, No. 2310-2313.

FIG. 6.1. ΙΟΥΔΑΙΑΣ ΕΑΛΩΚΥΙΑΣ FROM CAESAREA (81AD),
IM No. 93.2.14470.

Just like the *JUDEA CAPTA* coins from Rome, the ΙΟΥΔΑΙΑΣ ΕΑΛ*W*ΚΥΙΑΣ coins from Caesarea's were used by the Flavians to communicate the establishment of their new dynasty and the important victory over the Jews. The mint picked and translated the important theme of victory by immortalizing it on coins.[11] As Syme puts it, Titus' "sole claim to glory [was] the sack of Jerusalem,"[12] implying that his victory had to be celebrated as an empire-wide event worthy of imperial pursuits. Caesarea's ΙΟΥΔΑΙΑΣ ΕΑΛΩΚΥΙΑΣ series are then the most important emic expression of the Flavian victory over the Jews.

The Flavian coinage of Dora and Caesarea are material illustrations of the different cultural mélange of two cities which, although barely 10 miles apart, had very little in common in their social and political outlook. Dora's Flavian issues were part of the city's acceptance and celebration of the new dynasty, whereas Caesarea's coins were the means for the Flavians to become accepted, giving the city the same role as that of a mini-Rome.

Additionally, while Greek remained the only language appearing on Dora's coins throughout its minting history, Latin was the sole language of Caesarea's coins starting with Domitian, when the city's new title *COLONIA PRIMA FLAVIA AUGUSTA CAESAREA* first appeared on its coins.[13] Finally, the palm tree, which is not depicted on any of Dora's coins, appears next to Nike on the Caesarea's ΙΟΥΔΑΙΑΣ ΕΑΛΩΚΥΙΑΣ series, i.e., the captured Judea coins. Since the palm tree had previously appeared on Jewish iconography and coins, the Romans must have looked at that symbol as Jewish enough to represent the province of Judea.[14] By depicting a palm tree, Caesarea's coin iconography again translates the Roman concept of a province – the one whose defeat is being celebrated.

By studying selected coins from Caesarea using the same material culture approach used for Dora, it can be seen that coins are indeed the vehicles through which meaning was constructed in cities throughout the Roman Empire. The specific comparison between the Flavian period mints of Dora and Caesarea strengthens the reliability of the numismatic data as a medium through which the two cities expressed their civic pride differently. Each of the cities displayed loyalty to the Roman Empire and to the holders of the *imperium*, but the backgrounds of glorification of the city and the points of reference were depicted differently on their coins.[15] Dora drew its numismatic themes and forms from a repertoire that linked the city to its glorious Greek or Hellenized mythical past — hence Tyche or Zeus Doros. Caesarea, a more recent city, drew its numismatic repertoire from its historical Roman past, partaking, as seen in the case of the ΙΟΥΔΑΙΑΣ ΕΑΛΩΚΥΙΑΣ type coins, in the Roman discourse of military triumphs and dynastical legitimacy.

6.4. Conclusions

The connection between coins and cultural identity is a strong one. While assessing Dora's coins as vehicles of cultural identity, the changes that took place in the city from its Ptolemaic years, when the city began minting coins, until the mint's final issues under Caracalla have been evaluated. The earliest, the Ptolemaic coins, present a city that was no longer Phoenician, having been under Greek control for over one hundred years. However, the city is neither completely Ptolemaic nor Seleucid, but contested between the feuding parties. Its location on the coast and on the border between provinces made Dora the ideal 'border' town in a modern sense – a city in which identity must be formed in a transnational context. The Roman period coins, both autonomous and imperial, again offer the reality of a border city at the fringe of the province — neither important enough to play a major role in the geopolitics and economics of the area, i.e., minting its own silver, nor obscure enough to be ignored. In fact, as seen in our discussion, Dora's port, although small compared to Caesarea or Tyre, might have played an important enough role for the Roman military machinery to guarantee the city the title of **NAYAPXIC** under Trajan; again, however, the city was not important enough to earn the title of *METROPOLIS* under the Severans.[16]

This study of the distribution of Dora's coin finds shows that the city's minting was tied to the economic reality of the larger surroundings. Dora's civic coins were mostly of small value and therefore more suitable as a medium of exchange rather than as a store of wealth. In fact, the link between Dora's coin production and Roman military campaigns is evidence that the city must have made a profit from providing the small denomination coins necessary to exchange the Roman army's imperial gold and silver issues. Furthermore, the wide distribution of Dora's coins

---

[11] *JUDEA CAPTA* western coins were minted during the Flavian dynasty in Rome and Lugdunum. See Mattingly 1930.
[12] Syme 1929, 135.
[13] As explained in chapter 5 (5.3), the new title, *COLONIA PRIMA FLAVIA AUGUSTA CAESAREA* expressed the highest status reached by a city within the Roman Empire.
[14] The palm branch first appeared on the coins of Alexander Jannaeus (105-78 BCE) and henceforth appeared on all Jewish coins. See Madden 1976. According to de Saulcy, the palm tree is generally represented with seven branches to represent the seven branches of the sacred candelabrum. (Madden 1976, 241).

[15] Belayche 2009, 168.
[16] For explanation of the title NAYAPXIC, see Chapter 5.3. For *METROPOLIS*, see 6.1 for explanations.

in or around military encampments demonstrates that the coins' accidental losses came from legionary soldiers.

Although this study is, of course, limited by the restriction of the material resources available, the iconographical analysis of coins that span a 285-year period — the duration of Dora's Roman coinage — has provided a reliable view into Dora's visual culture. For example, the coins' religious iconography show that the images of Tyche and Zeus Doros on all autonomous and imperial coins undergo little or no change during the entire period, signifying a religious continuity with roots in the city's religious syncretism. The rise of these two gods and their assimilation of the roles and attributes of Tyche/Fortuna and Zeus/Poseidon are in fact symptomatic of the mixed cultural milieu and hybridization of Dora's Hellenistic and Roman worlds. Even under the Severans, during Dora's most Romanized period, the city's architectural-type coins, depicting Tyche inside her shrine, denote a religion that is politically neutral and accommodating to the city's multicultural system.

Furthermore, the depiction of Tyche inside an architectural structure on several Severan issues illustrates the city's response to its process of Romanization. By putting Tyche's temple on its coins, Dora carries out the long-standing Roman tradition of fixing images of existing monuments on coins and turning them into symbols of imperial power. Under the Severans, Dora was not resistant to the Roman notion of civic and cultic monumentality, but embraced it. The same Romanization process that puts Dora's monuments on the city's coinage is further evidenced by the portrayal of each member of the imperial family on the same coins and to the occurrence of imperial/imperial types. While the earliest Roman coins of Dora do have local imagery on both the obverse and the reverse (local/local), they eventually become imperial/local, with emperors on the obverse and local imagery on the reverse. Under the Severans, both the obverse and the reverse depict the royal family (No. 44), becoming the imperial/imperial types.

In a city such as Dora, the identity cannot have been a simple matter of choice between Phoenician or Jewish, Greek or Roman. On the contrary, each new identity must have been a superstructure that changed the city slowly, once the local élite assimilated the values and standards of the newcomers. The study shows, in fact, that Dora's imperial depictions on coins were not Rome's imposition of imperial power nor the city's acceptance of Rome's colonialism, but rather the result of both externally generated events (the Roman takeover) and localized actions with roots in the city's past. The people of Dora present the various emperors on their coins, using a traditional, symbolic system within the existing framework of beliefs that bestowed divine powers on each new ruler. In the collective imagination of Dora's citizens, emperors were thus visualized as divine rulers on the same footing with the earlier Hellenistic kings and with the local deities Tyche and Zeus Doros, who were usually depicted on the reverse of the same coins.

Other iconographical themes are further documentation of the city's historical, political and economic reality within the geopolitical structure of the Levant. The coins with nautical themes and galleys, for instance, demonstrate that the natural harbor and the sea contributed to the city's social, military, and economic fabric, which included the city's purple dye industry. Similarly, the representations of wheat and grapes, not visibly associated with the deities Demeter or Dionysos, seem to have less of a god-centered nature and more of an economically engaged one. Although it is impossible to completely exclude any sacred connotation of the symbols the wheat and grapes on Dora's coins, representing bread and wine — two very important year-round food items familiar to the people of Dora — qualify as those symbols of food production and eating that Goodenough refers to as symbols of "life urges," [17] i.e., the type of symbols that operate on and respond to the primordial needs of people.

Finally, by locating Dora's coins within the current discourse of material culture, cultural contacts, and language use, this epigraphical study has provided significant insights into Dora's notion of self-identity. The exclusive use of Greek on Dora's Roman coins, for example, is a clear indication of Dora's continuous notion of Greek self-identity, as well as a measure of the city's cultural allegiance to Rome. Dora's Greekness is not, of course, surprising, given our discussion of the Romanization of the East in general and the fact that the Greek and Latin languages remained sufficiently distinct throughout the area's changed political circumstances. Indeed, it can be seen that the Greek language is a defining characteristic of identity; by allowing the Greek language to be exclusively used on Dora's coins, the Romans therefore allowed the Greek-speaking citizens of Dora to remain Greeks. As Cicero wrote to his brother,

cum vero ei generi hominum praesimus, non modo in quo ipso sit, sed etiam a quo ad alios pervenisse putetur humanitas, certe iis eam potissimum tribuere debemus, a quibus accepimus.[18]

As in the rest of the Greek-speaking world, cultural fusion took place in a dynamic way that structured both Greek and Roman elements until the Christianization of the area. Additionally, this study has shown that although the city was under Hasmonean rule for a short time at the end of its Hellenistic period (104-64 CE), therefore allowing a potential increase of the Jewish population of Dora, Judaism never influenced the city's cultural milieu, which continued to be entirely Phoenician and Greek. Literary evidence does indicate that a Jewish community had its own synagogue in Dora during the Roman period and that conflicts arose between the Greek and Jewish populations of the city in 42 CE under Claudius' reign.[19]

---

[17] Goodenough 1953, 50; See Chapter 4, 136-7, especially footnote 205.
[18] Cicero, *Ad Quintum Fratrem* I.9.27. "But since indeed we have taken that very race of men in which there is not only *humanitas*, but from whom *humanitas* is believed to have spread to others, we ought to at least give them what they have given us."
[19] According to Josephus (*Antiquities* 9. 300-302), in 42-41 BCE "Certain young men of Dora, who set a higher value on audacity than

The literary claim is not, however, supported by the archaeological evidence unearthed at Tel Dor thus far. Dora's material culture does not in fact present the Jewish evidence commonly found in the cities with larger Jewish populations, such as neighboring Caesarea Maritima, Hamat Tiberias overlooking the Sea of Galilee, Beit Alpha in the Jezreel Valley, and Tzippori and Kfar Baram in the Galilee Mountains.[20] All religious artifacts of Dora, as well as coin evidence, point to a Greco-Roman pantheon.[21]

This study of Dora's Greek and Roman coins has enabled the exploration of the history and cultural identity of the city. However, the study is by no means exhaustive. A chemical analysis of the coins' metal content would provide further commentary on the economy of the city and the political decisions of those who authorized the minting. Likewise, a chemical analysis of Dora's coins might offer insight into Roman metallurgy, i.e., the process of minting low-denomination bronze coins and the elemental composition of the metal alloys used by the mint.[22] Additionally, the geochemical fingerprint of the coins could also shed light on the organizational aspects of the city's coinage: where the copper came from; how well it was refined; and whether neighboring cities employed the same copper ores as Dora.[23] Finally, a study of the coins as actual currency in a modern economic sense might shed light on the intrinsic value of Dora's coins and their actual purchasing power. Since, according to Harl, coins produced by the civic mints of the Roman East held their relative purchasing power, an economic study of Dora's coins would no doubt reveal information concerning prices, exchange rates, and imperial economic policies for the entire surrounding area.[24]

As currency, i.e., as a medium of exchange, Dora's coins provided the city with economic benefits. But, as this study has shown, the coins were also a medium of visual communication, and their role in influencing identity was therefore parallel to a written language. The analogy between language and money is, of course, not a new one, having its roots in the eighteenth-century German philosophers who studied the semantic commonalities of both coins and words, i.e., the notion of circulation, exchange, symbolism, counterfeiting, etc.[25] Indeed, as noted by Goux, "The term representing a concept and the coin representing a value are both universal equivalents, resulting from similar dialectal processes."[26] The goal of this study, however, has not been to prove the relationship between money and language, which has been long established, but to critically analyze Dora's coins within the city's material culture and cultural identity. By looking at the coins' visual imagery as a semantic system, it is possible to appreciate the cognitive dimensions of the coins as can be done for any other artifact (coins are, after all, miniature artistic creations), reaching the underlying principles that shaped the history of the city during the time in which its mint was operating. This study of Dora's coins has thus contributed to the construction and understanding of Dora's historical narrative in multiple ways.

---

on holiness and were by nature recklessly bold, brought an image of Caesar into the synagogue of the Jews and set it up. This provoked Agrippa exceedingly, for it was tantamount to an overthrow of the laws of his fathers. He went to Publius Petronius, the governor of Syria, and denounced the people of Dora." It seems that Petronius "was no less angry at the deed, for he too regarded the breach of law as sacrilege," and issued an edict, stating that the people of Dora "had sinned not only against the law of the Jews, but also against the emperor, whose image was better placed in his own shrine than in that of another, especially in a synagogue." For more on the account of the conflict between the Greek and Jewish populations in Dora, see Pucci Ben Zev 1998; Sherwin-White 1967. See also Chapter 1.

[20] Foester 1992, 289-319. After the two Jewish revolts and the final destruction of Jerusalem in 135 CE, most Jews resettled in Galilee, which became a Jewish religious, administrative and culture center. Remains of early synagogues are evidence of the large Jewish presence in the area. For a more in-depth study of Jewish Galilee, see Fine 1996. Caesarea, whose Jewish citizens started the first Jewish revolt in 68 CE, continued to be a center of Jewish life, becoming the seat of important rabbinical schools, including those of Rabbi Bar Qappara and Rabbi Hosheya. Remains of ancient synagogues are evident. See Avi-Yonah 1960, 44-48.

[21] After the 1980 and 1982 discoveries at Tel Dor of two *favissae*, i.e., pits containing votive figures datable to the end of the Jewish exile (fifth century BCE), there were speculations that perhaps the city had been settled by Jewish exiles who no longer tolerated cultic figures. The claim was, however, rebutted by Stern who claims that in order to prove the presence of Jews in Persian-period Dor, the name 'Yehud' must be found stamped on artifacts of the period (Stern 1989, 54). The presence of Jewish coins among the material culture excavated at Tel Dor was discussed in Chapter 1.

[22] External Proton-Induced X-ray Emission (PIXE) is the scientific method for non-destructive analysis of coin metals. The method has been used successfully on many of the coins at the IAA, including the Persian-period coins of Southern Palestine. See Gitler 2008. Laser Ablation (LA)-ICP-MS is another technique used for isotopic analysis of solid samples, and it was used to study the metal composition of the Roman coins at the Manchester Museum, UK (Talib 2004). Although chemical analyses of the sediments within and around industrial structures at Tel Dor were done in 2009, revealing high concentrations of copper and lead that indicated metallurgical activity in the city (Eliyahu-Behar 2009, 135-151), no microscopic and chemical analysis of the bronze was done. Chemical analysis of the bronze used for casting bronze objects might have shed some light on the coins as well. For a thorough discussion of chemical analyses of coins, see Hall and Metcalf 1972; Guerra 1995.

[23] As demonstrated by Talib (2004, 156-166), considerable variations in both the major and trace element signatures can be attributed to the availability of raw materials and manufacturing techniques of different time periods.

[24] Harl 1990, 128. The "power of the monetary unit to purchase quantities of various goods is called the purchasing power of the money unit … [which] consists of the array of all the given money prices on the market at any particular time, considered in terms of the prices of the goods per unit of money." See Rothbard 2009, 315. A study of the purchasing power of Dora's coins would take into consideration the coins and the economies of all cities in the area, and it is therefore beyond the scope of this study.

[25] Gray 1996, 1-14. Among the German philosophers who underwrite the analogy between money and language are Gottfried Leibniz (*Unvorgreifliche Gedanken, betreffend die Ausübung und Verbesserun der teutschen Sprache*, 1719), Johann Hamman (*Socratische Denkwürdigkeiten*, 1759), Johann Herder (*Uber die neuere deutsche Literatur*, 1767), Johann Büsch (*Abhandlung von dem Geldumlauf*, 1780), Johann Lavater (*Aussichten in die Ewigkeit*, 1768-1778), and Friedrich Gedike (*Bernilische Monatsschrift*, 1789). See also Harrison 1996, 1-7.

[26] Goux 1990, 96; he also notes that Zeno, the founder of Stoicism, made a reference to the analogy of words and coins, writing that words, like coins, are not always to be trusted at their face value and that "well-ordered speeches were like Alexandrian coins that, although well minted, were nonetheless base coins, whereas words that were incorrect but rich in meaning were like the Attic four-*drachma* coins" (101; footnote 26).

Bibliography

Adams, J., M. Janse, and S. Swain. 2003. *Bilingualism in Ancient Society: Language Contact and the Written Word*. Oxford: Oxford University Press.

Adler, H. 2008. "Herder's Concept of Humanität." In *A companion to the Works of Johan Gottfried Herder*, edited by H. Adler and W. Köpke, 93- 116. Rochester, NY: Boydell & Brewer Inc.

Aitchison, N. 1988. "Roman Wealth, Native Ritual: Coin Hoards within and Beyond Roman Britain." *World Archaeology* 20 (2): 270-284.

Albright, W. 1942. *Archaeology and the Religion of Israel*. Baltimore: Johns Hopkins University Press.

Albright, W. 1956. "John Garstang in Memoriam." *Bulletin of the American Schools of Oriental Research* 144: 7–8.

Albright, W. 1963. *The Archaeology of Palestine*. London: Penguin Books.

Albright, W. 1966. *Archaeology: Historical Analogy & Early Biblical Tradition*. Baton Rouge: Louisiana State University Press.

Alcock, S. and R. Osborne, eds. 1998, *Placing the Gods, Sanctuaries and Sacred Space in Ancient Greece*. Oxford: Oxford University Press.

Alexander, C. 1934. "A Portrait of Antoninus Pius." *The Metropolitan Museum of Art Bulletin* 29 (2): 28.

Allen, M. 2004. "Medieval English Die-Output." *The British Numismatic Journal* 74: 39-49.

Allen, T. W., and A. Rambaut. 1915. "The Date of Hesiod." *The Journal of Hellenic Studies* 35: 85-99.

Anderson, B. 1991. *Imagined Communities*. London: Verso.

Ando, C. 2000. *Imperial Ideology and Provincial Loyalty in the Roman Empire*. Berkeley: University of California Press.

Antonaccio, C. 2003. "Hybridity and the Cultures within Greek Culture." In *The Cultures within Greek Culture*, edited by C. Dougherty & L. Kurke, 57-74. Cambridge: Cambridge University Press.

Apostolos-Cappadona, D., ed. 1984. *Art, Creativity, and the Sacred: An Anthology in Religion and Art*. New York: Crossroads.

Arnold-Biucchi, C., L. Beer-Tobey, and N.M, Waggoner. 1988. "A Greek Archaic Silver Hoard from Selinus." *American Numismatic Society Museum Notes* 33: 1-35.

Arnold, M. 1883. *Culture and Anarchy: An Essay in Political and Social Criticism*. New York: MacMillan and Co.

Aubet, M. 1993. *The Phoenicians and the West: Politics, Colonies and Trade*. Cambridge: Cambridge University Press.

Avigad, N. 1962. " A Depository of Inscribed Ossuaries in the Kidron Valley." *Israel Exploration Journal* 12: 1- 12.

Avi-Yonah, M. 1960. "The Synagogue of Caesarea." *Bulletin Rabinowitz* 3: 44- 48.

Baldus, H.R. 1989. "Zur Münzprägung von Dora. Phönizien zu Ehren Kleopatras VII und Mark Antons." *Chiron* 19: 477- 480.

Balmuth, M. 1971. "Remarks on the Appearance of the Earliest Coins." In *Studies Presented to George M.A. Hanfmann*, edited by D. Mitten, 1-7. Cambridge, MA: Fogg Art Museum.

Bar-Kochva, B. *The Image of the Jews in Greek Literature: The Hellenistic Period*. Berkley, CA: University of California Press

Barag, D. and L. Kadman. 1983. *Proceedings of the International Numismatic Convention on Greek Imperials, Jerusalem, 2nd-5th January 1983*. Jerusalem: Israel Numismatic Society.

Barag, D. 1978. "The Palestinian Judea Capta Coins of Vespasian and Titus and the Era on the Coins of Agrippa II minted under the Flavians." *Numismatic Chronicle* 138: 14-23.

Barag, D.1996. "The Legal and Administrative Status of the Port of Sebastos during the Early Roman Period." In *Caesarea Martima: A Retrospective After Two Millenia*, edited by Avner Raban and Kenneth G. Holum, 609-614. Leiden, New York: Brill.

Barnard, F. 1983. "National Culture and Political Legitimacy: Herder and Rousseau." *Journal of the History of Ideas* 44 (2): 231-253.

Baron, I. M. Herslund, and F. S Sørensen (ed).. 2001. *Dimensions of Possession*. Copenhagen: John Benjamins Publishing Company

Barr, A. 1996. "Horse and Rider Plaques at Ilion: A Preliminary Study of the Hellenistic Hero Cult in Asia Minor." *Studia Troica* 6: 133-157.

Bartman, E. 2001. " Hair and the Artifice of the Roman Female Adornment." *American Journal of Archaeology* 105 (1): 1-25.

Basch, L. 1969. "Phoenician Oared Ships." The Mariners' Mirror 55:139-62, 227-45.

Bashkow, I. 2004 "A Neo-Boasian Conception of Cultural Boundaries." *American Anthropologist* 106 (3): 443-458.

Battezzato, L. 2009. Review of *Visualizing the Tragic. Drama, Myth, and Ritual in Greek Art and Literature*, by Chris Kraus. *Bryn Mawr Classical Review* 47 (2009). http://bmcr.brynmawr.edu/2009/2009-05-47. html (15 August 2010).

Baudrillard, J. 1981. *For a Critique of the Political Economy of Sign*. St. Louis: Telos Press Publishing.

Baudrillard, J. 1985. *Simulacra and Simulations*. Translated by S. Glaser. Ann Arbor, MI: University of Michigan Press.

Beckmann, M. 2009. "The Significance of Roman Imperial Coin Types." *Klio Beiträge zur alten Geschichte* 91 (1): 144 – 161.

Belayche, N. 2009. "Foundation Myths in Roman Palestine. Traditions and

Reworkings." In *Ethnic Constructs in Antiquity* edited by T. Derks and N. Roymans, 167-188. Amsterdam: Amsterdam University Press.

Belloni, G. 1976. "Monete Romane e Propaganda." In *I Canali della Propaganda nel Mondo Antico: Contributi dell'Istituto di Storia Antica,* edited by M. Sordi, 131-133. Milano: Università Cattolica del Sacro Cuore.

Ben-Sasson, H.H. 1976. *A History of the Jewish People.* Cambridge, MA: Harvard University Press.

Ben-Yehuda, N. 1995. *Masada Myth: Collective Memory and Mythmaking In Israel.* Madison, WI: The University of Wisconsin Press.

Ben-Yehuda. N. 2002. *Sacrificing Truth: Archaeology and The Myth of Masada.* Amherst, NY: Humanities Books.

Bennet, J. 1997. *Trajan: Optimus Princeps:A Life and Times.* London: Routledge.

Benvenisti, M. 2000. *Sacred Landscape. The Buried History of the Holy Land since 1948.* Berkley: University of Californian Press.

Berg, J. 1986. "The Temple at Dor, Israel." M.A. diss., California State University.

Berg, J. E., B. Zilberstein and I. Sharon. 2002. "The Water Supply, Distribution and Sewage Systems at Roman Dor." In *Ancient Aqueducts in Israel*, edited by D. Amit, Y. Hirschfeld, and Y. Patrich, 155-167. Portsmouth, RI: Journal of Roman Archaeology Supplementary Series, Vol 46.

Berlin, A. 1997. "Archaeological Sources for the History of Palestine: Between Large Forces: Palestine in the Hellenistic." *The Biblical Archaeologist* 60 (1): 2-51.

Bernstein, P. 2008. *A Primer on Money and Banking, and Gold.* New York: Wiley.

Betlyon, J. 1982. *The Coinage and Mints of Phoenicia. Harvard Semitic Monograph No. 26.* Chico, CA: Scholars Press.

Bhabha, H. 1994. *The Location of Culture.* London: Routledge.

Bijovsky G., W. Fischer-Bossert, D. Hendin, A. Meadows. 2013. *Coins of the Holy Land: The Abraham D. Sofaer Collection at the American Numismatic Society.* New York: American Numismatic Society

Blakely, J.,A., Robert Brinkmann, and Charles J. Vitaliano. 1996. "Toward a Study of Economics at Caesarea Maritima." In *Caesarea Martima: A Retrospective After Two Millenia*, edited by Avner Raban and Kenneth G. Holum. Leiden, New York: Brill.

Boardman, J. 1993. *Classical Art in Eastern Translation.* Oxford: Oxford University Press.

Boardman, J. 1999. *The Greek Overseas: Their Colonies and Early Trade.* 4th ed. London: Thames and Hudson.

Boardman, J. 2002b. "Greeks in Syria: Pots and People." In *Greek Settlements in Eastern Mediterranean and the Black Sea*, edited by G.R. Tsetskhladze and A.M. Snodgrass, 1-16. BAR International Series 1062. Oxford: Archaeopress.

Bodel, J. 2001. *Epigraphic Evidence: Ancient History from Inscriptions.* London: Routledge.

Bohannan, P. 1969. *Social Anthropology.* New York: Holt, Rinehart & Winston.

Boschung, D. 1993. *Das Römische Herrscherbild.* Vol 2, pt 1, *Die Bildnisse des Augustus.* Berlin: Mann.

Boschung, D. 1993b. "Die Bildnistypen derl iulisch-claudischen Kaiserfamilie: ein Kritischer Forschungsbericht." *Journal Roman Archaeology* 6: 39-79.

Bottomore, T and M. Rubel, eds. 1964. *Karl Marx Selected Writings in Sociology and Social Philosophy.* New York: McGraw-Hill.

Bourdieu, P. 1977. *Outline of a Theory of Practice*, trans. Richard Nice. Cambridge: Cambridge University Press.

Bowersock, G. 1983. *Roman Arabia.* Cambridge, MA: Harvard University Press.

Brah, A. and A. Coombes, eds. 2000. *Hybridity and its Discontents: Politics, Science, Culture.* London: Routledge.

Briant, P. 1978. Colonisation Hellénistique et populations indigènes: la phase d'installation." *Klio Beiträge zur Alten Geschichte* 60 (14): 57-92.

Briant, P. 2002. *From Cyrus to Alexander: A History of the Persian Empire.* Winona Lake: Eisenbrauns.

Brody, A. 1999. *Each Man Cried Out to His God. The Specialized Religion of Canaanite and Phoenician Seafarers.* Harvard Semitic Monographs. Atlanta, GA: Scholars Press

Broughton, T. R. 1968. *The Romanization of Africa.* Baltimore: John Hopkins University Press.

Brown, B. 1981. "Style in the Alexander Portraits on the Coins of Lysimachos." In *Coins, Culture and History: Studies in Honor of Bluma Trell*, edited by L. Casson and L. Price, 1-25. Detroit, MI: Wayne State University Press.

Brown, B. 1984. "Art History in Coins: Portraits issued by Ptolemy I." In *Alessandria e il Mondo Ellenistico. Studi in Onore di Achille Adriani*, edited by A. Adriani, 405-417. Rome : "L'Erma" di Bretschneider.

Brown, B. 1988. "Neo-Classicism in the Coin Portraits issued by Ptolemy." *Praktika Tou XII Diethnous Synedriou Kasikes Archaiologias* 12: 33-36.

Brown, B. 1995. *Royal Portraits in Sculpture and Coins: Pyrrhos and the Successor of Alexander the Great.* New York: Peter Lang Publishing Inc.

Bruit Zaidman, L. et al. 1993. *Religion in the Ancient Greek City.* Cambridge: Cambridge University Press.

Brunetti, L. 1963. *Aspetti Statistici della Metanumismatica.* Rome P & P Santamaria.

Brunt, P. 1976. "Local Ruling Classes in the Roman Empire." In *Assimilation et Résistance à la Culture Gréco-romaine dans le Monde Ancien*, edited by D. Pippidi, 160-173. Bucharest and Paris: Editura Academiei.

Buckingham, J. 1821. *Travels in Palestine through the Countries of Bashan and Gilead, East of the River Jordan: Including a Visit to the Cities of Geraza and*

Gamala, in the Decapolis. London : Longman, Hurst, Rees, Orme & Brown.

Budin, S. 2004. "A Reconsideration of the Aphrodite-Ashtart Syncretism." *Numen* 51 (2): 95-145.

Bull, R. and O. Storvick. 1993 "The Gold Coin Hoard at Caesarea." *Biblical Archaeologist* 56: 116-20.

Bullard, R. 1970. "Geological Studies in Field Archaeology." *The Biblical Archaeologist* 33 (4): 98-132.

Buraselis, C. 2001. "Kos Between Hellenism and Rome: Studies on the Political, Institutional, and Social History of Kos from Ca. the Middle Second Century." *Transactions of the American Philosophical Society* 90 (4): 1-189.

Burckhardt, J. 1943. *Force and Freedom. Reflections on History.* Edited by James H. Nichols. New York: Pantheon Books.

Burckhardt, J. 1955. *Letters.* Selected, edited and translated by Alexander Dru. New York: Pantheon Books.

Burckhardt, J. 1998. *The Greeks and Greek civilization.* Translated by S. Stern. Edited by O. Murray. New York: St. Martin's Press.

Burnett, A. 1987. *Coinage in the Roman World.* London: Seaby.

Burnett, A. 1990. "Marco Baldanza's Instruttione Sopra le Medaglie degli Imperatori Antichi Romani." In *Medals and Coins from Budé to Mommsen,* edited by M. H. Crawford, C. R. Ligota, J. B. Trapp, 73-85. London: Warburg Institute, University of London.

Burnett, A. 1993. "Roman Provincial Coins of the Julio-Claudian." In *Essays in Honour of Robert Carson and Kenneth Jenkins,* edited by M. Price, A. Burnett, and R. Bland, 145-153. London: Spink.

Burnett, A. 1999. "Building and Monuments on Roman Coins." In *Roman Coins and Public Life under the Empire: E. Togo Salmon papers II,* edited by G. Paul and M. Ierardi, 137- 64. Ann Arbor, MI: University of Michigan Press.

Burnett, A. 2002. "Syrian Coinage and Romanisation from Pompey to Domitian." In *Les Monnayages Syriens: Quel apport pour l'Histoire du Proche-Orient Hellénistique et Romain? Actes de la table ronde de Damas, 10-12 novembre 1999,* edited by C. Augé and F. Duyrat, 115-122. Beirut: Institut Français d'archéologie du Proche-Orient.

Burnett, A. 2005. "The Roman West and the Roman East." In *Coinage and Identity in the Roman Provinces,* edited by C. Howgego, V. Heuchert and A. Burnett, 171-180. Oxford: Oxford University Press.

Burrell, B. 1996 "Palace to Praetorium: The Romanization of Caesarea." Pp. 228-247 in *Caesarea Martima: A Retrospective After Two Millenia,* edited by A. Raban and K. Holum, 228-247. Leiden, New York: Brill.

Burrell, Barbara. 2004. *Neokoroi: Greek Cities and Roman Emperors.* Leiden: Brill.

Butcher, K. 1988. *Roman Provincial Coins. An Introduction to the Greek Imperials.* London: Seaby.

Butcher, K. 2003. *Roman Syria and the Near East.* London: British Museum Press.

Butcher, K., 2004. *Coinage in Roman Syria, Northern Syria, 64 BC– AD 253.* London: The Royal Numismatic Society (Special Publications 34).

Butcher, K. 2005. "Information, Legitimation, or Self-Legitimation? Syria." In *Coinage and Identity in the Roman Provinces,* edited by C. Howgego, V. Heuchert and A. Burnett, 143-156. Oxford: Oxford University Press.

Buttrey, T. 1954. "Thea Neotera: On coins of Anthony and Cleopatra*." American Numismatic Society Museum Notes* 6: 95- 109.

Buttrey, T.V. 1972. "Vespasian as Moneyer. The Numismatic Chronicle 12:89-109.

Buttrey, T. 1993. "Calculating Ancient Coins Production: Facts and Fantasies." *The Numismatic Chronicle* 153: 334-351.

Buttrey, T. 1994. "Calculating Ancient Coins Production II: Why It Cannot Be Done." *The Numismatic Chronicle* 154: 341-352.

Cahn, H. 1948. *Frühhellenistiche Münzkunst.* Basel: Mainz.

Caley, E. R. 1964. *Orichalcum and Related Alloys. Origin, Composition and Manufacture with Special Reference to Coinage of the Roman Empire.* New York: The American Numismatic Society.

Çalık, A. 1996. "A New Head of Hadrian from Pompeiopolis." *Anatolian Studies* 4: 83-89.

Carpenter, R. 1941. "Observation on Familiar Statuary in Rome." *Memoirs of the American Academy in Rome* 18: 73-81.

Carr, C., and J. Neitzel. 1995. *Style, Society and Person: Archaeological and Ethnological Perspectives.* New York: Springer-Verlag.

Carrier, D. 1987. "Ekphrasis and Interpretation: Two Modes Of Art History Writing." *The British Journal of Aesthetics* 27 (1): 20-31.

Carrithers, M., S. Collins, and S. Lukes (eds.). 1985. *The Category of the Person: Anthropology, Philosophy, History.* Cambridge: Cambridge University Press.

Carson, R. 1978. *Principal Coins of the Romans.* Vol. 1, *The Republic.* London: British Museum Publications.

Casey, J. 1986. *Understanding Ancient Coins: Introduction for Archaeologists and Historians.* Norman, OK: University of Oklahoma Press.

Càssola, F. 1993. *Scritti di storia antica. Istituzioni e politica. Grecia.* Napoli: Jovene Editore

Càssola, F. 1996. "Chi erano i Greci?" In *I Greci. Storia Cultura Arte Società,* edited by S. Settis, 5-23. Torino: Luigi Einaudi Editore.

Casson, L. 1967. The Emergency Rig of Ancient Warships." *Transactions and Proceedings of the American Philological Association* 98: 43-48.

Casson, L. 1991. *The Ancient Mariners: Seafarers and Sea Fighters of the Mediterranean in Ancient Times.* Princeton, NJ: Princeton University Press.

Casson, L. 1995. *Ships and Seamanship in the Ancient World.* Baltimore, MD: The John Hopkins University Press.

Casson, L. and M. Price, eds. 1981. *Coins, Culture and History in the Ancient World: Numismatic and Other*

Studies in Honor of Bluma L. Trell. Detroit, MI: Wayne State University Press.

Caubet, A. 2007. "Le monde perse 600 avant-600 après J.C., Perspective." *La Revue de l'INHA*. Actualités de la Recherche en Histoire de l'Art 1: 45-48.

Childe, V.G. 1929. *The Danube in Prehistory*. Oxford: Oxford University Press.

Childe, V.G. 1930. *The Bronze Age*. Cambridge: Cambridge University Press.

Childe, V.G. 1956. *Society and Knowledge*. New York: Harper and Brothers.

Chilton, E. 1999. *Material Meanings: Critical Approaches to the Interpretation of Material Culture*. Salt Lake City: University of Utah Press.

Cipolla, C. 1967. *Money, Price, and Civilization in the Mediterranean World: Fifth to Seventh Century*. New York: Gordian.

Clifford J. and G. Marcus. 1986. *Writing Culture. The Poetics and Politics of Ethnography*. Berkley: University of California Press.

Clifford, R. 1990. "Phoenician Religion." *Bulletin of the American Schools of Oriental Research* 279: 55-64.

Coarelli, F. 1985. *Roma*. Rome: Laterza.

Cobley, P., ed. 2001. *The Routledge Companion to Semiotics and Linguistics*. London: Routledge.

Cohen, B. 2000. *Not the Classical Ideal: Athens and the Construction of the Other in Greek Art*. Leiden: Brill.

Colledge, M. 1987. "Greek and non-Greek Interaction in the Art and Architecture of the Hellenistic East." In *Hellenism in the East*, edited by A. Kuhrt and S. Sherwin-White, 143-175. Berkley: The University of California Press.

Collingwood, R. 1932. *Roman Britain*. Oxford: Clarendon Press.

Codere, H. 1968. "Money-Exchange Systems and a Theory of Money." Man, *New Series* 3: 557-77.

Coogan, M. 1978. *Stories from Ancient Canaan*. Philadelphia: The Westminster Press.

Cook, R. 1958. *"Speculations on the Origins of Coinage." Historia: Zeitschrift für Alte Geschichte* 7 (3): 257-262.

Cotton, H. 1997. "The New Province of Arabia in the Papyri from the Judean Desert." *Zeitschrift für Papyrologie und Epigraphik* 116: 206-207.

Cotton, H. 2000. "The Legio Sexta Ferrata between 106 and 136." In *Les Légions de Rome sous le Haut-Empire: Actes du Congrès de Lyon septrembre 1998*, edited by Y. Le Bohec, 351-357. Paris: E. de Boccard.

Crawford, M. 1969. *Roman Republican Coin Hoards*. London: Royal Numismatic Society.

Crawford, M. 1970. "Money and Exchange in the Roman World." *Journal of Roman Studies* 60:40-48.

Crawford, M. 1983. "Roman Imperial Coin Types and the Formation of Public Opinion." In *Studies in Numismatic Method Presented to Philip Grierson*, edited by C.N.L. Brooke, B.H.I.H Stewart, J.G. Pollard and R. Volk. 47-64. Cambridge: Cambridge University Press.

Crawford, H. M. 1985. *Coinage and Money under the Roman Republic*. Berkeley: University of California Press.

Crawford, M. 1982. *La Moneta in Grecia e a Roma*. Bari: Laterza.

Crump, G. 1985. "Coinage and Imperial Thought." In *The Craft of the Ancient Historian: Essays in Honor of Chester G. Starr*, edited by J. Eadie and J. Ober, 425-441. New York: University Press of America.

Csikszenmihalyi, M. and E. Rochberg-Halton. 1981. *The Meaning of Things: Domestic Symbols and the Self*. Cambridge: Cambridge University Press.

Dahl, G. 1915. "The Materials for the History of Dor." *Transactions of the Connecticut Academy of the Arts and Science* 20: 1-181.

Dalby, A. 2000. "To Feed a King – Tyrants, Kings, and the Search for Quality in Agriculture and Food." In *Paysage et Alimentation dans le Monde Grec*, edited by J. M. Luce, 133-144. Toulouse: Presses Universitaires du Mirail.

Damaskos, D. and D. Plantzos (eds.). 2008. *A Singular Antiquity: Archaeology and the Hellenic Identity in the Twentieth Century*. Athens: Benaki Museum.

Dauphin, C. 1981. "Dor Byzantine Church." *Israel Exploration Journal* 31 (1-2): 117-119.

Dauphin, C. 1982. "On the Pilgrims Way to the Holy City." *Bulletin of the Anglo- Israel Archaeological Society* 1: 25-31.

Dauphin, C. 1984. "Dor, Byzantine Church." *Israel Exploration Journal* 34: 271-274.

Dauphin, C. 1986. "Temple Grec, Église Byzantine et Cimetière Musulman: la Basilique de Dor en Israël." *Proche-Orient Chrétien* 36: 14-22.

Dauphin C. and S. Gibson 1994. "The Byzantine City of Dor/Dora Discovered." *Bulletin of the Anglo-Israel Archaeological Society* 14: 9-37.

Dauphin, C. 1999. "From Apollo and Asclepius to Christ." *Liber Annuus* XLIX: 397-425. Jerusalem: Studium Biblicum Franciscanum.

Davies, J. K. 1984. "Cultural, Social and Economic Features of The Hellenistic World." In *The Cambridge Ancient History*, Vol. 7, pt 1, The Hellenistic World, edited by F. Walbank, 257-320. Cambridge: Cambridge University Press.

Deely, J. 2003. "The Semiotic Foundations of The Human Sciences From Augustine to Peirce." Recherche Sémiotique / Semiotic Inquiry 23: 3-29.

De Jong, L. 2007. "Becoming a Roman Province: An Analysis of Funerary Practices in Roman Syria in the Context of Empire." Ph.D. diss. Stanford University.

De Jong, J. 2007. "The Employment of Epithets in the Struggle for Power: A Case Study." In *Crisis and the Roman Empire. Proceedings of the Seventh Workshop of the International Network Impact of Empire, Nijmegen, June 20-24, 2006*, edited by O. Hekster, G. de Kleijn, and D. Slootjes, 311-326. Leiden: Brill.

Den Boer, W., ed. 1973. *Le Culte des Souverains dans l'Empire Romain*. Geneva: Fondation Hardt.

DeRose Evans, J. 1993. *The Art of Persuasion: Political Propaganda from Aeneas to Brutus*. Ann Arbor: Michigan University Press.

Derrida, J. 1982. *Margins of Philosophy*. Translated by A. Bass. Chicago: University of Chicago Press.

De Saulcy, F. 1874. *Numismatique de la Terre Sainte*. Paris: Didier.

Dever, W. 2005. *Did God Have a Wife? Archaeology and Folk Religion in Ancient Israel*. Grand Rapids, MI: Wm. B. Eerdmans Publishing Company.

Dewsnap, M. 1997. "Roman Jerusalem: Hadrian. A Portrait in Bronze." *Biblical Archaeological Society* 23: 1-6.

Dimitrova, N. 2002. "Inscriptions and Iconography in the Monuments of the Thracian Rider." *Hesperia* 71 (2): 209-229.

Diplock, P. 1973. "Further Comment on 'An Identification of the Caesarea Statues'." *Palestine Exploration Quarterly* 105: 165-66.

Di Segni, L. 1993 "A Jewish Greek Inscription from the Vicinity of Caesarea Maritima." *Atiqot*, English series 22: 133-36.

Di Segni, L. 1994. "The Date of the Binyamina Inscription and the Question of Byzantine Dora." *Atiqot* xxv: 183-186.

Dohrn, T. 1960. *Die Tyche Von Antiochia*. Berlin: Verlag Greb.

Donaldson, T. L. 1859. *Architectura Numismatica*. London: Day & Son, Lithographers.

Donaldson, T. 2000. *Religious Rivalries and the Struggle for Success in Caesarea Maritima*. Waterloo, ON: Wilford Laurier University Press.

Dougherty, C. and L Kurke, eds. 2003. *The Cultures within Ancient Greek Culture: Contact, Conflict, Collaboration*. Cambridge: Cambridge University Press.

Downey, G. 1961. *A History of Antioch In Syria: From Seleucus to the Arab Conquest*. Princeton: Princeton University Press.

Downey, S. 1988. *Mesopotamian Religious Architecture. Alexander through the Parthians*. Princeton: Princeton University Press.

Drijvers, H. 1980. "Romeinen in Syrië." *Phoenix* 26:73-93.

Durand, J. and F. Lissarague. 1980. "Un Lieu d'Image? L'Espace du Louterion." *Hephaistos* 2: 89-106.

Dvorjetski, E. 1994. "Nautical Symbols on the Gadara Coins and their Link to the Thermae of the Three Graces at Hammat-Gader." *Mediterranean Historical Review* 9 (1):100 – 115.

Dyer, A. W. 1989. "Making Semiotic Sense of Money as a Medium of Exchange." *Journal of Economic Issues* 23 (2): 503-510.

Eck, W. 2007. *Rom und Judaea : Fünf Vorträge zur Römischen Herrschaft in Palaestina*. Tübingen: Mohr Siebeck.

Eckhel, J. 1798. *Doctrina Nummorum Veterum*, Vol. 8, pt 2. Vindobonae (Vienna): Sumptibus Iosephi Comesina et Soc.

Eco, U. 1994. *The Limits of Interpretation. Advances in Semiotics*. Bloomington: Indiana University Press.

Edelman, M. 1996. *From Art to Politics: How Artistic Creations Shape Political Conceptions*. Chicago: University of Chicago Press.

Edward, C. 1990. "Tyche at Corinth." *Hesperia* 59 (3): 529-542.

Ehrhardt, C. 1984. "Roman Coin Types and the Roman Public." *Jahrbuch für Numismatik und Geldgeschichte* 34: 41– 54.

Ehrich, A. 2003. "Response on the Article by E. Stern 'Goddesses and Cults at Tel Dor.'" *Qadmoniot* 125:55-56 (Hebr.).

Ehrlich, A. 2010. "Hellenistic and Roman Terracotta Figurines from Tel Dor: Production, Imports and Imitation." *Michmanim* 22: 15-26 (Hebrew).

Elayi, J. 1980. "The Phoenician Cities in the Persian Period." *Journal of the Ancient Near East Society* 12: 13-28.

Elayi, J. 1982. "Studies in Phoenician geography during the Persian period." *Journal of Near Eastern Studies* 41 (83): 91-2.

Elayi, J. ed. 1993. *Trésors de Monnaies Phéniciennes et Circulation Monétaire*. Paris: Gabalda.

Elayi, J. and A.G. Elyai. 2004. *Le monnayage de la cite phenicienne de Sidon a l 'epoque perse (Ve-IVe s. av. J.-C.)*. Paris: Gabalda.

Elsner, J. 1996. "Image and Ritual: Reflections on the Religious Appreciation of Classical Art." *The Classical Quarterly* 46 (2): 515-531.

Elsner, J. 1997. "The Origin of the Icon: Pilgrimage, Religion and Visual Culture in the Roman East as Resistance to the Culture." In *The Early Roman Empire in the East,* edited by S. F. Alcock, 178-99. Oxford: Oxford University Press.

Elsner, J. 1998. *Imperial Rome and Christian Triumph: The Art of the Roman Empire AD 100-450*. Oxford: Oxford University Press.

Eliyahu-Behar, A., L. Regev, S. Shilstein, S. Weiner. 2009. "Identifying a Roman Casting Pit at Tel Dor, Israel: Integrating Field and Laboratory Research." *Journal of Field Archaeology* 34 (2): 135-151.

Engelmann, H. 1985. "Wege Griechischer Geldpolitik." Zeitschrift für Papyrologie und Epigraphik 60: 165-176.

Erskine A., ed. 2003. *A Companion to the Hellenistic World*. Oxford: Blackwell.

Esty, W. 1986. "Estimation of the Size of a Coinage: Survey and Comparison of Methods." *The Numismatic Chronicle* 146: 185-215.

Esty, W. 1990. "The Theory of Linkage." *The Numismatic Chronicle* 150: 205-221.

Evans, T. 1982. "William Morris and the Study of Material Culture." *Folklore Forum* 15 (1): 69-86.

Evers, C. 1994. *Les portraits d' Hadrien: Typologie et Ateliers*. Bruxelles: Académie Royale de Belgique.

Fejfer, J. 2008. *Roman Portraits in Context*. New York: Walter de Gruyter.

Feliu, L. and W. Watson. 2003. *The God Dagan in Bronze Age Syria*. Leiden: Brill Academic Publishers.

Figueira, T. 2006. "Colonization in the Classical Period." In: *Greek Colonisation: An Account of Greek Colonies and other Settlements Overseas*, edited by G.Tsetskhladze, 427-521. Leiden: Brill Academic Publishers.

Fine, S., ed. 1996. Sacred Realm: The Emergence of the Synagogue in the Ancient World. New York: Oxford University Press and Yeshiva University Museum.

Finley, M. 1973. *The Ancient Economy.* Los Angeles: University of California Press.

Fisch, M. 1978. "Peirce's General Theory of Signs." In *Sight, Sound, and Sense,* edited by T. A. Sebeok, 31-70. Bloomington: Indiana University Press.

Fishwick, D. 1965. "Vae Puto Deus Fio." *The Classical Quarterly* 15 (1): 155-157.

Flannery K. and J. Marcus. 1996. "Cognitive Archaeology." In *Contemporary Archaeology in Theory: A Reader,* edited by R. Preucel and I. Hodder, 350-363. New York: Wiley-Blackwell.

Foerster, G.1975 "The Early History of Caesarea." In *Studies in the History of Caesarea Maritima,* edited by C. T. Fritsch, 9-22. Missoula, Montana: Scholars Press.

Foester, G. 1992. "The Ancient Synagogues of the Galilee." In *The Galilee in Late Antiquity,* edited by L. Levine, 289-319. New York: Jewish Theological Seminary.

Forsythe, G.2005. *A Critical History of Early Rome: From Prehistory to the First Punic War.* Los Angeles: University of California Press.

Frankfurter, D. 2010. Religion in Roman Egypt: Assimilation and Resistance. Princeton: Princeton University Press.

Freedman, L. 1995. "Cinquecento Mythographic Descriptions of Neptune." *International Journal of the Classical Tradition* 2 (1): 44-53.

Freeman, P. 1993. Romanization and Roman material culture." *Journal of Roman Archaeology* 6: 438-45.

Freeman, P. 1996. "The Annexation of Arabia and Imperial Grand Strategy." *Journal of Roman Archaeology* 18: 91-118.

Fritsch, C. ed. 1975 *Studies in the History of Caesarea Maritima.* Bulletin of the American Schools of Oriental Research, Supplemental Studies No. 19. Scholars Press: Missoula, MT.

Fromm, E. 2004. Reprint. *Marx's Concept of Man.* London: Continuum International Publishing Group. Original edition, New York: F. Ungar, 1961.

Frova, A., G. Dell'Amore, D. Adamesteanu, V. Borroni. 1966. *Scavi di Caesarea Maritima.* Rome: L'Erma di Bretschneider.

Frova, A., A. Calderini; L. Crema.1959 "Caesarea Maritima (Israele), Rapporto preliminare della I campagna di scavo della Missione Archeologica Italiana,"

Rendiconti dell'Istituto Lombardo, Classe di lettere, scienze morali e storiche 1-33.

Fullerton, M. 1990. *The Archaistic Style in Roman Statuary.* Leiden: Brill Academic Publishers.

Gais, R. M. 1978. "Some Problems of River-God Iconography." *Amerian Journal of Archaeology* 82: 355-370.

Gamble, C. 2001. *Archaeology: the Basics.* New York: Routledge.

Gardin, J-C. 1992."Semiotic Trends in Archaeology." In *Representations in Archaeology,* edited by J-C. Gardin and C. Peebles, 251-275. Bloomingdale: Indiana University Press.

Gardner, R. ed. 1995. *The Age of the Galley: Mediterranean Oared Vessels since Pre- classical.* Annapolis, MD: Naval Institute Press.

Gauthier, P. 1987-89. "Grandes et Petites Cités: Hégémonie et Autarcie." *Opus* 6-8: 187-202.

Gauthier, P.1993. "Les Cités Hellénestiques." *University of California Publications in Classical Archaeology* 1: 211-31.

Geertz, C. 1973. *The Interpretation of Cultures: Selected Essays by Clifford Geertz.* New York: Basic Books.

Gera, D. 1995. "Tryphon's Sling Bullet from Dor." In *Qedem Reports: Excavation at Dor* Vol. 1B, edited by E. Stern, 491-6. Jerusalem: The Institute of Archaeology of the Hebrew University.

Gera, D. and H. Cotton. 1995. "A Dedication from Dor to a Governor of Syria." In *Qedem Report: Excavation at Dor,* Vol 1B, edited by E Stern, 497-500. Jerusalem: The Institute of Archaeology of the Hebrew University.

Gersht, R. 1984 "The Tyche of Caesarea Maritima." *Palestinian Exploration Quarterly* 116: 110-14.

Gersht, R. 1996. "Presentations of Deities and the Cults of Caesarea." In *Caesarea Martima: A Retrospective After Two Millenia,* edited by A. Raban and G. Holum, 305-324. Leiden, New York: Brill.

Ghedini, F. 1984. *Giulia Domna tra Oriente e Occidente: le Fonti Archeologiche.* Milano: L'Erma di Bretschneider.

Gibson, J. 1982. *Textbook of Syrian Semitic inscriptions.* Volume 3: Phoenician Inscriptions. Oxford: Clarendon Press.

Gilbert, E. 2005. "Common Cents: Situating Money in Time and Place." *Economy and Society* 34 (3) 357-388.

Gilboa, A., I. Sharon and E. Boaretto. 2009. "Tel Dor and the Chronology of Phoenician "Pre-Colonization" Stages." In *Beyond the Homeland: Markers in Phoenician Chronology,* edited by C. Sagona, 113-204. Leuven: Peeters.

Gitler H, M. Ponting and O. Tal. 2008. "Metallurgical Analysis of Southern Palestinian Coins of the Persian Period." *Israel Numismatic Research* 3: 13-28.

Goldberg, H. 1984. *Judaism Viewed from Within and from Without: An Anthropological Study.* New York: State University of New York Press.

Goodenough, E. 1953-68. *Jewish Symbols in the Greco-Roman Period.* 11 vols. Princeton: Princeton University Press.

Gordon, M. 1964. *Assimilation in American Life. The Role of Race, Religion, and National Origins.* Oxford: Oxford University Press.

Gordon, R. 1990. "Religion in the Roman Empire: the Civic Compromise and its Limits." In *Pagan Priests. Religion and Power in the Ancient World,* edited by M. Beard and J. North, 235-255. London: Duckworth.

Gosden, C. 2001. "Post-colonial in Archaeology: Issues of Culture, Identity and Knowledge." In *Archaeological Theory Today,* edited by I. Hodder, 241-61. Cambridge: Cambridge University Press.

Goux, J-J. 1990. *Symbolic Economies: After Marx and Freud.* Translated by J. Gage. Ithaca: Cornell University Press.

Graf, D. 1992. "Hellenisation and the Decapolis." *ARAM Society for Syro-Mesopotamian Studies* 4:1-48.

Graf, D. 1994. "The Nabataean Army and the Cohortes Ulpiae Petraeorum." In *The Roman and Byzantine Army in the East*, edited by E. Dabrowa, 265-311. Kraków: Drukarnia Uniwersytetu Jagiellońskiego.

Grainger, J. 1992. *Hellenistic Phoenicia*. New York: Oxford University Press.

Grant, M. 1984. *The History of Ancient Israel*. New York: Charles Scribner's Sons.

Gray, J. 1949. "The Canaanite God Horon." *Journal of Near Eastern Studies* 8 (1): 27-34.

Gray, J. 1964. *The Canaanites. Ancient Peoples and Places Series*. New York: Frederick A. Praeger Publishers.

Gray, R. 1996. "Buying into Signs: Money and Semiosis in Eighteenth-Century German Language Theory." *The German Quarterly* 69 (1): 1-14.

Green, A. 2003. *The Storm-God in the Ancient Near East*. Winona Lake: Eisenbrauns.

Green, P. 1996. *The Greco-Persian Wars*. Los Angeles: University of California Press.

Große, J. 1999. "Reading History: On Jacob Burckhardt as Source-Reader." *Journal of the History of Ideas* 60: 525-47.

Gruen, E. 2005. *Cultural Borrowings and Ethnic Appropriations in Antiquity*. Stuttgart: F. Steiner.

Guarducci, M. 1967. *Epigrafia Greca*. Rome: Istituto Poligrafico dello Stato.

Guerra, M. F. 1995. "Elemental Analysis of Coins and Glasses." *Applied Radiation and Isotopes* 46 (6-7): 583-588.

Gury F. 1986. "Dioskouroi/*Castores*." LIMC III: 608-635. Zurich-Munchen.

Hackett, J. A. 1989. "Can a Sexist Model Liberate Us? Ancient near Eastern 'Fertility' Goddesses." *Journal of Feminist Studies in Religion* 5 (1): 65-76.

Hall E. T. and D. M. Metcalf, eds. 1972. *Methods of Chemical and Metallurgical Investigation of Ancient Coinage*. London: Royal Numismatics Society, Special Publication No. 8.

Hall, J. 1997. *Ethnic Identity in Greek Antiquity*. Cambridge: Cambridge University Press.

Hall, J. 2002. *Hellenicity. Between Ethnicity and Culture*. Chicago: University of Chicago Press.

Hall, J. 2003. "Culture or Cultures? Hellenism in the Late Sixth Century." In *The Cultures within Ancient Greek Culture: Contact, Conflict, Collaboration*, edited by C. Dougherty and L. Kurke, 23-34. Cambridge: Cambridge University Press.

Hall, J. 2004a. "How Greek Were the Early Western Greeks?" In *Greek Identity in the Western Mediterranean*, edited by K. Lomas, 35-54. Leiden: Brill Academic Press.

Hall, J. 2004b. "Culture, Cultures and Acculturation." In *Griechische Archaik: Interne Entwicklungen – Externe Impulse*, edited by R. Rollinger and C. Ulf, 5-50. Innsbruck: Akademie Verlag.

Hamburger, H. 1955 "Minute Coins from Caesarea." *Atiqot*, English series 1: 115-38.

Hamburger, H. 1968 "Gems from Caesarea Maritima." *Atiqot*, English series 8: 1-38.

Hamburger, H.. 1971. "The Coins Issue of the Roman Administration from the Mint of Caesarea." *Israel Exploration Journal* 21: 81- 91.

Hammond, M. 1957. " Imperial Elements in the Formula of the Roman Emperors during the first two and a half Century of the Empire." *Memoirs of the Academy in Rome* 25: 19-64.

Handler, S. 1971. "Architecture on the Roman Coins of Alexandria." *American Journal of Archaeology* 75 (1): 57-74.

Hanson, A. 2003. *Meaning in Culture*. New York: Routledge.

Hardy, H. G. 1911. *Six Roman Laws*. Oxford: The Clarendon Press.

Harl, K. 1987. *Civic Coins and Civic Politics in the Roman East. A. D. 180-275*. Berkley: University of California Press.

Harl, K. 1990. *Coinage in the Roman Economy, 300 B.C. to A. D. 700*. Baltimore: The Johns Hopkins University Press.

Harland, P. 2003. "Imperial Cults within Local Cultural Life: Associations in Roman Asia." Zeitschrift für Alte Geschichte 17: 85-107.

Harris, JW. 1989. *Ancient Literacy*. Cambridge, Ma: Harvard University Press.

Harrison, H.1996. *Pistoles/Paroles: Money and Language in Seventeenth-Century French Comedy*. Charlottesville, VA: Rookwood Press.

Hartog, F. 1998. *The Mirror of Herodotus: The Representation of the Other in the Writing of History*. Berkeley, CA: University of California at Berkeley.

Hasenmueller, C. 1978. "Panofsky, Iconography, and Semiotics." *The Journal of Aesthetics and Art Criticism* 36 (3): 289-301.

Haverfield, F. 1923. *The Romanization of Roman Britain*, 4th ed. Oxford: Clarendon Press.

Hawadi, S. 1970. *Village Statistics, 1945: A classification of Land and Area Ownership in Palestine*. Beirut: Palestine Liberation Organization Research Center.

Hazzard, R. 1995. "Theos Epiphanes: Crisis and Response." *The Harvard Theological Review* 88 (4): 415-436.

Head, B. 1887. *Historia Numorum: A Manual of Greek Numismatics*. Oxford: Clarendon Press.

Heckster, O. 2003. " Coins and Messages. Audience Targeting on Coins of Different Denominations." In *The Representation and Perception of Roman Imperial Power: Proceedings of the Third Workshop of the International Network Impact of Empire*, edited by L. de Bois, 20-35. Amsterdam: Brill Academic Publishers.

Hedlund, R. 2008. "...Achieved Nothing Worthy of Memory". Coinage and Authority in the Roman Empire c. AD 260-295. Uppsala: Uppsala Universitet.

Helleiner, F. 1998. "National Currencies and National Identities." *American Behavioral Scientist* 41 (10): 1409-36.

Hendin D. and I. Shachar. 2008. "The Identity of YNTN on Hasmonean Overstruck Coins and the Chronology of the Alexander Jannaeus Types." *Israel Numismatic Research* 3:87-94.

Hengel, M.. 1980. *Jews, Greeks, and Barbarians: Aspects of the Hellenization of Judaism in the Pre-Christian Period.* Translated by John Bowden. Philadelphia: Fortress Press.

Henig, M. 1970. "The Veneration of Heroes in the Roman Army: The Evidence of Engraved Gemstones." *Britannia* 1: 249-265.

Henrichs, A. 1984. "Loss of Self, Suffering, Violence: The Modern View of Dionysus from Nietzsche to Girard." *Harvard Studies in Classical Philology* 88: 205-240.

Hermary, A. 1986. "Dioskouroi." LIMC III: 567–93. Zurich-Munchen.

Heuchert, V. 2004."The Chronological Development of Roman Provincial Coin Iconography." In *Coinage and Identity in the Roman Provinces*, edited by C. Howgego, V. Heuchert and A. Burnett, 143-156. Oxford: Oxford University Press.

Hides, S. 1996. "The Genealogy of Material Culture and Cultural Identity." In *Cultural Identity and Archaeology: The Construction of European Communities*, edited by P. Graves-Brown, S. Jones, and C. Gamble, 25-61. New York: Routledge.

Hiesinger, U.W. 1969. "Julia Domna: Two Portraits in Bronze." *American Journal of Archaeology* 73 (1): 39-44.

Hill, G. 1910. *Catalogue of the Greek Coins of Phoenicia.* London: British Museum.

Hodder, I. 1982. *Symbols in Action. Ethnoarchaeological Studies Of Material Culture.* Cambridge: Cambridge University Press.

Hodder, I. 1987. *The Archaeology of Contextual Meanings.* Cambridge: Cambridge University Press.

Hodder, I. 1999. *The Archaeological Process. An Introduction.* Oxford: Wiley-Blackwell.

Hodder, I. and S. Hutson. 2004. *Reading the Past: Current Approaches to Interpretation in Archaeology.* 3rd ed. Cambridge: Cambridge University Press.

Hodos, T. 2006. *Local Responses to Colonization in the Iron Age Mediterranean.* Abingdon: Routledge.

Hohlfelder, R. 1984. "Caesarea Maritima in Late Antiquity: An Introduction to the Numismatic Evidence." In *Ancient Coins of the Graeco-Roman World*, edited by W. Heckel and R. Sullivan, 261-85. Waterloo, Ontario: Wilfrid Laurier University Press.

Hohlfelder, R., J. P. Oleson, A. Raban, and R. Lindley Vann. 1992. "Hadrian and Caesarea: An Episode in the Romanization of Palestine." *Ancient World* 23: 51-61.

Holdcroft, D. 1991. *Saussure: Signs, System, and Arbitrariness.* Cambridge: Cambridge University Press.

Hölscher, T. 1971. *Ideal und Wirklichkeit in den Bildnissen Alexanders des Grossen.* Heidelberg: Heidelberg AWA.

Hölscher, T. 1980. "Die Geschichtsauffassung in der Römischen Repräsentationskunst." *Jahrbuch des Deutschen Archäologischen Instituts* 95: 265-321.

Hölscher, T. 1987. *Römische Bildsprache als semantisches System. Vorgetragen am 16. Juni 1984.* Heidelberg: C. Winter.

Hölscher, T. 2003. "Images of War in Greece and Rome: between Military Practice, Public Memory, and Cultural Symbolism." *Journal of Roman Studies* 93: 1-17.

Hölscher, T. 2004. *The language of Images in Roman Art.* Translated by A. Snodgrass and A. Künzl-Snodgrass. Cambridge: Cambridge University Press.

Højte, J. M. 2000. "Imperial Visits as Occasion for the Erection of Portrait Statues?" *Zeitschrift für Papyrologie und Epigraphik* 133: 221-235.

Hopkins, K. 1980. "Taxes and Trade in the Roman Empire (200 B.C.–A.D. 400)." *Journal of Roman Studies* 70: 101-125.

Hornborg, A. 1999. "Money and the Semiotics of Ecosystem Dissolutions." *Journal of Material Culture* 4 (2): 143-162.

Horsley, G. 1999. *The Rider God Steles at Burdur Museum in Turkey.* Armidale, N.S.W., Australia: The University of New England Press.

Horster, M. 2003. "Multiple Portraits of the Roman Imperial Families in Provincial Coinage." *Proceedings of International Congress of Numismatics* 1: 863-865.

Howgego, C. 1985. *Greek Imperial Countermarks. Studies in the Provincial Coinage of the Roman Empire.* London: Royal Numismatic Society.

Howgego, C. 1990. "Why Did Ancient States Strike Coins?" *The Numismatic Chronicle* 150: 1- 25.

Howgego, C. 1994. "Coin circulation and the integration of the Roman economy." Journal of Roman archaeology 7: 5-21.

Howgego, C. 1995. *Ancient History from Coins.* London: Routledge.

Howgego, C., V. Heuchert and A. Burnett. eds. 2005. *Coinage and Identity in the Roman Provinces.* Oxford: Oxford University Press.

Hunt, J. 1993. "The Sign of the Object." In *History from Things: Essays on Material Culture*, edited by Steven Lubar & David Kingery, 293-298. Washington: Smithsonian Institution Press.

Huot, P. 1996. "The Emperor, the Army, and the Coinage: Four Quantitative Studies." M.A., diss., University of Ottawa.

Huskinson, J. 2000. *Experiencing Rome: Culture, Identity and Power in the Roman Empire.* New York: Routledge.

Ingham, G. 2006. *Concepts of Money: Interdisciplinary Perspectives from Economics, Sociology And Political Science.* Northampton, MA: Edward Elgar Publishing.

Irvine, J. and S. Gal. 2000. "Language Ideology and Linguistic Differentiation." In *Regimes of Language*, edited by P. V. Kroskrity, 35-84. Santa Fe, NM: School of American Research Press.

Isaac, B. 1998. "Ethnic Groups in Judea under Roman Rule." In *The Near East under Roman Rule: Selected Papers*, edited by B. Isaac, 257- 283. Leiden: Brill Academic Publishers.

Isaac, B. 2004. *The Invention of Racism in Classical Antiquity.* Princeton: Princeton University Press.

Isserlin, R. 1998. "A Spirit of Improvement? Marble and the Culture of Roman Britain." In *Cultural Identity in the Roman Empire*, edited by R. Laurence and J. Berry, 125-150. London: Routledge.

Jeffery, A. 1990. Reprint. *The Local Scripts of Archaic Greece: A Study of the Origin of the Greek Alphabet and Its Development from the Eighth to the Fifth Centuries B.C.* Oxford: Clarendon Press. Original Edition, Oxford, 1961.

Jenkins, G. K. 1967. "The Monetary Systems in the Early Hellenistic Time with Special Regard to the Economic Policy of the Ptolemaic Kings." In *International Numismatic Convention, Jerusalem 1963*, edited by A. Kindler, 53-72. Tel Aviv: Israel Numismatic Society.

Jenkins, G. 1990. *Ancient Greek Coins*. London: Seaby.

Jensen, L. 1963. "Royal Purple of Tyre." *Journal of Near Eastern Studies* 22 (2): 104-118.

Jidejian, N. 1969. *Tyre through the Ages*. Beirut: Dar El-Mashreq Publishers.

Johnston, A. 1974. "New Problems for Old: Konrad Kraft on Die-sharing in Asia Minor." *Numismatic Chronicle* 14: 203-207.

Johnston, A. 2007. *Greek Imperial Denominations, ca. 200-275: A Study of the Roman Provincial Bronze Coinages of Asia Minor.* London: Royal Numismatic Society.

Jones, A. 1956. "Numismatic and History." In *Essays in Roman Coinage Presented to Harold Mattingly*, edited by R. Carson and C. Sutherland, 13-33. London: Oxford University Press.

Jones, T.B. 1965. "Greek Imperial Coins." *The Voice of the Turtle* 4 (12): 295-301.

Jones, T.B. 1963. "A Numismatic Riddle: The So-Called Greek Imperials." *Proceedings of the American Philosophical Society* 107 (4): 308-347.

Jongeling, K. 2003. "Deos Deasque." In *Hamlet on a Hill: Semitic and Greek Studies Presented to Professor T. Muraoka on the Occasion of His Sixty-Fifth Birthday*, edited by M. Baasten and W. Van Peursen, 309-340. Dudly, MA: Peeters Publishers.

Kadman, L. 1957. *The Coins of Caesarea Maritima*. Tel-Aviv and Jerusalem: Schoken Publishing House.

Kadman, L. 1961. *The Coins of Akko Ptolemais. Corpus Nummorum Palaestinensium.* Vol 4. Tel-Aviv: Schocken.

Kadman, L. 1963. *Coins in Palestine throughout the Ages*. Tel Aviv: Lada'ath Publisher.

Kagan, D. 1982. "The Dates of the Earliest Coins." *American Journal of Archaeology* 86 (3): 343-360

Karmon, N. and E. Spanier. 1988. "Remains of a Purple Dye Industry Found at Tel Shiqmona." *Israel Exploration Journal* 38 (3): 184-186.

Karwiese, S. 1991. "The Artemisium Coin Hoard and the First Coins of Ephesus." *Revue Belge de Numismatique* 137:1-28.

Kasher, A. 1990. *Jews and Hellenistic Cities in Eretz-Israel*. Tübingen: Siebeck.

Keane, W. 2003. "Semiotics and the Social Analysis of Material Things." *Language and Communication* 23:409-423.

Keel, 0., and C. Uehlinger. 1998. *Gods, Goddesses, and Images of God in Ancient Israel.* Minneapolis: Fortress Press.

Keen, A. 1998. *Dynastic Lycia: A Political History of the Lycians and Their Relations With Foreign Powers. 545-362 B.C.* Leiden: Brill Academic Publishers.

Kennedy, D. 1999. "Greek, Roman and Native Cultures in the Roman Near East." In *The Roman and Byzantine Near East.* Vol. 2. *Some Recent Archaeological Research*, edited by J. H. Humphrey, 77-106. Portsmouth, RI: Journal of Roman Archaeology.

Kenrick, J. 1855. *Phoenicia.* London: B. Fellowes

Kent, J. 1993. "Coins Inscriptions and Language." In *The Later Roman Empire Today: Paper Given in Honour of Professor John Mann*, edited by D. Clark et al., 9-18. London: Institute of Archaeology.

Kenyon, K. 1970. "Some Aspects of the Impact of Rome on Palestine." *The Journal of the Royal Asiatic Society of Great Britain and Ireland* 2: 181-191.

Kertzer, D. I. 1988. *Ritual, Politics, and Power.* New Haven: Princeton University Press.

Ketner, K. and C. Kloesel, eds.1986. *Peirce, Semeiotic, and Pragmatism. Essays by Max H. Fisch.* Bloomington, IN: Indiana University Press.

Khalidi, W. 1992. *All That Remains: The Palestinian Villages Occupied and Depopulated by Israel in 1948.* Beirut: Institute for Palestine Studies.

Kindler, A. 1967. *The Patterns of Monetary Development in Phoenicia and Palestine in Antiquity.* Jerusalem: Israel Numismatic Society.

Kindler, A. 1974. *Coins of the Land of Israel: Collection of the Bank of Israel, a Catalogue.* Jerusalem: Keter Publishing House.

Kindler, A. 1982. "The Status of Cities in the Syro-Palestinian Area as Reflected by Their Coins." *Israel Numismatic Journal* 6-7: 79-87.

Kindler, A. and A. Stein. 1987. *A Bibliography of the City Coinage of Palestine: from the 2nd Century BC to the 3rd Century AD.* Oxford: British Archaeological Reports, 374.

King, C. 1999. "Roman Portraiture: Images of Power." In *Roman Coins and Public Life under the Empire*, edited by G. Paul and M. Ierardi, 123-136. Ann Arbor, MI: University of Michigan Press.

King, G., and R. Hedges. 1974. "An Analysis of some Third-Century Roman Coins for Surface Silvering and Silver Percentage of their Alloy." *Archaeometry* 16:2: 189-200.

King P., and E. Lawrence. 2001. *Life in Biblical Israel.* Louisville: Westminster John Knox Press.

Kingsley, S., and K. Raveh. 1994. "The Dor D Shipwreck and Holy Land Wine Trade." *International Journal of Nautical Archaeology* 23 (1): 1 – 12.

Kleiner, D. 2005. *Cleopatra and Rome.* Cambridge, MA: Harvard University Press.

Kleiner, F. 2006. *A History of Roman Art.* Belmont, CA: Wadsworth Publishing.

Kleiner, F. and S. Noe. 1977. *The Early Cistophoric Coinage.* New York: American Numismatic Society.

Klose, D. 2004. "Festivals and Games in the Cities of the East during the Roman Empire." In *Coinage and Identity in the Roman Provinces*, edited by C. Howgego, V. Heuchert and A. Burnett, 125-133. Oxford: Oxford University Press.

Knappett, C. 2005. *Thinking Through Material Culture: An Interdisciplinary Perspective*. Philadelphia: University of Pennsylvania Press.

Knight, R. 1892. *The Symbolical Language of Ancient Art and Mythology*. New York: J. W. Bouton.

Kraay, C. 1964. "Hoards, Small Change and the Origin of Coinage." *The Journal of Hellenic Studies* 84: 76-91.

Kraay C. 1976. *Archaic and Classical Greek Coins*. Berkeley, CA: University of California Press.

Kraft, K. 1972. *Das System der Kaiserzeitlichen Münzprägung in Kleinasien: Materialen und Entwürfe*. Berlin: Gebr. Mann.

Kreitzer, L. 1996. *Striking New Images: Roman Imperial Coinage and the New Testament World*. Sheffield, UK: Sheffield Academic Press.

Kroeber, A. 1945. "The Ancient Oikoumene as an Historic Culture Aggregate." *The Journal of the Royal Anthropological Institute of Great Britain and Ireland* 75 (1/2): 9-20.

Kuhn, A. 1974. *The Logic of Social Systems*. San Francisco: Jossey-Bass.

Kurke, L. 1999. *Coins, Bodies, Games, and Gold: The Politics of Meaning in Archaic Greece*. Princeton: Princeton University Press.

Kurke, L. 2003. *The Cultures within Ancient Greek Cultures*. Cambridge: Cambridge University Press.

Kushnir-Stein, A. 2008. "City Eras on Palestinian Coins." *In Coinage and Identity in the Roman Provinces*, edited by C. Howgego, V. Heuchert, and A. Burnett, 157-162. Oxford: Oxford University Press.

Langdon, S. 1930. "The Semitic Goddess of Fate, Fortuna-Tyche." *The Journal of the Royal Asiatic Society of Great Britain and Ireland* 1: 21-29.

Lash, W. 1996. "Iconography and Iconology." *The Grove Dictionary of Art* 15: 89-98.

Lauritis, B. 1998. "The Portraits of Julia Domna." *The Celator* 12 (1): 10-16.

Lendon, J. E. 2006. *Soldiers and Ghosts: A History of Battle in Classical Antiquity*. New Haven: Yale University Press.

Le Rider, G. 1986. "Les Alexandres d'Argent en Asie Mineure et dans l'Orient Séleucide au IIIe siècle a. J.C. (c. 275-c.225): Remarques sur le système monétaire des Séleucides et des Ptolémées." *Journal des Savants* 1: 3-57.

Le Rider, G. 1995. "La Politique Monétaire des Séleucides en Coelé Syrie et en Phénicie." *Bulletin de Correspondance Hellénique* 119: 391-404.

Le Rider, G. and F. de Callataÿ. 2006. *Les Séleucides et les Ptolémées : L'Héritage Monétaire et Financier d'Alexandre le Grand*. Paris: Editions du Rocher.

Le Rider, G., C. M. Kraay, O. Mørkholm, eds. 1985. *Kraay-Mørkholm Essay. Numismatic Studies in Memory of C. M. Kraay and O. Mørkholm*. Louvain-La-Neuve: Institut Supérieur d'Archéologie et d'Histoire de l'Art.

Learsi, R. 1949. *Israel, A History of the Jewish People*. Cleveland and New York: The World Publishing Company.

Leick, G. 2002. *The Babylonians: An Introduction*. New York: Routledge.

Lele, V. 2006. "Material Habits, Identity, Semeiotic." Journal of Social Archaeology 6: 48-70.

Leverton, D. 1966. Architectura Numismatica. Ancient Architecture on Greek and Roman Coins and Medals. Chicago: Argonaut Publishers.

Levick, B. 1982. "Propaganda and Imperial Coinage." *Antichthon* 16:104-116.

Levick B. 1999. "Message on the Roman Coinage: Types and Inscriptions." In *Roman Coins and Public Life under the Empire: E. Togo Salmon*, edited by G. Paul and M. Ierardi, 41- 49. Ann Arbor: University of Michigan Press.

Levine, L. 1974 "The Jewish-Greek Conflict in First-Century Caesarea." *Journal of Jewish Studies* 25: 381-97.

Levine, L.. 1975. *Caesarea Under Roman Rule*. Leiden: Brill Academic Publishers.

Levine, L. 1998. *Judaism and Hellenism in Antiquity: Conflict or Confluence?* Seattle: University of Washington Press.

Lévi-Strauss, C. 1976. *Structural Anthropology*. 1st ed. New York: Basic Books Inc.

Lévi-Strauss, C. 1979. *Myth and Meaning*. New York: Schocken Books.

Lévi-Strauss, C. 1987. *Introduction to the Work of Marcel Mauss; translated by Felicity Baker*. London : Routlege & Kegan Paul.

Lewis, D. M. "Public Property in the City." In *The Greek City from Homer to Alexander,* edited by S. Price, 245-263. Oxford: Clarendon Press.

Lieu, J., J. North, and T. Rajak, eds. 1992. *The Jews Among Pagans and Christians in the Roman Empire*. New York: Routledge.

Lightfoot, C. 1990. "Trajan's Parthian War and the Fourth-Century Perspective." *The Journal of Roman Studies* 80: 115-126.

Lissarrague, F. 2001. *Greek Vases: The Athenians and their Images*. Translated by K. Allen. New York: Riverside Book Company.

Lissarrague, F. 2007. "Looking at Shield Devices: Tragedy and Vase Painting" In *Visualizing the Tragic. Drama, Myth, and Ritual in Greek Art and Literature. Essays in Honour of Froma Zeitlin*, edited by C. Kraus et al., 151-164. Oxford: Oxford University Press.

Littman, R.J. 1995. "Athens, Persia, and the Book of Ezra." *Transactions of the American Philological Association* 125:251-59

Littman, R. J. 2001. "Dor and the Athenian Empire." *American Journal of Ancient History* 15: 155-176.

Lo Cascio, E. 1981. "State and Coinage in the Late Republic and Early Empire." *Journal of Roman Studies* 71: 76-86.

MacDonald, W. 1986. *The Architecture of the Roman Empire*. Vol 2, *An Urban Appraisal*. New Haven: Yale University Press.

MacCormack. 1975. "Roma, Constantinopolis, the Emperor, and His Genius." *The Classical Quarterly* 25 (1): 131-150.

MacMullen, R. 1968. "Rural Romanization." *Phoenix* 22: 337-341.

MacMullen, R. 1984. "Notes on Romanization." *Bulletin of the American Society of Papyrologists* 21: 161-177.

MacMullen, R. 2000. *Romanization in the Time of Augustus*. New Haven and London: Yale University Press.

Madden, F. 1976. *Coins of the Jews*. New York: Olms Verlag. Original edition, London:

Trübner & Co., 1881.

Maineke, A. 2010. Reprint. *Analecta Alexandrina*. Whitefish, MT: Kessinger Publishing LLC. Original Edition, Berolini (Berlin): Sumptibus Th. Chr. Fr. Enslini, 1843.

Mairs, R. 2012. Hellenization. In *The Encyclopedia of Ancient History, First Edition,* edited by R. Bagnall, K. Brodersen, C. Champion, A. Erskine, S. Huebner, 144. Oxford: Blackwell Publishing Ltd.

Maisler (Mazar) B. 1946. "Canaan and the Canaanites." *Bulletin of the American Schools of Oriental Research* 102: 7-12

Manders, E. 2002. "Mapping the Representation of Roman Imperial Power in Times of Crisis." In *Crisis and the Roman Empire,* edited by O. Hekster, 275 -290. Leiden: Brill Academic Publishers.

Mart, Y., and I. Percman. 1996. "Neotectonic Activity in Caesarea and the Mediterranean Coast of Central Israel." *Tectonophysics* 254 (1-2): 139-153.

Martin, R. 2007. "Hellenization" and Southern Phoenicia: Reconsidering the Impact of Greece before Alexander." Ph.D. diss., University of California.

Martin, T. 1985. *Sovereignty and Coinage in Classical Greece*. Princeton: Princeton University Press.

Martin, T. 1996. "Why Did the Greek '*Polis*' Originally Need Coins?" *Historia: Zeitschrift für Alte Geschichte* 45 (3): 257-283.

Martini, R. 1991. *Monetazione Provinciale Romana. Prontuario delle Zecche Provinciali*. Milano: Edizioni Ennerre.

Mastino, A. 1981. *Le Titolature di Caracalla e Geta Attraverso le Iscrizioni*. Bologna: Editrice Clueb.

Mattingly, D. 1996. "From One Colonialism to Another: Imperialism and the Maghreb." In *Roman Imperialism, Post-Colonial Perspectives*, edited by J. Webster and N. Cooper, 49-69. Leicester: School of Archaeological Studies.

Mattingly, D. 2004. "Being Roman. Expressing Identity in a Provincial Setting." *Journal of Roman Archaeology* 17: 5 - 25.

Mattingly, H. 1921. "The Mints of the Empire: Vespasian to Diocletian." *The Journal of Roman Studies* 11: 254-264.

Mattingly, H. B. 1997. "The Date and Significance of the Lex Antonia De Termessibus." *Scholia* 6: 68-78.

Mattingly, H. B. 1977. "Coinage and the Roman State." *Numismatic Chronicle* 17: 199-201.

Mattingly, H. B. 2004. *From Coins to History: Selected Numismatic Studies*. Ann Harbor: University of Michigan Press.

Mauss, M. 1931. *Instructions Summaires Pour Les Collectuers d'Objets Ethnographiques*. Paris: Musée d'Ethnographie Trocadéro.

Ma'zov, Z. U. 2008. "Ships on Roman Provincial Coins in the Southern Levant: Voyages on the River Styx." *Israel Numismatic Research* 3: 147-162.

Mazza, F. 1988. "The Phoenician as seen by the Ancient World." In *The Phoenicians,* edited by S. Moscati, 548- 567. Milan: Bompiani.

McGuire, R. 1992. *A Marxist Archaeology*. San Diego: Academic Press.

Meadows, A. 2001. "Money, Freedom, and Empire in the Hellenistic World." In *Money and Its Uses in the Ancient Greek World*, edited by A. Medows and K. Shipton, 53-64. Oxford: Oxford University Press.

Meadows, A. and K. Shipton, eds. 2001. *Money and Its Uses in the Ancient Greek World*. Oxford: Oxford University Press.

Meadows, A. and J. Williams. 2001. "Moneta and the Monuments: Coinage and Politics in Republican Rome. The Journal of Roman Studies 91: 27-49.

Meadows, A. and J. Williams. 2007. "Coinage." In *The Edinburgh Companion to Ancient Greece and Rome*, edited by E. Bispham, T. Harrison, and B. Sparks, 173-182. Edinburgh: Edinburgh University Press.

Meischner, J. 1967. *Das Frauenporträt der Severerzeit*. Berlin: Ernst-Reuter-Gesellschaft.

Menger, C. 1892. "On the Origin of Money." *Economic Journal* 2: 239-255.

Meshorer, Y. 1967. *Jewish Coins of the Second Temple Period*. Tel Aviv: Am Hassefer.

Meshorer, Y. 1982. *Ancient Jewish Coinage. 2 Vols*. New York: Amphora Books.

Meshorer, Y. 1985. *City Coins of Eretz-Israel and the Decapolis in the Roman Period*. Jerusalem: The Book Gallery.

Meshorer, Y. 1995a. "Coins from Areas A and C." *In Qedem Reports: Excavation at Dor,* vol. 2b, edited by E. Stern, 461-472. Jerusalem: The Institute of Archaeology of the Hebrew University.

Meshorer, Y. 1995b. "The Coins of the Mint of Dora." In *Qedem Report: Excavation at Dor.* Vol 1a, edited by Y. Stern and J. Berg, 355-365. Jerusalem: The Institute of Archaeology of the Hebrew University.

Meshorer, Y. 1996. "Coins from Areas A and C." In *Qedem Reports. Excavation at Dor: Final Report.* Vol. 1b, *Areas A and C: the Finds,* edited by E. Stern, 355-372. Jerusalem: The Institute of Archaeology.

Meshorer, Y. 2001. *A Treasury of Jewish Coins from the Persian Period to Bar-Kochba*. Jerusalem: Yad Ben-Zvi Press.

Metcalf, W. 1975. "The Tell Kalak Hoard and Trajan's Arabian Mint." *American Numismatic Society Museum Notes* 20:104.

Meyer, E. 1999. Review of Asylia: *Territorial Inviolability in the Hellenistic World*, by J. Rigsby, *American Journal of Philology* 120 (3): 460-464.

Migliorati, G. 2003. *Cassio Dione e l'Impero Romano da Nerva ad Antonino Pio: alla Luce dei Nuovi Documenti.* Milano: Università Cattolica del Sacro Cuore.

Millar, F. 1983. "The Phoenician Cities: A Case Study of Hellenisation." *Proceedings of the Cambridge Philological Society* 209 (3): 55-71.

Millar, F. 1990. "The Roman *Coloniae* of the Near East: A Study of Cultural Relations." In *Roman Eastern Policy and Other Studies in Roman History*, edited by H. Solin and M. Kajava, 1-23. Helsinki: Finnish Society of Science and Letters.

Millar, F. 1993. The Roman Near East: 31 BC- AD 337. Cambridge, MA: Harvard University Press.

Millar, F. 2002. *Rome, The Greek World, and the East.* Vol. 1, *The Roman Republic and the Augustan Revolution.* Chapel Hill: University of North Carolina Press

Miller, J. 1965. "Living Systems: Basic Concepts." *Behavioral Science* 10 (3): 193-237.

Miller, J. 1986. *A History of Ancient Israel and Judah.* 1st ed. Philadelphia: Westminster John Knox Press.

Miller, M.C. 1997. *Athens and Persia in the Fifth Century B.C.: A Study in Cultural Receptivity.* Cambridge: Cambridge University Press.

Mionnet, T. E. 1807-1837. *Description de Médailles Antiques Grecques et Romaines.* 15 Vols. Paris.

Mitchell, S. 1995. *Anatolia: Land, Men, and Gods in Asia Minor.* Vol. 1, *The Celts and the Impact of Roman Rule.* Oxford: Oxford University Press.

Modood, T., and P. Werbner, eds. 1997. *The Politics of Multiculturalism in the New Europe: Racism, Identity and Community.* London: Zed Books.

Moggi, M. 2007. "La polis e le altre organizzazioni politico-territoriali: formazione e sviluppi." In *Storia d'Europa e del Mediterraneo*, Vol. 3, edited by M. Giangiulio, 93-130. Roma: Bompiani.

Momigliano, A. 1970. "J.G. Droysen. Between Greek and Jews." *History and Theory* 9 (2):139-53.

Momigliano, A. 1975. *Alien Wisdom: The Limits of Hellenization.* Cambridge: Cambridge University Press.

Mommsen, T. 1996. A History of Rome under the Emperors. *Based on the Lecture Notes of Sebastian and Paul Hensel, 1882-6.* Translated by C. Krojzl. Edited, with the Addition of a New Chapter by T. Wiedemann. London: Routledge.

Montalbano, F. 1951. "Canaanite Dagan: Origin, Nature*."* *Catholic Biblical Quarterly* 13: 381-397.

Mørkholm, O. 1965. "The Municipal Coinage with Portraits of Antiochus IV of Syria." In *Congresso Internazionale di Numismatica, Roma 11-16 Settembre* 1961: 63-7. Rome: Istituto Italiano di Numismatica.

Mørkholm, O. 1967. "The Monetary System of the Seleucid Kings until 129 BC." In *The Patterns of Monetary Development in Phoenicia and Palestine in Antiquity,* edited by A. Kindler, 82-6. Tel Aviv: Schocken.

Mørkholm, O. 1980. "A Group of Ptolemaic Coins from Phoenicia and Palestine." *Israel Numismatic Journal* 4: 4-7.

Mørkholm, O. 1981. "Some Coins of Ptolemy V from Palestine." *Israel Numismatic Journal* 5: 5-10.

Mørkholm, O. 1982. "Some Reflections on the Production and Use of Coinage in Ancient Greece." *Historia: Zeitschrift für Alte Geschichte* 31 (3): 290-305.

Mørkholm, O. 1985. "The Monetary System of the Seleucid Empire after 187 BC." In *Ancient Coins of the Graeco-Roman World: The Nickle Numismatic Papers*, edited by W. Heckel and R. Sullivans, 93-113. Waterloo, ON: Wilfrid Laurier University Press.

Mørkholm, O. 1991. *Early Hellenistic Coinage. From the Accession of Alexander to the Pease of Apamea (336-188 BC).* Cambridge: Cambridge University Press.

Morris, B. 1994. *1948 and After: Israel and the Palestinians.* Oxford: Oxford University Press.

Moscatti, S.1968. *The World of the Phoenicians.* New York: Frederick A. Praeger.

Motta, R. 2010. Greek and Roman Coins of Tel Dor: A Study of Material Culture and Cultural Identity. Ph.D. diss., University of Virginia.

Motta, R. 2011. "Zeus on Dora's Coins." *Israel Numismatic Research* 6: 79-92.

Müller, V. 1941. "The Date of the Augustus from Prima Porta." *The American Journal of Philology* 62 (4): 496-499.

Murray, O. 1993. *Early Greece.* 2nd ed. Cambridge: Harvard University Press.

Murray, O. 1999. Introduction to *The Greeks and Greek Civilization*, by Jacob Burckhardt, ix-xxi. New York: St. Martin's Press.

Mylonopoulos, J. 2009. *Divine Images and Human Imaginations in Ancient Greece and Rome.* Leiden: Brill.

Newell, E. T. 1937. *Royal Greek Portrait Coins.* New York: Wayte Raymond.

Newell, T. 2010. Reprint. *The Seleucid Mint of Antioch.* Whitefish, MT: Kessinger Publishing, LLC . Original edition, New York: The American Journal of Numismatics, 1915.

Newton, D. 2006. "Found Coins as Indicators of Coins in Circulation: Testing Some Assumptions." *European Journal of Archaeology* 9 (2-3): 211-227.

Nilsson, M. 1948. *Greek Piety.* Oxford: Oxford University Press.

Nilsson, M. 19161. *Geschichte der Griechischen Religion*, 2nd ed. Munich: Bech.

Nitschke, J., R. S. Martin and Y. Shalev. 2011. "Between the Carmel and the Sea – Tel Dor: The Later Periods." *Near Eastern Archaeology* 74:132-54.

Nitschke, J.L. 2013. "Interculturality in Image and Cult in the Hellenistic East: Tyrian Melqart Revisited." In *Shifting Social Imaginaries in the Hellenistic Period: Narrations, Practices, and Images*, edited by E. Stavrianopoulou, 253-282. Leiden, Boston: Brill.

Nock, A. 1947. "The Emperor's Divine Comes." *The Journal of Roman Studies* 37: 102-116.

Nodelman, S. 1965. Severan Imperial Portraiture, AD 193-217. Ph.D. diss., Yale University.

Nodelman, S. 1982. "A Portrait of the Empress Plautilla." *The J. Paul Getty Museum Journal* 10: 105-120.

Notley, R. and Z. Safrai. 2005. *Eusebius, Onomasticon. The Place Names of Divine Scripture.* Boston and Leiden: Brill.

O'Driscoll, G. 1986. "*Money:* Menger's Evolutionary Theory." History of Political Economy 18 (4): 601-616.

Opper, T. 2008. *Hadrian: Empire and Conflict.* Cambridge, MA: Harvard University Press.

Oppert, J. 1877. "Inscription on the Sarcophagus of King Eshmunazar." In *Records of the Past. Being English Translations of the Assyrian and Egyptian Monuments.* Vol. 9, 109-114. London: Samuel Bagster and Sons.

Orlinsky H. 1981. *Israel Exploration Journal Reader.* New York: Ktav Publishing House.

Orni, E and E. Efrat. 1971. *Geography of Israel.* Philadelphia: The Jewish Publication Society of America.

Ortner, S. 1984. "Theory in Anthropology since the Sixties." *Comparative Studies in History and Society* 26: 126-66.

Osborne, R.1997. "Early Greek Colonization? The Nature of Greek Settlement in the West." In *Archaic Greece: New Approaches and New Evidence*, edited by N. Fisher and H.Van Wees, 251-69. London: Duckworth

Panofsky, E. 1939. *Studies in Iconology.* New York: Oxford University Press.

Panofsky, E. 1982. *Meaning in the Visual Art.* Chicago: University of Chicago Press.

Parker, H. 1966. *A History of the Roman World from A.D. 138 to 337.* London: Methuens & Co. Ltd.

Parker, K. 1998. *The Continuity of Peirce's Thought.* Nashville: Vanderbilt University Press.

Parra, M. C. 1978. "A Proposito di un Rilievo con Statua di Silvano (Leptis Magna)." *Mélanges de l'Ecole Française de Rome. Antiquité* 90 (90-2): 807-828.

Paul, G. and M. Ierardi, eds. 1999. *Roman Coins and Public Life under the Empire: E. Togo Salmon Papers II.* Ann Arbor: University of Michigan Press.

Pearce, S. 1986. "Objects as Signs and Symbols." *Museums Journal* 85: 131- 135.

Peckham, B. 1987. "Phoenicia and the Religion of Israel: the Epigraphic Evidence." In *Ancient Israelite Religion: Essays in Honor of Frank Moore Cross*, edited by P. D. Miller, Jr., D. Hanson, and S. McBride, 79-99. Philadelphia: Fortress Press.

Peirce, B. 1995. "Social Identity, Investment, and Language Learning. *TESOL Quarterly 29* (1): 9-31.

Petersen, W. 1925. "The Adnominal Genitive." *The American Journal of Philology* 46 (2): 128-160.

Petsas, P. 1978. "Some Pictures of Macedonian Riders as Prototypes of the Thracian Rider." *Pulpudeva* 2: 192-204.

Pike, K. 1967. "Etic and Emic Standpoints for The Description Of Behavior." In *Language and Thought: An Enduring Problem in Psychology*, edited by D. Hildum, 32-39. Princeton: D. Van Norstrand Company.

Pike, K. 1990. "On the Emics and Etics of Pike and Harris." In *Emics and Etics: The Insider/Outsider Debate*, edited by T. Headland, K. Pike and M. Harris, 28-47. Newbury Park: Sage.

Pike, K. 1993. *Talk, Thought and Thing: The Emic Road Toward Conscious Knowledge.* Dallas: Summer institute of Linguistics.

Pike, K. 1996. *The Mystery of Culture Contacts, Historical Reconstruction, and Text Analysis: An Emic Approach.* Washington DC: Georgetown University Press.

Polanyi, K. 1968. *Primitive, Archaic, and Modern Economies: Essays of Karl Polanyi* edited by G. Dalton. Garden City, NY: Beacon Press.

Pollini, J. 1984. "Damnatio Memoriae in Stone: Two Portraits of Nero Re-cut to Vespasian in American Museums." *American Journal of Archaeology* 88 (4): 547-555.

Pollini, J. 2005. "A Portrait of Caracalla from the Mellerio Collection and the Iconography of Caracalla and Geta." *Revue Archéologique* 1: 55-78.

Pollitt, J. 1986. *Art in the Hellenistic Age.* Cambridge: Cambridge University Press.

Pomeroy, S., S.M. Burstein, W. Donlan and J.Tolbert Roberts. 1988. *Ancient Greece: A Political, Social, and Cultural History.* Oxford: Oxford University Press.

Prag, J. 2006. Poenus Plane Est – But Who Were the 'Punickes'? *Papers of the British School at Rome* 74: 1-37.

Préaux, C. 1965. *Réflexions sur l'Entité Hellénistique.* Paris: Presses Universitaires De France.

Préaux, C. 1978. Le Monde Hellénistique. La Grèce Et L'orient *(323-141 Avant JC).* Paris: Presses Universitaires De France.

Preston, R. 2007. "Roman Question, Greek Answers: Plutarch and the Construction of Identity." In *Being Greek Under Rome: Cultural Identity, the Second Sophistic and the Development of Empire*, edited by S. Goldhill, 86-122. Cambridge: Cambridge University Press

Preucel, R. 2010. *Archaeological Semiotics.* Hoboken, NJ: Wiley-Blackwell.

Price, M. and B. Trell. 1977. *Coins and their Cities.* London: Friary Press Ltd.

Price, S. 1985. *Rituals and Power: the Roman Imperial Cult in Asia Minor.* Cambridge: Cambridge University Press.

Pritchard, J. 1969. *Ancient Near Eastern Texts Relating to the Old Testament.* Princeton: Princeton University Press.

Prown, J. 1982. "Mind in Matter, An introduction to Material Culture Theory and Method." *Winterthur Portfolio* 17 (1): 1-19.

Prown, J. 1990. "The Power of Things: The Role of Domestic Objects in the Presentation of Self." In *Beyond Goffman: Studies on Communication, Institution, and Social Interaction,* edited by S. Riggins, 341-367. New York: Mouton de Gruyter.

Prown, J. 1993. "The Truth of Material Culture: History or Fiction?" In *History from Things: Essays on Material Culture*, edited by S. Lubar & W. Kingery, 1-19. Washington: Smithsonian Institution Press.

Pucci Ben Zeev, M. 1998. *Jewish Rights in the Roman World. The Greek and Roman Documents Quoted by Josephus Flavius.* Leinen: Mohr Siebeck.

Qedar, S. 2002. "Tissaphernes at Dor?" *Israel Numismatic Journal* 14: 9-14.

Raban, A. 1988. "The Constructive Maritime Role of the Sea People in the Levant." In *Society and Economy in the Eastern Mediterranean (1500-1000 BC)*, edited by M. Helzer and E. Lipinski, 261-294. Leuven: Uitgeverij Peeters.

Raban, A. and K. Holum. 1996. *Caesarea Maritima: A Retrospective After Two Millennia*. Leiden: Brill Academics.

Raeder, J. 1992. "Herrscherbild und Munzpropaganda . Zur Deutung des Serapistypus des Septimius Severus." *Jahrbuch des Deutschen Archäologischen Instituts* 107: 175-196.

Raveh, K., and S. Kingsley. 1991. "The Status of Dor in Late Antiquity: A Maritime Perspective." *The Biblical Archaeologist* 54 (4): 198-207.

Ray, L. and J. Berry, eds. 1998. *Cultural Identity in the Roman Empire*. New York: Routledge.

Reece, R. 1988. "Interpreting Roman Hoards. *World Archaeology* 20 (2): 261-269.

Reece, R. 1993. "Coins as Minted and Coins as Found." *Acta Numismatica* 21-22: 57-62.

Reekmans, L. 1958. "La 'Dextrarum Iunctio' dans l'Iconographie Romaine et Paleochretienne." *Bulletin de l'Institut Historique Belge de Rome* 31: 69 – 73.

Renfrew, C. 1972. *The Emergence of Civilisation: The Cyclades and the Aegean in The Third Millennium BC*. London: Methuen and Co. Ltd.

Renfrew, C., 2001a. "Symbol Before Concept: Material Engagement and the Early Development of Society." In *Archaeological Theory Today*, edited by I. Hodder, 122-40. Cambridge: Polity Press.

Renfrew, C., 2001b. Commodification and institution in group-oriented and individualizing societies. *Proceedings of the British Academy* 110: 93-117.

Renfrew, C., 2003. *Figuring It Out: the Parallel Visions of Artists and Archaeologists*. London: Thames & Hudson.

Renfrew, C. 2004. "Towards a Theory of Material Engagement." In Rethinking Materiality: The Engagement of Mind with the Material World, edited by E. DeMarrais, C. Gosden, and C. Renfrew, 23-31. Cambridge: McDonald Institute for Archaeological Research.

Renfrew, C. and J. Cherry, eds. 1986. *Peer Polity Interactions and Socio-political Change*. Cambridge: Cambridge University Press.

Revell, L. 2009. *Roman Imperialism and Local Identities*. Cambridge: Cambridge University Press.

Riccardi, L. A. 2000. "Uncanonical Imperial Portraits in the Eastern Roman Provinces: The Case of the Kanellopoulos Emperor." Hesperia 69 (1): 105-132.

Richter, G. 1940. "A Portrait of Caracalla." *The Metropolitan Museum of Art Bulletin* 35 (7): 139-142.

Rigsby, K. 1996. *Asylia: Territorial Inviolability in the Hellenistic World*. Berkley: University of California Press.

Ringel, J. 1988. "Literary Sources and Numismatic Evidence of Maritime Activity in Caesarea during the Roman Period." *Mediterranean Historical Review* 3 (1): 63-73.

Robb, J. 1998. "The Archaeology of Symbols." *Annual Review of Anthropology* 27: 329-46.

Robinson, E. 1951. "The Coins from the Ephesian Artemision Reconsidered." *Journal of Hellenic Studies* 71: 159.

Rodan, S. 2005. "Maritime Related Cults in the Coastal Cities of Philistia during the Roman Period: Legacy and Change." Ph.D. diss., University of Haifa.

Rogers, M. 1862. *Domestic Life in Palestine. Reprinted in 1989*. London: Kegan Paul International Limited.

Roller, D. 2010. *Cleopatra: A Biography*. Oxford: Oxford University Press.

Romanoff, P. 1943. "Jewish Symbols on Ancient Jewish Coins." The Jewish Quarterly Review 33 (4): 435-444.

Romm, J. 1992. *The Edges of the Earth in Ancient Thought: Geography, Exploration, and Fiction*. Princeton, NJ: Princeton University Press.

Rose, C. B. 1997a. *Dynastic Commemoration and Imperial Portraiture in the Julio-Claudian Period*. Cambridge: Cambridge University Press.

Rose, C. B. 1997b. "The Imperial Image in the Eastern Mediterranean." In *The Early Roman Empire in the East*, edited by S. Alcock, 108-120. Oxford: Oxford University Press.

Rosenberg, M. 1975. *The Rosenberg Israel Collection*. Vol. 2, *Caesarea, Diospolis, Dora, Eleutheropolis*. Jerusalem: Israel Numismatic Society.

Rothbard, M. 2009. *Man, Economy, and the State with Power and Market*. 2nd ed. Auburn, Ala: Ludwig von Mises Institute.

Rutherford, I. 2003. "Interference or Translationese? Some Patterns in Lycian-Greek Bilingualism." In *Bilingualism in Ancient Society: Language Contact and the Written Word*, edited by J. Adams, M. Janse and S. Swain. 197-245. Oxford: Oxford University Press.

Rutter, N. 1997. *Greek Coinages of Southern Italy and Sicily*. London: Spink & Son.

Sackett, J. 1977. "The Meaning of Style in Archaeology: A General Model." *American Antiquity* 42 (3): 369-380.

Sami H. 1970. *Village Statistics of 1945: A Classification of Land and Area Ownership in Palestine*. Beirut: Palestinian Liberation Organization Research Center.

Sartre, M. 2005. *The Middle East under Rome*. Cambridge, MA: Harvard University Press.

Saul, M. 2005. "The Circulation of Coins and The Roman Periphery." *Archaeological Dialogues* 12 (1): 31-34. Cambridge University Press

Saussure, F. 1998. Reprint. *Course in General Linguistics*. Translated by R. Harris. Chicago: Open Court Publishing. Original Edition, Paris: Payot, 1916.

Sayles, G. 1998. *Ancient Coin Collecting*. Vol. 4, *Roman Provincial Coins*. New York: Krause Publications.

Scarre, C. 1995. *Chronicle of the Roman Emperors*. New York: Thames and Hudson.

Schaps, D. 2004. *The Invention of Coinage and the Monetization of Ancient Greece*. Ann Harbor, MI: The University of Michigan Press.

Schlereth, T. 1983. "Material Culture Studies and Social History Research." *Journal of Social History* 16: 111-143.

Schlereth, T. 1991. "Material Culture or Material Life: Discipline or Field? Theory or Method?" In *Living in a Material World: Canadian and American Approaches to Material Culture,* edited by G. Pocius, 231-240. St. John's, Newfoundland: Institute of Social And Economic Research.

Schnapp, A. 1994. "Are Images Animated? The Psychology of Statues in Ancient Greece." In *The Ancient Mind: Elements of Cognitive Archaeology*, edited by C. Renfrew and E. Zubrow, 40-44. Cambridge: Cambridge University Press.

Schürer, E. 1979. *The History of the Jewish People in the Age of Jesus Christ*. Vol. 2. Edinburgh: T. & T. Clark Ltd.

Schwartz, D. 1992. *Studies in the Jewish Background of Christianity*. Tübingen: J.C.B. Mohr.

Scott, S and J. Webster. 2003. *Roman Imperialism and Provincial Art*. Cambridge: Cambridge University Press.

Scrinari, V. 1953-55. "Le Donne dei Severi nella Monetazione dell'Epoca." *Bullettino della Commissione Archeologica Comunale di Roma* 75: 117-135.

Sear, F. 1983. *Roman Architecture*. Ithaca, NY: Cornell University Press.

Sellwood, D.G. 1963. "Some Experiments in Greek Minting Technique." *The Numismatic Chronicle* 3: 217-231.

Seltman, C. 1933. *Greek Coins*. London: Methuen & Co., Ltd.

Seltman, C. 1949. *Masterpieces of Greek Coinage*. Oxford: Bruno Cassirer

Seltman, C. 1955. Greek Coins: *A History of Metallic Currency and Coinage Down to the Fall of the Hellenistic Kingdoms*. London: Methuen and Co. Ltd.

Sewell, W. 1999a. "The Concept of Culture(s)." "In *Beyond the Cultural Turn: New Directions in the Study of Society and Culture*, edited by V. Bonnell and L. Hunt, 35-61. Berkeley: University of California Press.

Sewell, W. 1999b. "Geertz, Cultural Systems, and History: from Synchrony to Transformation." In *The Fate of Culture: Geertz and Beyond*, edited by S. B. Ortner, 35-55. Berkley: University of California Press.

Seyrig, H. 1963. "Antiquités Syriennes." *Syria* 40: 19-28.

Seyrig, H. 1972. "La Tyché de Cesaree de Palestine." *Syria* 49: 112-115.

Shalev Y. and S. R. Matin, 2012. "Crisis and Opportunity: Phoenician Urban Renewal after the Babylonians. *Transeuphratène* 41: 81-100.

Shank, M. and C. Tilley. 1993. *Reconstructing Archaeology: Theory and Practice*. London: Routledge.

Sharon, I. 1987. "Phoenician and Greek Ashlar Construction Techniques at Tel Dor, Israel." *Bulletin of the American School of Oriental Research* 267: 21-42.

Sharon, I. 2009. "Ashlar Construction at Dor: Four Comments on the State of Research." *Eretz Israel* 29: 362-382 (Hebrew).

Shell, M. 1978. *The Economy of Literature*. Baltimore: John Hopkins University Press.

Sherwin-White, A. 1967. *Racial Prejudice in Imperial Rome*. Cambridge: Cambridge University Press.

Sherwin-White, A. N. 1973. *The Roman Citizenship*, 2nd ed. Oxford: Oxford University Press.

Shin, U. 1990. "Panofsky, Polanyi, and Intrinsic Meaning." *Journal of Aesthetic Education* 24 (4): 17-32.

Short, T. 2007. *Peirce's Theory of Signs*. Cambridge: Cambridge University Press.

Sigurdson, R. 2004. *Jacob Burckhardt's Social and Political Thought*. Toronto: University of Toronto Press.

Silberman, N. 1989. *Between Past and Present: Archaeology, Ideology, and Nationalism in the Modern Middle East*. 2nd ed. New York: Random House.

Singer, I. 1992. "Towards the Image of Dagon the God of the Philistines." *Syria* 69 (3/4): 431-450.

Small, J. P. 2003. *The Parallel Worlds of Classical* Art and Text. Cambridge: Cambridge University Press.

Smallwood, E. M. 1976. *The Jews under Roman rule: From Pompey to Diocletian*. Leiden: Brill Academic Publishers.

Smith, A. 2003, 18 January. "Athenian Political Art from the Fifth and Fourth Centuries BCE: Images of Political Personifications. " Dēmos: Classical Athenian Democracy. http://www.stoa.org.

Smith, R. 1999. "Cultural Choice and Political Identity in Honorific Portrait Statues in the Greek East in the Second Century A.D." *The Journal of Roman Studies* 88: 56-93.

Smith, M. S. 2002. *The Early History of God: Yahweh and the Other Deities in Ancient Israel*. 2nd ed. Grand Rapids, MI: William B. Eerdmans Pub.

Smith, R.R. 1987. "The Imperial Relief from the Sebasteion at Aphrodisias." *The Journal of Roman Studies* 77: 88-138.

Smith, T. J. 2003. "Black-Figure Vases in the Collection of the British School at Athens." *The Annual of the British School at Athens* 98: 347-368.

Smith, T. J. 1997. "Votive Reliefs from Balboura and Its Environs." *Anatolian Studies* 47: 3-49.

Schnapp, A. 1994. "Are Images Animated? The Psychology of Satues in Ancient Greece." In *The Ancient Mind: Elements of Cognitive Archaeology*, edited by C. Renfrew and E. Zubrow, 40-44. Cambridge: Cambridge University Press.

Snodgrass. A. 1986. "Interaction by Design: the Greek City State" In *Peer Polity Interactions and Socio-political Change*, edited by C. Renfrew and J. Cherry, 47-58. Cambridge: Cambridge University Press.

Sourvinou-Inwood, C. 1990. "What is Polis Religion?" In *The Greek City from Homer to Alexander*, edited by O Murray and S. Price, 295-322. Oxford: Clarendon Press.

Speidel, M. 1992. "Roman Army Pay Scales." *The Journal of Roman Studies* 82: 87-106.

Sperber, D. 1998. *The City in Roman Palestine*. Oxford: Oxford University Press.

Spolsky, B. 1999. "Second-language Learning." In *Handbook of Language and Ethnic Identity*, edited by J. Fishman, 181-192. Oxford: Oxford University Press.

Stanwick, E. P. 2002. *Portraits of the Ptolemies: Greek Kings as Egyptian Pharaohs*. Austin: University of Texas Press.

Starr, C. 1977. *The Economic and Social Growth of Early Greece 800-500 B.C.* New York and Oxford: Oxford University Press.

Starr, C. 1983. *The Expansion of the Greek World, Eight to Sixth Century B.C.* Cambridge: Harvard University Press.

Stazio, A. ed. 1993. *La Monetazione Ccorinzia in Occidente: Atti del IX Convegno del Centro internazionale di Studi Numismatici, Napoli, 27-28 ottobre 1988*. Rome: Istituto Italiano di Numismatica.

Stern, E. 1985. Dor, Tel - 1984. *Excavations and Surveys in Israel* 4: 21-24.

Stern, E.1989. "What Happened to the Cult Figures?" *Biblical Archaeological Review* 15 (4): 22-29, 53-54.

Stern, E. ed.. 1995a. *Qedem Report: Excavations at Dor, Final Report*. Vol. 1a, *Areas A and C: Introduction and Stratigraphy*. Jerusalem: Institute of Archaeology of the Hebrew University.

Stern, E. ed. 1995b. *Qedem Reports Excavations at Dor, Final Report*. Vol. 1b, *Areas A and C: The Finds*. Jerusalem: Institute of Archaeology of the Hebrew University.

Stern, E. 2000. *Dora, Ruler of the Sea*. Jerusalem: Israel Exploration Society.

Stern, E. 2006. "Goddesses and Cults at Tel Dor." In *Confronting the Past: Archaeological and Historical Essays on Ancient Israel in Honor of William G. Dever*, edited by S. Gitin, E. Wright and J. Dessel, 177-180. Winona Lake, IN: Eisenbrauns.

Stern, E. 2013. *The Material Culture of the Northern Sea People in Israel*. Winona Lake, IN: Eisenbrauns.

Stevenson, S. 1964. *A Dictionary of Roman Coins, Republican and Imperial*. London: B.A. Seaby Ltd.

Stewart, A. and Martin, R. S. 2005. "Attic Import Pottery at Tel Dor, Israel: An Overview." *Bulletin of the American Schools of Oriental Research* 337: 79-94.

Stinespring, W. 1939. "Hadrian in Palestine, 129/130 AD." *Journal of the American School of Oriental Society* 59 (3): 360-365.

Stocking, F. W. 1968. *Race, Culture and Evolution. Essays in the History of Anthropology*. New York: Free Press.

Storey, J., ed. 1998. *Cultural Theory and Popular Culture: A Reader*. Atlanta: University of Georgia Press.

Stuckey, J. H. 2002. "The Great Goddesses of the Levant." *Bulletin of the Canadian Society for Mesopotamian Studies* 37:27-48.

Sutherland, C. 1956. "The Intelligibility of Roman Imperial Coin Types." *The Journal of Roman Studies* 49: 46-55.

Sutherland. 1966. *RIC* Vol. VII. *From Constantine to Licinius. AD 313-337*. London: Spink and Son Ltd.

Sutherland, C. H. 1970. *The Cistophori of Augustus*. London: Royal Numismatic Society.

Sutherland, C. H. 1986. "Compliment or Complement? Dr. Levick on Imperial Coin Types." *The Royal Numismatic Society* 146: 85-93.

Syme, R. 1929. "The Argonautica of Valerius Flaccus." *The Classical Quarterly* 23 (3/4): 129-137.

Svoronos, J. N. 1926. *Les Monnaies d'Athènes*. Munich: F. Bruckmann.

Swain, S. 1998. *Hellenism and Empire: Language, Classicism, and Power in the Greek World, AD 50-250*. Oxford: Oxford University Press.

Swift, E. H. 1923. "Imagines in Imperial Portraiture." *American Journal of Archaeology* 27 (3): 286-301

Taylor, G. 1971. *The Roman Temples of Lebanon*. Beirut: Dar el-Machreq Publishers

Thomas, R. 2000. *Herodotus in Context: Ethnography, Science and the Art of Persuasion*. Cambridge: Cambridge University Press.

Thompson, C. 2003. "Sealed Silver in Iron Age Cisjordan and the 'Invention of Coinage.'" *Oxford Journal of Archeology* 22 (1): 67-107.

Thomson, W. 1859. *The Land And The Book: Or, Biblical Illustrations Drawn From The Manners And Customs, The Scenes And Scenery of The Holy Land*. New York: Harper & Brothers.

Tilley, C. 1991. "Interpreting Material Culture." In *The Meaning of Things: Material Culture and Symbolic Expression*, edited by Ian Hodder, 185-194. London: Routledge.

Tilley, C. 1999. *Metaphor and Material Culture*. Oxford: Blackwell.

Tod, M. 1945-7. "The Progress of Greek Epigraphy." *The Journal of Hellenic Studies* 67: 90-127.

Townsend, P. 1938. "The Significance of the Arch of the Severi at Lepcis." *American Journal of Archaeology* 42 (4): 512-524.

Trigger, B. 1980. *Gordon Childe: Revolution in Archaeology*. London: Thames and Hudson.

Tsetskhladze, G. 2006. *Greek Colonisation: an Account of Greek Colonies and Other Settlements Overseas*. Leiden: Brill Academic Publishers.

Tuck, S. 2005. "The Origins of Roman Imperial Hunting Imagery: Domitian and the Redefinition of *Virtus* under the Principate." *Greece and Rome* 52 (2): 221-245.

Tylor, E. 1920. *Primitive Culture*. New York: J.P. Putnam's Sons.

Vagi, D. 2000. *Coinage and History of the Roman Empire*. Vol. 1, *The History*. London : Fitzroy Dearborn.

Van Henten, J. 2005. "Cleopatra in Josephus: From Herod's Rival to the Wise Ruler's Opposite." In *The Wisdom of Egypt: Jewish, Early Christian, and Gnostic Essays in Honour of Gerard P. Luttikhuizen*, edited by A. Hilhorst and G.H. van Kooten, 113-132. Leiden: Brill Academic Publishers.

Van Straten, R. 1986. "Panofsky and Iconoclass." *Artibus et Historiae* 13: 165-181.

Varner, E. 2004. *Mutilation and Transformation: Damnatio Memoriae and Roman Imperial Portraiture*. Leiden: Brill Academic Publishers.

Vermeule, C. 1962. "Egyptian Contributions To Late Roman Imperial Portraiture." *Journal of the American Research Center in Egypt* 1: 63-68

Vermeule, C. 2002. "Roman Provincial Coins: the Statues in the Temples and Shrines." *Celator* 16 (1): 6-18.

Vila, P. 1999. "Constructing Social Identities in Transnational Contexts: The Case of the Mexico-US Border." *International Social Science Journal* 51 (159): 75-87.

Von Reden, S. 1995. *Exchange in Ancient Greece.* London: Duckworth.

Von Reden, S. 1997. "Money, Law, and Exchange: Coinage in the Greek Polis." *Journal of Hellenistic Studies* 117: 154-176.

Von Reden, S. 2001. "Monetization in Third-Century BC Egypt." In *Money and Its Uses in the Ancient Greek World*, edited by A. Meadows and K. Shipton, 65-76. Oxford: Oxford University Press.

Von Reden, S. 2002. "Money in the Ancient Economy. A Survey of Recent Research." *Klio* 84: 141-74.

Von Reden, S. 2007. *Money in Ptolemaic Egypt: from the Macedonian Conquest to the End of the Third Century BC.* Cambridge: Cambridge University Press.

Wailes, B., ed. 1996. *Craft Specialization and Social Evolution: In Memory of V. Gordon Childe.* Philadelphia: University of Pennsylvania Press.

Weiss, Z. 1996 "The Jews and the Games in Roman Caesarea." In *Caesarea Martima: A Retrospective After Two Millenia*, edited by A. Raban and K. Holum, 443-453. Leiden, New York: Brill.

Wallace, R. 1987. "The Origin of Electrum Coinage." *American Journal of Archeology* 91 (3): 385-397.

Wallace-Hadrill, A. 1981a. "Galba's Aequitas." *Numismatic Chronicle* 141: 20-39.

Wallace-Hadrill, A. 1981b. "The Emperor and his Virtues. *Historia, Zeitschrift für Alte Geschichte* 30 (3): 298-323.

Wallace-Hill, A. 1986. "Image and Authority in the Coinage of Augustus." *The Journal of Roman Studies* 76: 66-87.

Walter, C. 1979. "The *Dextrarum Junctio* of Leptis Magna in Relation to the Iconography of Marriage." *Antiquités Africaines* 14: 271-283.

Webster, J. 1997a. "A Negotiated Syncretism: Readings in the Development of Roman- Celtic Religion." In *Dialogues in Roman Imperialism: Power, Discourse, and Discrepant Experience in the Roman Empire*, edited by D. J. Mattingly, 165-184. Portsmouth, RI: Journal of Roman Archaeology.

Webster, J. 1997b. "Necessary Comparisons: A Post-Colonial Approach to Religious Syncretism in the Roman Provinces." *World Archaeology* 28 (3): 324-338.

Webster, J. 2001. "Creolizing the Roman Provinces." *American Journal of Archaeology* 105 (2): 209-225.

Webster, J. and N. Cooper. 1996. *Roman Imperialism, Post-Colonial Perspectives.* Leicester: School of Archaeological Studies.

Wegner, M. 1956. *Hadrian, Plotina, Marciana, Matidia, Sabina. Das Römische Herrscherbild.* Vol. 2, pt. 3. Berlin: Deutsches Archäologisches Institut.

Weiss, P. 2005. "The Cities and their Money." In *Coinage and Identity in the Roman Provinces*, edited by C. Howgego, V. Heuchert and A. Burnett, 57-68. Oxford: Oxford University Press.

Wells, P. 1999. *The Barbarians Speak. How the Conquered People Shaped Roman Europe.* Princeton: Princeton University Press.

Wennerling, C. 2001. "Money Talks, but What Is It Saying? Semiotics of Money and Social Control." *Journal of Economic Issues* 35 (3): 557-574.

Wessel, F. 1946-7. Römische Frauen-frisuren von der Severischen bis zur Konstantinischen Zeit." *Archäologischer Anzeiger* 61: 62-76.

Winter, I. 1995. "Homer's Phoenicians: History, Ethnography, or Literary Trope? (A Perspective on Early Orientalism)." In *The Age of Homer: A Tribute to Emily Townsend Vermeule*, edited by J.B. Carter and S. P. Morris, 247-71. Austin: University of Texas Press.

Whitmarsh, T. 2007. "Greece is the World: Exile and Identity in the Second Sophist." In *Being Greek under Rome: Cultural Identity, the Second Sophistic and the Development of Empire*, edited by S. Goldhill, 269-305. Cambridge: University of Cambridge Press.

Wittkower, C. 1955. " Interpretation of Visual Symbols in the Arts." In *Studies in Communication: Contributed to the Communication Research Centre, University College, London*, edited by I. Evans, 109-124. London: Secker & Warburg.

Whittaker, C. 1974 "The Western Phoenicians: Colonization and Assimilation." *Proceedings of the Cambridge Philological Society* 200: 58- 79.

Wittkower, R. 1978. *Idea and Image: Studies in the Italian Renaissance.* New York: Thames and Hudson.

Wood, S. 1997. *Roman Portrait Sculpture 217-260 A.D: The Transformation of an Artistic Tradition.* Leiden: Brill.

Wood , M. and F. Queiroga, eds. 1992. *Current Research on the Romanization of the Western Provinces.* Oxford: Oxford University Press.

Wolf, E. 1982. *Europe and the People Without History.* Berkley: University of California Press.

Woolard, K. and B. Schieffelin. 1994. "Language Ideology." *Annual Review of Anthropology* 23: 55 - 82.

Woolf, G. 1994. "Becoming Roman, Staying Greek: Culture, Identity and the Civilizing Process in the Roman East." *Proceedings of the Cambridge Philological Society* 40:116-43

Woolf, G. 1997. "Polis-Religion and Its Alternatives in The Roman Provinces." In *Römische Reichsreligion und Provinzialreligion*, edited by H. Cancik, and J. Rüpke, 71-84. Tübingen: Mohr Siebeck GmbH & Co.

Woolf, G. 1998. *Becoming Roman. The Origins of the Provincial Civilization in Gaul.* Cambridge: Cambridge University Press.

Wyatt, N. 1980. "The Relationship of the Deities Dagan and Hadad." *Ugarit-Forschungen* 12:375-379.

Young, R. 1995. *Colonial Desire: Hybridity in Theory, Culture and Race.* London: Routledge.

Zangemeister, K. 1890. "Inschrift der Vespasianische Colonie Caesarea in Palestina." ZDPV - Deutscher Verein zur Erforschung Palästinas 13: 25-30.

Zanker, P. 1983. *Provinzielle* Kaiserporträts. Munich: Bayerische Akademie der Wissenschaften.

Zanker, P. 1988. *The Power of Images in the Age of Augustus.* Ann Arbor, MI: University of Michigan Press.

Zeitlin, F. 2001 "Visions and Revisions of Homer's." In *Being Greek Under Rome,* edited by S. Goldhill, 195-266. Cambridge: Cambridge University Press.

Ziegler, R. 1996. "Civic Coins and Imperial Campaigns." In *The Roman Army in the East,* edited by D.L. Kennedy, 119-227. Ann Arbor, MI: Journal of Roman Archaeology.

Coin Catalogue

205-199 BCE

1. Silver *tetradrachm*; 13.75 gr. Svoronos, No. 1262; Meshorer, No. 1; Israel Museum Jerusalem.
   Obv: Bust of Ptolemy V r., wearing royal diadem; dotted circle.
   Rev: Eagle standing l. on thunderbolt; ΠΤΟΛΕΜΑΙΟΥ ΒΑΣΙΛΕΩΣ; in l. field ΔΩ; dotted circle.

64/63 BCE = LA (year 1)

2. Bronze, 5.50 gr. Meshorer No. 4; Fichman Collection.
   Obv: Bust of Tyche r. laureate and veiled, wearing dangling earrings and necklace. Coin is slightly off flan.
   Rev: Prow of galley, l., Dioscuri caps above, and date *LA* on both side of caps; below ΔΩ.
3. Bronze, 10.00 gr. Meshorer No. 2; Fichman Collection.
   Obv: Bust of Zeus Doros, bearded, laureate, r.
   Rev: Tyche standing to l., holding palm branch with r. hand and caduceus with l. hand; date L A; in l. field ΔΩΡΙ/ΤΩΝ.
4. Bronze, 7.52 gr. Meshorer No. 3; Fichman Collection.
   Obv: Bust of Tyche r., laureate and veiled.
   Rev: Tyche standing l., resting her r. hand over tiller; holding cornucopia with l. hand; in field date *LA* and ΔΩ.
5. Bronze, 2.86 gr. Meshorer No. 5; Fichman Collection.
   Obv: Bust of Tyche, r., laureate and veiled.
   Rev: Ear of grain; date *LA*, and ΔΩ on two lines, with one letter on each field.
6. Bronze, 1.2 gr. Meshorer No. 8; attributed to 64/3 BCE; Fichman Collection.
   Obv: Bust of Tyche r., laureate and veiled.
   Rev: Bunch of grapes; the letters ΔΩ divided between the fields.

Undated

7. Bronze, 2.70 gr. Meshorer No. 10; undated; Fichman Collection.
   Obv: Bust of Tyche r., laureate and veiled.
   Rev: Bunch of grapes with stem and large vine leaf; ΔΩ PIT.

Conflicting Dates:

8. Bronze, 7.30 gr. Meshorer No. 11; *RPC* 4752; Israel Museum Jerusalem.
   Obv. Jugate busts of Antonius and Cleopatra (?) r.
   Rev: Tyche standing l., holding palm branch with r. hand and caduceus with l. hand; in l. field *L* ΘΙ ΔΩ.

34/33 BCE = L ΛΑ (year 31)

9. Bronze, 5.41 gr. Meshorer No. 12; *RPC* 4753; Sofaer Collection.
   Obv: Jugate bust of Antony and Cleopatra or Dioscuri, r. surrounded by wreath.
   Rev: Tyche standing l., holding rudder with her r. hand and cornucopia with l. hand; in r. field *LΛΑ*.

7/6 BCE = NZ (year 57)

10. Bronze, 9.91 gr. Meshorer No. 30; Israel Antiquities Authority.
    Obv: Head of Augustus, r., laureate (inscription worn).
    Rev: Tyche standing l., holding palm branch with r. hand, and caduceus with l. hand; in l. field *L NZ*; in r. field: ΔΩΡΙ/ΤΩΝ in two lines.

64/65 CE = PKH (year 128)

11. Bronze, 22 mm, 11. 28 gr. Meshorer No. 16; *RPC* 4757; Fichman Collection.
    Obv: Head of Zeus Doros, bearded, laureate, r.
    Rev: Tyche standing to front, looking r., holding standard with r. hand and cornucopia with l hand; on r. ΔΩΡΙΤΩΝ; date on l. field *L PKH*.
12. Bronze, 6.11. Meshorer No. 17; Fichman Collection.
    Obv: Bust of Tyche, r., veiled and turreted.
    Rev: Tyche standing to front, looking r., holding standard with r. hand and cornucopia with l. hand; date, *L PKH* upwards on l.; ΔΩΡΙΤΩΝ on r.
13. Bronze, 3.11 gr. Meshorer No. 18; Fichman Collection.
    Obv: Bust of Tyche, r.; veiled and turreted.
    Rev: Galley sailing l.; above it in two lines ΔΩΡΙΤΩΝ and *PKH*.

66/67 CE = ΛΡ (year 131)

14. Bronze, 12.48 gr. Meshorer 19b; *RPC* 4758; Fichman Collection.
    Obv: Head of Zeus Doros, bearded, laureate, r.
    Rev: Tyche standing to front, looking r., holding a standard with r. hand and cornucopia with l. hand; ΔΩΡΙΤΩΝ on r.; year ΛΡ in left field; murex shell on r. field.
15. Bronze, 2.72; Meshorer No. 21; Fichman Collection.
    Obv: Bust of Tyche r., veiled and turreted.
    Rev: Galley with railing, sailing l., above ΔΩΡΙΤΩΝ and date *LΛΡ*.
16. Same as 15 with Legion X mark in r. field of obverse.

67/68 CE = AΛP (year 131)

17. Bronze, 22 mm, 9.48; Meshorer 23; *RPC* 4759; Israel Antiquities Authority.
    Obv: Head of Zeus Doros, bearded, laureate, r.
    Rev: Tyche standing to front, looking l., holding standard with r. hand and cornucopia with l. hand; in l. field date: AΛP; from right: ΔΩPITΩN.

68/69 CE = BΛP (year 132)

18. Bronze, 2.28; Meshorer No. 27; *RPC* I 4764; Fichman Collection.
    Obv: Bust of Tyche, l., veiled and turreted.
    Rev: Galley sailing l., above: ΔΩPITΩN and date BΛP.
19. Bronze, 14.08 g.; Meshorer No. 31; RIC II, 2088. Fichman Collection.
    Obv: Bust of Vespasian, r., laureate; *AYTOKPATΩP OYEΣΠAΣIANOΣ.*
    Rev: Tyche standing to front, looking r., holding standard with r. hand and cornucopia with l. hand; ΔΩPITΩN on right inside; dotted border; date BΛP on l. field.
20. Bronze, 7.65; Meshorer No. 31a; Israel Antiquities Authority.
    Obv: Bust of Vespasian, r.; laureate; a round countermark depicting a head. *AYTOKPATΩP OYEΣΠAΣIANOΣ.*
    Rev: same as 17.
21. Bronze, 10.50 gr. Meshorer No. 32; RIC II, 2089. Israel Museum Jerusalem.
    Obv: Bust of Titus, r., laureate; *T.ΦΛAYIOYEΣΠ KAIΣ ETOY NEOY IEP*
    Rev: Tyche standing to front, looking r., holding standard with r. hand and cornucopia in l. hand; ΔΩPITΩN on right; date BΛP on l. field.

75/76 CE = ΘΛP (year 139)

22. Bronze, 5.53 gr. Meshorer No. 29; *RIC* II, 2091. Israel Museum Jerusalem.
    Obv: Bust of Tyche r., laureate, veiled.
    Rev: Tyche standing to l., holding standard with r. hand and cornucopia with l. hand; on l. of standard ΘΛP; ΔΩPITΩN on right.
23. Bronze, 12.60 gr. Meshorer No. 28; RIC II, 2090. Fichman Collection.
    Obv: Head of Zeus Doros, r.; aphlaston in r. field.
    Rev: Tyche standing to front, looking r., supporting standard with r. hand and holding cornucopia with l. hand; date on l. field, divided between ΘΛ on l. of standard and P on r.; ΔΩPITΩN on r, along the dotted circle.

111/112 CE = POE (year 175)

24. Bronze, 26 mm, 12.58 gr. Meshorer No. 33. Israel Antiquities Authority.

Obv: Bust of Trajan, r., laureate, undraped, in r. field star; *AYTOK KAICAP TPAIANOC CEB ΓEPM ΔAK.*
Rev: Bust of Zeus Doros, bearded, laureate, r.; aphlaston in r. field; *POE ΔΩP IEP ACYΛ AYTON NAYAP.*

25. Bronze, 4.86; Meshorer No. 35; Israel Museum Jerusalem.
    Obv: Bust of Trajan, r., laureate, undraped; AYTOK KAICAP TPAIANOC *CEB ΓEPM ΔAK.*
    Rev: Tyche standing to front, looking l., holding standard with r. hand and cornucopia with l. hand; on r. ΔΩPITΩN; date on l. upward *POE.*
26. Bronze, 10.93; Meshorer No. 34; Israel Museum Jerusalem.
    Obv: Bust of Trajan, r., laureate, undraped; AYTOK KAICAP TPAIANOC *CEB ΓEPM ΔAF.*
    Rev: Bust of Tyche r. turreted and veiled, surrounded by wreath of wine leaves; across fields ΔΩPI; below *POE.*
27. Bronze, 3.55; Meshorer No. 36; Fichman Collection.
    Obv: Bust of Trajan, laureate, undraped; *NEP TPA KAIC.*
    Rev: Galley sailing l. above it: ΔΩPA IEPA in two lines; below galley: POE.
28. Bronze, 14.7 gr. Meshorer No. 33; Fichman Collection.
    Obv: Bust of Trajan, r., laureate, undraped, in r. field star; *AYTOK KAICAP TPAIANOC CEB ΓEPM ΔAK.*
    Rev: Bust of Zeus Doros r.; longer, curlier beard; *POE ΔΩP IEP ACYΛ AYTON NAYAP.*
29. Bronze, 3.54; Meshorer No. 36; Fichman Collection.
    Obv: Bust of Trajan, laureate, undraped; star in r. field; *NEP TPA KAIC.*
    Rev: Galley sailing l. above it: ΔΩPA IEPA in two lines; below galley: POE.

117/118 CE = ΠP (year 180)

30. Bronze, 12.88 gr.; Meshorer No. 37; Fichman Collection.
    Obv: Bust of Hadrian, r., laureate and cuirassed; *AYTO TRA.AΔPIANΩ KAIC.*
    Rev: Bust of Zeus Doros, bearded, laureate, r.; ΔΩP IEP ACYΛ. AYT *NAYAP*; date below ΠP.
31. Bronze, 9.98 gr. Meshorer No. 38; Fichman Collection.
    Obv: Bust of Hadrian, r., laureate, cuirassed; *AYTO TRA.AΔPIANΩ KAIC.*
    Rev: Bust of Tyche r. turreted and veiled, surrounded by wreath of wine leaves; across fields ΔΩPI; date below in r. ΠP.
32. Bronze, 6.21; Meshorer No. 39; Fichman Collection.
    Obv: Bust of Hadrian, r., laureate, cuirassed; *AYTO TRA.AΔPIANΩ KAIC.*
    Rev: Tyche standing to front, looking l., holding standard with r. hand and cornucopia with l. hand; on r. *ΔΩPITΩN*; date on l. upward ΠP.
33. Bronze, 3.70; Meshorer No. 40. Fichman Collection.

Obv: Bust of Hadrian, r., laureate, cuirassed; *AYTO TRA.AΔPIAN*

Rev: Galley sailing l. above it: ΔΩPA IEPA in two lines; date below galley: ΠP.

34. Bronze, 11.81 gr. Meshorer No. 38; Eretz Museum, Tel Aviv.

Obv: Bust of Hadrian, r., laureate; *AYTO TRA. AΔPIANΩ KAIC.*

Rev: Bust of Zeus Doros, bearded, laureate, r.; ΔΩP IEP ACYΛ. AYT *NAYAP*; date below ΠP.

143/144 CE = CZ (year 207)

35. Bronze, 12.57 gr. Meshorer No. 41; Fichman Collection.

Obv: Bust Antoninus Pius, r., laureate, draped; small star in r. field; *AYT KAI ANTΩNEINOC CEBEY.*

Rev: Head of Zeus Doros, bearded, laureate, r.; ΔΩP IEP AC AYT *NAYAPXIC*; date L CZ.

36. Bronze, 9.84 gr. Meshorer No. 42; Fichman Collection.

Obv: Bust Antoninus Pius, r., laureate, draped; small star in r. field; *AYT KAI ANTΩNEINOC CEBEY.*

Rev: Bust of Tyche r. turreted and veiled, surrounded by wreath of grape leaves; across fields ΔΩPI.

37. Bronze, 5.35 gr. Meshorer No. 43; Fichman Collection. *RPC* 6791.

Obv: Bust Antoninus Pius, r., laureate, draped; small star in r. field; *AYT KAI ANTΩNEINOC CEB EY.*

Rev: Tyche standing to front with head turning l., holding standard with r. hand and cornucopia with l. hand; on r. ΔΩPITΩN; date on l. upward L ZC.

201/202 CE = EΞC (year 265)

38. Bronze, 30 mm, 18.35 gr. Meshorer No. 44. Israel Antiquities Authority.

Obv: Bust of Septimius Severus, r., laureate, draped; *AYT KAI Λ CEΠ CEOYHPOC CEB.*

Rev: Caracalla and Geta, togated, facing each other in *dextrarum junctio* act; *AYT K M AYP ANT KAI Π EΠ ΓET KAI;* ex: ΔΩPI and date EΞC.

39. Bronze, 23 mm, 10.55 gr. Meshorer No. 45; Israel Antiquities Authority.

Obv: Bust of Julia Domna, r., draped; *IOYΛ ΔOMNA CEB*

Rev: Bust of Tyche r., turreted, veiled, inside dotted circle; in r. field prow of galley; ΔΩP N AY EΞC.

40. Bronze, 16.08 gr. Meshorer No. 48; Fichman Collection.

Obv: Bust of young Caracalla, r.; laureate, draped; *AYT K M AYP ANTΩ CEB.*

Rev: Tyche standing to front, looking r., inside arched aedicule, holding standard with r. hand and cornucopia with l. hand; ex: ΔΩPA; on l. field upward IEPA; on r. field downward EΞC.

41. Bronze, gr. 4.35; Meshorer No. 52; Israel Museum Jerusalem.

Obv: Bust of Plautilla, r. draped; *ΠΛA YTIΛΛ AYT.*

Rev: Galley sailing l.; above ΔΩPA/NAYA in two lines; date EΞC below.

42. Bronze, 9.28 gr. Meshorer No. 47; Fichman Collection.

Obv: Bust of young Geta, r.; Π (P?) *CEΠ ΓETA K.*[1]

Rev: Head of Zeus Doros, bearded, laureate, r.; ΔΩPA IEPA EΞC; in r. field aphlaston.

210/211 CE = ΔOC

43. Bronze, 14.16 gr. Meshorer No. 49; Israel Museum Jerusalem.

Obv: Bust of Caracalla, r., laureate, undraped; *M AYP ANTΩNEINOC CEB.*

Rev: Tyche standing inside tetrastyle temple, facing to front, looking l., holding standard with r. hand and cornucopia with l. hand; ex: ΔΩPA; on r. downward IEPA; on l. upward ΔOC.

44. Bronze, 18.46 gr. Meshorer No. 50; Bijovsky No. 44. Sofaer Collection.

Obv: Bust of Caracalla, r., laureate, undraped; (*M AYP ANTΩNEINOC CEB*).

Rev: Emperor galloping on horse, r., holding spear with r. hand; l. upwards: ΔΩPA IEP ACY ΔOC.

45. Bronze, gr. 11.64. Meshorer No. 51; Bijovsky No. 45; Fichman Collection.

Obv: Bust of Caracalla, r., laureate, undraped; *M AYP ANTΩNEI CEB.*

Rev: Bust of Zeus Doros, bearded, laureate, r.; on r. field aphlaston; l. upwards: ΔΩPA IEP ACY ΔOC.

46. Bronze, 15.4; unpublished; Fichman Collection.

Obv: Bust of Caracalla, r., laureate, undraped; *(M AYP ANTΩNEINOC CEB).*

Rev: Tyche standing to front, looking l., inside arched aedicula, holding standard with r. hand and cornucopia with l. hand; ex: ΔΩPA; on l. upward IEPA; on r. downward EΞC.

47. Bronze, gr. 4.22; unpublished; Fichman Collection.

Obv: Bust of Caracalla, r. laureate, undraped; *M AYP ANTΩNEINOC CEB.*

Rev: Galley sailing l.; inside dotted circle; *ΔΩPA IEPA* above boat.

211/212 CE = EOC (year 275)

48. Bronze, gr. 5.02; Meshorer No. 46; Fichman Collection.

Obv: Bust of Julia Domna, r.; *IOYΛIA ΔOMNA.*

Rev: Galley sailing l.; above: *ΔOPA*; below: *NAYA/ EOC* in two lines.

49. Bronze, 23 mm; gr. 7.45. Israel Antiquities Authority.[2]

Obv: Bust of Julia Domna, r; *(IOY)ΛIA (ΔOMNA).*

---

[1] The first letter of the legend appears to be a *Rho* rather than a *Pi*, suggesting a possible engraver's error (Dobbins, 11/5/2010).

[2] The original cataloguing at the IAA claimed that the depiction represented Aquilea Severa.

Rev: Tyche standing to front, looking l., holding rudder with r. hand and cornucopia with l. hand; *(ΔΩΡΙ)ΤΩΝ.*

50. Bronze, gr. 7.9; unpublished; Fichman Collection.

Obv: Bust of Julia Domna, r.*; ΙΟΥΛΙΑ ΔΟΜΝΑ.*

Rev: Bust of Tyche, turreted and veiled, r.; ΔOPA NAYA EOC.

Coin Plates

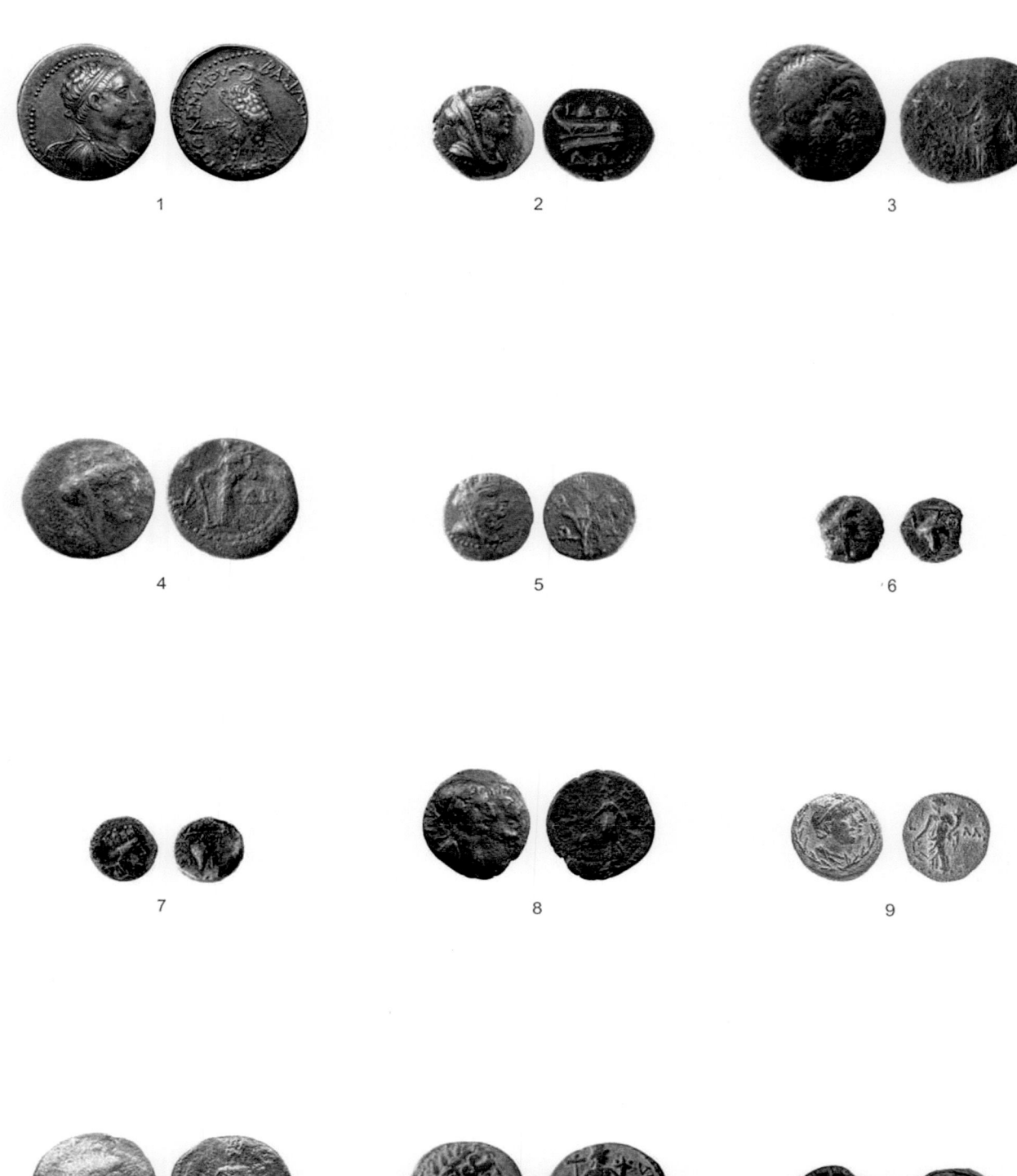

1

2

3

4

5

6

7

8

9

10

11

12

PLATE 1

100

13

14

15

16

17

18

19

20

21

22

23

24

25

Plate 2

101

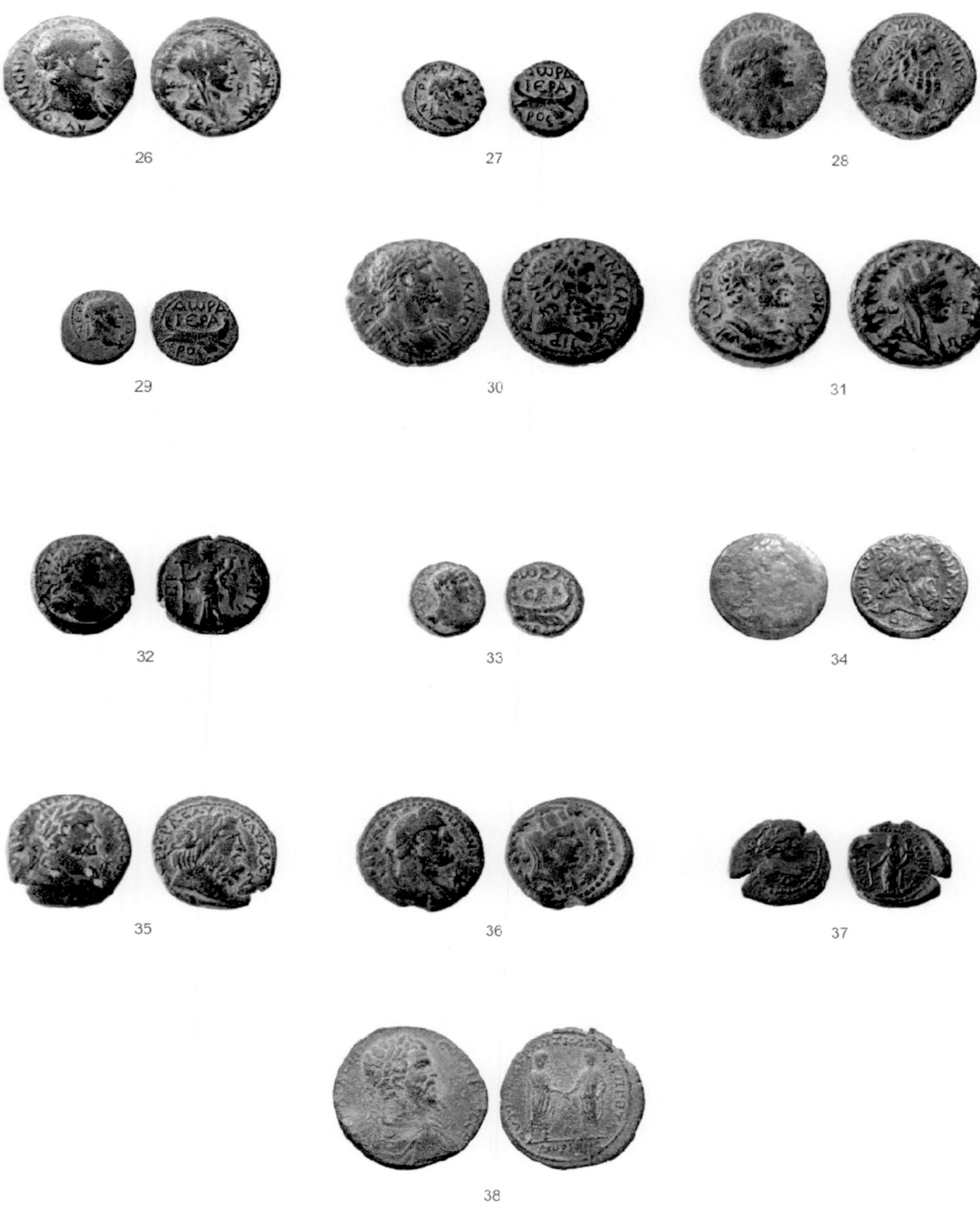

26

27

28

29

30

31

32

33

34

35

36

37

38

PLATE 3

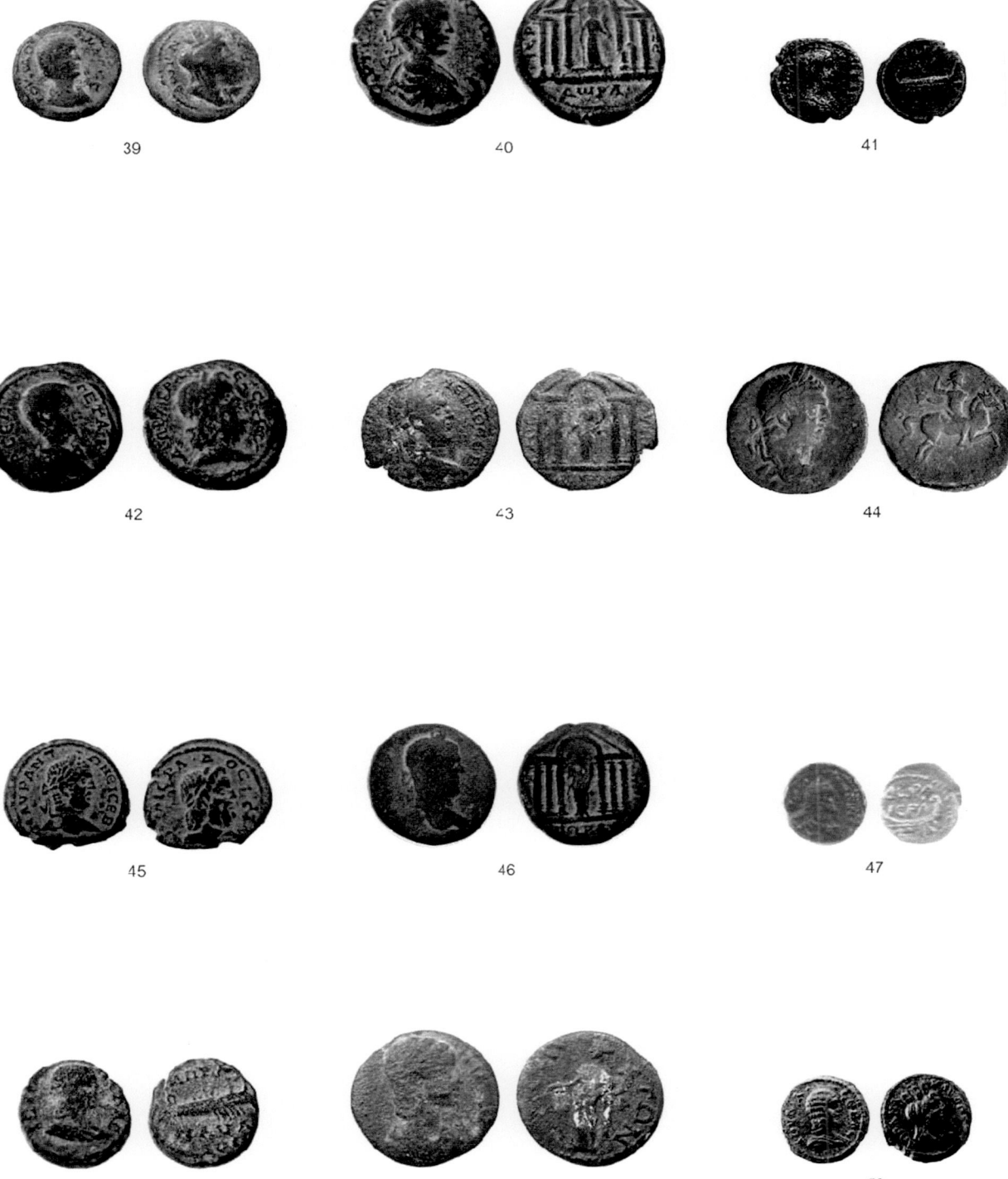

39   40   41

42   43   44

45   46   47

48   49   50

PLATE 4